CHAPTER 1

Introduction: The Problem and the Approach

Evil facts . . . are a genuine portion of reality; and they may after all be the best key to life's significance and possibly the only openers of our eyes to the deepest levels of truth.

—WILLIAM JAMES, *Varieties of Religious Experience*

1.1 What Is Evil?

Evil has an ominous connotation that goes beyond badness. It is perhaps the most severe succinct condemnation our moral vocabulary affords, so it should not be used casually and the conditions of its justified ascription should be made clear. Evil involves serious harm that causes fatal or lasting physical injury, as do, for instance, murder, torture, and mutilation. Serious harm need not be physical. But since judging the seriousness of nonphysical harm, such as loss of honor, happiness, or love, involves complex questions, I shall concentrate on simple cases of physical harm whose seriousness is as obvious as it is of losing life, limb, or eyesight, or suffering prolonged excruciating pain. Serious harm may be caused by natural disasters, animals, or viruses; and human beings may cause serious harm to the fauna or the flora. Nevertheless, evil has primarily to do with serious harm caused by human beings to other human beings. This may be excusable on moral grounds as self-defense, deserved punishment, necessary for averting worse harm, or as resulting from non-culpable ignorance, unavoidable accident, or unforeseeable contingencies. Part of what makes human actions evil, then, is that they cause serious harm and lack excuse.

The harm involved in evil actions is not just serious but also excessive. This is part of the reason why such actions are worse than morally bad. To rob someone at gunpoint is morally bad, but after having gotten the money, to torture, mutilate, and then murder the victim is evil. Evildoers cause more serious harm than is needed for achieving their ends. They are not just unscrupulous in their choice of means, but motivated by malevolence to gratuitous excesses. They treat their victims with ill will, rage, or hatred. This may be shown by the sheer quantity of the harm they do, as in the murder of thousands of innocent victims, or by the quality of their actions, such as torturing children. Evil actions go beyond breaking some ordinary moral rule; they show contempt for and flaunt fundamental moral prohibitions.

The evil of an action, therefore, consists in the combination of three components: the malevolent motivation of evildoers; the serious, excessive harm caused by their actions; and the lack of morally acceptable excuse for the actions.[1] Each of these components is necessary, and they are jointly sufficient for condemning an action as evil. An action may cause serious, excessive harm and not be evil if, for instance, it is accidental, coerced, or morally justified. Nor is malevolent motivation enough to make an action evil because as a result of unexpected circumstances—the bomb failed to explode, the gun misfired—the action may fail to cause any harm. Furthermore, an action prompted by malevolent motivation and causing serious, excessive harm may still not be evil if it is morally excusable by being, for example, justified punishment or necessary for avoiding even greater harm. The justified ascription of evil to an action requires, therefore, motive, consequence, and lack of excuse.

Each of these components allows for degrees: malevolent motives may range from short-term blind rage to a lifelong hatred of humanity; serious, excessive harm may involve the torture and murder of one innocent victim or doing the same to thousands; and a morally inexcusable action may fall anywhere on a continuum from culpable ignorance or weakness to deliberately and knowingly doing evil for its own sake. The justified ascription of evil to actions, therefore, allows for a distinction between levels of evil. People can be said to be evildoers if they habitually perform evil actions, and they can be greater or lesser evildoers depending on the level of evil they do. And institutions, societies, and other collectives are evil derivatively twice over if they lead their participants to cause various degrees of evil.

Evil actions violate their victims' physical security and thus transgress fundamental moral prohibitions that protect minimum conditions of human well-being. One essential task of morality is to safeguard these conditions. Evildoers or their defenders sometimes attempt to excuse evil actions by appealing to religious, political, aesthetic, scientific, or prudential considerations. Such excuses are morally unacceptable because the malevolent motivation and the excessive harm of evil actions go far beyond what is needed to pursue any reasonable nonmoral aim. Fundamental moral prohibitions are nevertheless routinely violated by evildoers. The reason for condemning such people and actions as evil, then, is the moral commitment to human well-being. It is a lamentable fact of life that undeniable cases of evil abound. Those in doubt have only to watch the news or read the newspapers or consult the books that catalog some of the atrocities of the past century.[2] Nor is it deniable that most of this evil is caused by human beings. The problem is to explain why they cause it.

1.2 Approaches to Explanation

There is no shortage of attempts to provide an explanation. My reason for adding to their number is that the most influential previous ones—those inspired by the religious and the Enlightenment world views—try to explain evil by explaining it away. They deny what the epigraph rightly asserts, namely, that "evil facts . . . are a genuine portion of reality." Both begin with a world view and then try to fit evil into it. But evil does not fit, and that is why they try to explain it away. A detailed discussion of these explanations and their shortcomings will follow, but a brief indication of what they are is needed here to contrast my approach with theirs.

A dominant tendency in the religious world view is to assume that a morally good order permeates the scheme of things and human lives go well to the extent to which they conform to it. The problem of evil, then, becomes the problem of explaining the failure to conform. There are various religious explanations, but most of them assume that the failure results from the misuse of the evildoers' reason or will. Evil is thus seen as a defect in evildoers rather than in the scheme of things. This explanation faces two difficulties its defenders have not succeeded in overcoming despite many centuries of trying. One is to justify the belief that although experience and history provide abundant contrary evidence, there is a morally good order in the scheme of things. The other is that since human beings are part of the scheme of things, any defect in evildoers is a defect in the scheme of things. The very existence of evil thus constitutes a reason against believing in a morally good order.

A central thread in the Enlightenment world view is the belief that human beings are basically good and their well-being depends on living according to reason. The more reasonable lives are, the better they are supposed to become. The problem of evil is thus the problem of explaining our failure to be more reasonable when it is in our interest to be so. The explanation is that external influences, usually in the form of bad political arrangements, corrupt our basic goodness. Evil is thus explained as the result of interference with our basic goodness. But what reason is there for supposing that human beings are basically good? There obviously are many bad human propensities, and they often overwhelm the good ones. Why suppose that good ones are basic and bad ones are not? Furthermore, if the corruption of our supposed basic goodness is the result of bad political arrangements, it needs to be explained how these arrangements become bad. They are made and maintained by human beings. If they are bad, it is because those who make and maintain them are bad. The ubiquity of bad political arrangements is thus a reason for doubting basic human goodness, not an explanation of evil.

These two approaches differ in many ways, but they share the assumption that the good is basic and evil is derivative because it is some kind of interference with the good. The explanation they seek, therefore, is of the nature and cause of the interference. In my view, this is to seek the explanation of evil in the wrong place because the assumption underlying the search is mistaken. I shall argue that there is no convincing reason for supposing that the good is basic and evil is derivative and there is no more reason to think that evil is interference with the good than that good is interference with evil.

1.3 Toward an Adequate Explanation

A first approximation of the explanation I shall defend emerges against the background of another questionable assumption on which previous explanations rest. Most of the explanations given in the framework of the religious or the Enlightenment world view assume that evil has a single cause. Evil, however, has many causes: various human propensities; outside influences on their development; and a multiplicity of circumstances in which we live and to which we must respond. Because these causes vary with person, time, and place, an attempt to find *the* cause of evil is doomed. There is no explanation that fits all or even most cases of evil. Weakness of will, ignorance of the good, defective reasoning, human destructiveness, bad political arrangements, excessive self-love, immoderate pleasure-seeking, revenge, greed, boredom, enjoyment, perversity, provocation, stupidity, fear, callousness, indoctrination, self-deception, negligence, and so forth may all explain some cases of evil. None, however, explains all or even most cases. This is not because the right explanation has not been found, but because the search for it is misguided.

Some who have given serious thought to evil have concluded from the failure of single explanations that evil is ultimately incomprehensible. Kant was neither the first nor the last in believing that "the rational origin of . . . the propensity to evil remains inscrutable to us."[3] This leads to the desperate measure of abandoning the attempt to cope with evil. For if evil is inscrutable, then we are helpless in trying to prevent it. The realization that evil has many causes, however, will lead one to expect the failure of attempts to find its single cause and to seek a better explanation rather than pronounce it a mystery. The best argument against the incomprehensibility of evil is to provide the supposedly impossible explanation. And that is what I shall attempt to do.

This explanation does not share the assumption of the religious world view that a morally good order permeates the scheme of things. The alternative is not that the order is bad, but that there is no moral order in the scheme of things; there are only impersonal, unmotivated, purposeless, natural processes. If the scheme of things were to have a point of view, then from that point of view human well-being would not matter at all. Not because something else would matter more, but because nothing would matter. Things can matter only to fairly complex sentient beings, and the scheme of things is an abstract idea, not a sentient being. Human well-being certainly matters to us. That, however, should not lead to the age-old religious mistake of projecting human concerns onto the scheme of things. Good and evil are human values, human ways of judging whether our well-being is favorably or unfavorably affected. From the human point of view, natural processes, including our own actions, may be good, evil, mixed, or indifferent. Our judgments about whether they are one or the other can be objectively true or false because we can be right or wrong about how some natural process affects our well-being. But the effects we find good or bad are equally natural, and neither is more basic than the other.

The alternative to the religious view, then, is that the scheme of things is the context in which human life must be lived, but that scheme is nonmoral. It is, therefore, unreasonable to have any moral attitude toward or moral expectation from it. It is not for or against human well-being because it is incapable of being for or against anything. Natural processes, of course, affect human well-being, but that is a consequence of the intersection of undirected causal chains, not of design. Human life, unlike the scheme of things, is value-laden. It is the repository of possibilities and limits with which we all start out and which have important effects on our well-being. But their effects, although important, are not decisive because there is a gap between what we must and can do. We cannot transgress our limits, yet we can often decide which among several possibilities we should try to realize. There are many ways of making such decisions, and reason is one of them.

The assumption of the Enlightenment world view is that human beings are basically good and if we use reason to make such decisions, we shall decide in favor of possibilities that contribute to human well-being. This is not so much wrong as superficial and half-true. It fails to recognize that we also have other propensities, such as aggression, fear, envy, and ambition. They are no less basic than reason, and they often prompt evil actions. The explanation I favor, unlike the Enlightenment one, recognizes that acting in accordance with our propensities may lead to either good or evil, so it rejects the view that human beings are basically good.

A dominant tendency in the Enlightenment world view is to explain evil as a failure of reason. This assumes that reason requires us to pursue our well-being and prohibits evil actions because they are detrimental to it. Evildoers are supposed to fail to see this as a result of some external interference with the development or the exercise of their reasoning capacity. Coping with evil depends on removing the interference so that people can reason without impediments. And then, it is supposed, they will promote human well-being and refrain from jeopardizing it.

This may well be called the Enlightenment faith because it continues to be held in the face of overwhelming evidence against it. Its reference to "our well-being" is crucially ambiguous. It may mean the "well-being of individual human beings" or the "well-being of human beings collectively." It matters which is meant because individual well-being often conflicts with collective well-being, and there are reasons for favoring both. Individuals may be perfectly reasonable in resolving such conflicts in favor of their own or their loved ones' well-being, even if it damages collective well-being. As we shall see later in some detail, evildoers often have reasons for their actions and they need not be handicapped in reasoning. It has been well said that "if you are committed to secular ethics, it really does seem that all the king's horses and all the king's men couldn't put reason and ethics together again in a way that shows individual wickedness to be necessarily irrational."[4] The supposition that people who reason well will promote collective well-being and those who do not must be unreasonable is wishful thinking that sustains hope at the cost of denying plain facts of human psychology. Explaining evil depends on recognizing that self-interest and the conditions of human life often make evil actions reasonable. The key to coping with it is to provide stronger reasons against doing evil than there are reasons for doing it.

Another significant difference between explanations derived from the religious or the Enlightenment world view and the one I favor concerns responsibility. All agree that evildoers should be held responsible for the evil they do, unless excused. The problem is to specify the excusing conditions. It is widely held that evildoers should be held responsible only for their intentional actions. I disagree. Evildoers may be rightly held responsible for unintentional actions if they lack knowledge they ought to have, act out of habits they ought not to have developed, or follow conventions they ought to have rejected. Responsibility depends not only on the motivation of evildoers, but also on whether they have the motivation they ought to have, on the prevailing moral sensibility that forms part of the context of their actions, and on the foreseeable consequences of their actions. This has important implications for how we explain and try to cope with evil.

The problem of evil is deep because human well-being depends on coping with it, but basic human propensities both cause evil and corrupt attempts to cope with it. Our basic good and evil propensities thus perpetually motivate us to follow incompatible courses of action. Sometimes one prevails, sometimes the other. Contrary to the religious world view, we have no reason to rely on resources external to humanity. And contrary to the Enlightenment world view, reason may favor not just good but also evil actions, depending on our characters and circumstances. Characters and circumstances can be changed, of course, but changing them guarantees nothing. For the effort to change them is as liable to corruption by evil propensities as the conditions were that we try to change. Furthermore, since our evil propensities are as basic as the good ones, if we succeed in preventing their expression in one way, they may just be expressed in some other way. This is why evil is a permanent adversity and coping with it is formidably difficult. An initial characterization of my approach, then, is that it combines the following claims: evil has many causes; the scheme of things is nonmoral; we have basic propensities for both good and evil actions, and thus we are ambivalent toward good and evil; evil actions may be reasonable; and evildoers may be held responsible for both intentionally and unintentionally evil actions.

1.4 The Approach

My aim is to provide a causal explanation of why evildoers do evil. There are excellent recent works giving historical accounts of past explanations,[5] but they are relevant to my aim only insofar as they contribute to the right explanation or illustrate mistakes. The facts I appeal to are psychological propensities familiar to normally intelligent people, not the fruits of research or deep reflection. Common knowledge of them makes it possible for novelists, playwrights, biographers, and historians to write about the character, motivation, and actions of people at places and times other than their own and feel confident about being understood. I have in mind such propensities as desiring a meaningful life, needing to be loved, having conflicting motives, deceiving oneself, wanting to appear other than one is, being ignorant of some of one's motives, resenting injustice, embellishing the past, fearing the unknown, minding defeat, caring about the opinion of others, and so forth. These propensities are commonplaces of human psychology, but they also have moral significance. They may be thought of as basic elements of moral psychology. It is to them that I shall appeal in order to explain the causes of evil actions. The most significant fact about evil, however, is not psychological but the serious physical harm it causes to innocent people. Evil matters because of the loss and suffering of its victims. This should be kept in mind throughout the book, even though much of the discussion will focus on psychological propensities that motivate evildoers. The reason for seeking an explanation of evil is to make it less widespread, but its causes will be found partly in the moral psychology of evildoers.

The argument has two parts. Part One comprises chapters 2–7, each being a detailed consideration of a concrete, indubitable, and conspicuous case of evil, and chapter 8, which draws tentative conclusions derived from these cases and formulates conditions an adequate explanation must meet. Part Two consists of chapters 9–14. The first three show that explanations of evil inspired by the religious or the Enlightenment world view are inadequate partly because they cannot account for all the cases discussed in Part One. Yet each of these explanations contributes some components to what I shall offer as a better explanation. The next three chapters provide this better explanation. It accounts for all the cases in Part One, incorporates the salvageable components of the inadequate explanations, identifies causes of evil, shows the conditions under which evildoers should be held responsible, and indicates what should be done to cope with evil. Finally, chapter 15 is a brief summary of the conclusions reached in the preceding chapters.

Part One

FORMS OF EVIL

CHAPTER 2

The Sleep of Reason

The sleep of reason brings forth monsters.

—FRANCISCO GOYA, *Caprichos* inscription

2.1 Crusade against the Cathars

The Cathars lived in Languedoc in southern France during the decades before and after A.D. 1200. They formed a religious sect based on the belief that there was a radical difference between the spiritual and material worlds. The spiritual world was created and ruled by God, and it was good. The material world was created and ruled by the Demiurge, and it was evil. In human beings, these two worlds met. The soul was potentially good because God implanted in it consciousness of the good. But the body and all its functions were evil, as a result of being the creation of the Demiurge, who made human beings in his own likeness. They believed that salvation depended on renouncing material possessions and on living as much as one could a spiritual life. The Cathars realized that such a life was demanding and difficult. Those who had committed themselves to it were called Perfects. They were celibate, vegetarian, propertyless, and ascetic. Most Cathars were sympathizers, not Perfects, because although they accepted the truth of the beliefs, they did not act on them consistently. Nevertheless, Cathars were noted for the simplicity of their lives and the honesty and kindness of their dealings with everyone. The name, Cathar, derived from the Greek *katharoi,* meaning "the pure ones."[1]

The implications of Cathar beliefs were profoundly at odds with the prevailing Christian orthodoxy. Cathars were committed to denying that God created everything and was omnipotent, for the material world was

10

created by the Demiurge, and God had no power over it. Nor could Jesus be the son of God because he had a body, which was evil, and God could not be evil. Moreover, since everything in the material world was evil, so was the church, its hierarchy, its practices; as well as sex and procreation, wealth, power, war, social status, and so on.

Most of the Cathars were simple, unreflective, illiterate, and scrabbling hard to make a living. They just happened to be influenced by the preaching and example of a wandering Perfect, and they were unaware of the unorthodox implications of their beliefs. It is doubtful that many of the Perfects themselves fully realized these implications. The more articulate ones saw themselves as rejecting the worldliness and corruption of many priests and thus upholding the true spirit of Christianity. They certainly did not want to change the world since they believed it to be irremediably evil. They had no theological or political interests. They sought salvation for themselves and others by living in preparation of a better life in the spiritual world.

The ecclesiastical authorities, first in Languedoc and later in Rome, were fully aware, however, that the Cathar creed was at odds with their most basic beliefs. They saw the Cathars as subverting the very foundation of Christianity. It also worried them that the Cathars were quite popular in Languedoc because people found the Perfects admirable and they could not but compare them favorably with priests and bishops whose manner of living deviated far more from the Christian ideal than the Perfects' own.

The church, therefore, was moved to take action. At first, local priests preached against the Cathars and emphasized their denial of the faith. But this was not effective. The Cathars then were maligned by lies, according to which they were Devil-worshipers who believed that Satan was the creator and ruler of heaven and earth; repudiated sexual restraint; denied that the Perfects could sin and thus encouraged them to do whatever they pleased; and derived their name from the Latin *catus*, meaning cat, which is the form in which Lucifer appears to them and whom they adore by kissing the cat's anus.[2] When even these absurd lies failed to put a dent in the Cathars' popularity, the pope—Innocent III—stepped in and declared Catharism to be a heresy.

This was an extremely serious matter with fatal consequences. "Far graver than the unbeliever was the case of the heretic, who accepted the same revelation as his orthodox neighbour but gave it a different interpretation, distorting and corrupting it, leading men away from their salvation. Heresy was a spreading poison and a community which tolerated it invited God to withdraw his protection" (AC 41). As Aquinas put the point: "Heresy is a sin which merits not only excommunication but also death, for it is worse to corrupt the Faith which is the life of the soul than to issue counterfeit coins which minister to the secular life. Since counterfeiters are justly killed by princes as enemies to the common good, so heretics deserve the same punishment."[3] The pope's declaration thus doomed the Cathars.

A powerful ecclesiastical machinery was set in motion to extirpate Catharism. It eventually produced the Albigensian Crusade, named after the town of Albi, where many Cathars lived. The stage was set for one of the most deplorable episodes in the history of Christianity. "No one doubts . . . the homicidal passions at work during the Albigensian Crusade. Even in an era commonly considered barbarous . . . the campaign against the Cathars and their supporters stands out for its stark cruelty" (PH 6). A very fair-minded medievalist says that "those who bore authority in the church . . . were responsible for some terrible acts of violence and cruelty, among which the Albigensian Crusade holds a position of peculiar horror" (WSC 19). It was "one of the most savage of all medieval wars. Faith ultimately prevailed, as Innocent III had predicted, but the consequences of the Albigensian Crusade went far beyond its aims" (AC 16). Among these consequences were that "the eleventh and twelfth centuries saw what has turned out to be a permanent change in Western society. Persecution became habitual. That is to say not simply that individuals were subject to violence, but that deliberate and socially sanctioned violence began to be directed, through established governmental, judicial and social institutions, against groups of people defined by general characteristics such as race, religion or way of life; and that membership of such groups in itself came to be regarded as justifying these attacks."[4]

Having no troops, Innocent III had to persuade others to mount the crusade. This he did by promising the king of France, Philip Augustus, the right to dispose of all the territories conquered in Languedoc, a substantial portion of the future revenues of the church in France, and last but not least the remission of the sins of the crusaders obtained by the personal appeal of Innocent III to God. Finding these terms acceptable, Philip Augustus recruited knights with their retinues for the crusade. Noteworthy among them was Simon de Montfort, a landless English warrior who eventually became the secular leader of the crusade. He was to receive from Philip Augustus all the land he won by the force of arms. Montfort "hated heresy with a fierce hatred, and genuinely regarded his own advancement as part of the design of Providence to encompass its destruction. He believed that 'My work is the work of Christ.' He was 'an athlete of Christ,' an instrument of God's anger. . . . He was an ascetic, a fanatic" (AC 101).

The crusade also had a religious leader, Arnold Amaury, the head of the Cistercian order of monks, to whom the pope gave total authority to conduct the crusade as he saw fit, so long as Catharism was destroyed. But the pope made clear the general line Amaury was to follow. In his letters Innocent III spoke of Catharism as a "hateful plague," a "spreading canker," and "vile wolves among the Lord's flock" (AC 67). He wrote to the crusaders: "Forward, volunteers of the Army of God! Go forth with the church's cry of anguish ringing in your ears. Fill your souls with godly rage to avenge the insult done to the Lord" (AC 77). And to Amaury he wrote: "Use cunning and deception as weapons, for in the circumstances deceit is no more than prudence" (AC 81).

The crusade began in 1209. Its initial size was estimated at twenty thousand, which made it enormous by the standards of the time, when warring forces rarely numbered over one thousand. The crusade was wildly unpopular in Languedoc because it meant the imposition of French rule over the hitherto more or less independent principality and because the crusaders lived off the land, causing great damage and commandeering resources that deprived the natives of their livelihood. The nobility and the general population alike sided with the Cathars, who were their fellow citizens, often neighbors, known to be peaceful, pure, and harmless. The people of Languedoc gave the Cathars refuge and protection, resisted the crusaders, with dreadful consequences for themselves and the Cathars.

Breziers was the first town the crusaders besieged. When the knights asked Amaury how they could tell the difference between Catholics and Cathars among the defenders, the priest told them: "Kill them all, God will know his own" (PH 5, 84). And that is what they did. The Army of God massacred about twenty thousand men, women, and children, faithful Catholics and heretical Cathars, and then, for good measure, burned down the town. Amaury wrote to the pope: "Nearly twenty thousand of the citizens were put to the sword, regardless of age and sex. The workings of divine vengeance have been wondrous" (PH 87).

The crusaders then marched to Carcassone. Its defender, Viscount Trancavel, wanting to avoid the fate of Breziers, proposed to negotiate terms of surrender. He was promised safe-conduct, and he rode out alone from his town to the crusaders' camp to negotiate the terms of surrender. But there was no negotiation. He was put in chains and later "manacled to the wall of his own dungeon," where "three months later, the once healthy Trancavel was found dead" (PH 100–101). The people of Carcassone were allowed to leave, provided they left all their goods behind. The town and their goods became the property of Montfort, who also succeeded Trancavel as ruler. Amaury, for his part, faithfully followed the pope's advice when, in contravention of the established rules of war, he violated the promise of safe-conduct, using "cunning and deception as weapons, for . . . deceit is no more than prudence" (AC 81). The town of Bram came next. The people of the nearest town learned Bram's fate from "a stumbling procession of about 100 men in single file. . . . The exhausted, whimpering men were Bram's defeated defenders; each trudged . . . with his face downcast, an arm outstretched to touch the shoulder of the man ahead in line. . . . The men have been blinded, their eyes gouged out by the wrathful victors. . . . Each man's nose and upper lip had been sliced off. . . . Their leader . . . had been left one eye to guide his companions" (PH 106). The crusaders were truly imbued with the "godly rage to avenge the insult done to the Lord" (AC 77) that the pope had encouraged them to vent. Just so that there would be no ambiguity about it, the pope renewed the call for the crusade every year (PH 109).

Many of the Cathar Perfects took refuge in the fortress of Minerva. It was taken by Montfort in 1210. He offered the Perfects a choice between dying and renouncing their beliefs. Of the 140 Perfects, three chose to live. The rest were "tied to stakes planted in great piles of wood and kindling. The fire was lit." A chronicler sympathetic to the crusade says that "afterwards their bodies were thrown out and mud shoveled over them so that no stench from these foul things could annoy our foreign forces" (PH 116).

In 1211 Montfort laid siege to the town of Lavaur. He was again successful. "The 80 knights who had commanded the defense . . . were all hanged, in an egregious flouting of the rules of warfare," as was Aimery, who led them. But that was only the beginning. Geralda, Aimery's sister, was "thrown down a well, then stoned to death," an act that "even by the standards of the day . . . was shocking." Furthermore, Montfort and Amaury "found 400 Perfects in Lavaur. As . . . Te Deum [was sung], the Cathars were . . . burned, in the largest bonfire of humanity in the Middle Ages" (PH 130–31).

The last mass murder of Cathars took place in 1244. The fortress of Montsegur surrendered, and the two hundred Cathar Perfects sheltered there were given two weeks to renounce their beliefs or be burned. Not one chose renunciation. All died in the fire that was lit to defend the faith against these harmless people whose belief in the material world being evil was so well confirmed by the church.

After this the military campaign slowly came to an end, but the extermination of the Cathars did not. The pope entrusted the persecution of suspected heretics to the newly founded order of Dominican friars (one of whose renowned members was Aquinas). The following is an example of how they proceeded. An old woman, suspected of being a Cathar, lay dying. Her traitorous servant summoned the Dominican bishop of the town, who, pretending to be a Cathar Perfect, elicited from the dying woman a profession of her Cathar beliefs. Then he revealed his true identity, pronounced the woman an unrepentant heretic, had her lashed to her bed since she was too feeble to move on her own, and ordered that she be thrown into the flames he had lit. A Dominican eyewitness notes: "This done, the bishop, together with monks . . . returned to the refectory and, after giving thanks to God and St. Dominic, fell cheerfully upon the food set before them" (PH 192–93). The Dominicans were later put in charge of the Inquisition, which began just about this time, but by then they were concentrating on other targets, since very few suspected Cathars were known to be left. The Albigensian Crusade thus achieved its purpose, and so did the French king, since from then on Languedoc has been a department of France.

2.2 Possible Excuses

If evil is serious, excessive, malevolent, and morally inexcusable harm caused by human beings to other human beings, then what was done to the Cathars was evil. Obviously, however, none of the crusaders thought so. They seem to have believed sincerely that what they did or arranged to have done was good, not evil. We need to understand what was behind this belief. No reasonable person can deny that the crusaders caused serious, excessive, malevolent harm to others. But that may be excused—as just punishment, self-defense, or the prevention of even greater harm—and perhaps this was the belief that motivated the persecutors of the Cathars. So the question whether what was done was good or evil turns on the question whether it was excusable on moral grounds. What could be the excuse for the torture, mutilation, and mass murder that was done?

One possibility is to appeal to the Bible and cite from it passages such as the following: "If thou shalt hear say in one of thy cities . . . Let us go and serve other gods . . . Then shalt thou enquire and make search, and ask diligently; and, behold, if it be truth, and the thing certain, that such abomination is wrought among you; Thou shalt surely smite the inhabitants of that city with the edge of the sword, destroying it utterly, and all that is therein. . . . And then thou shalt . . . burn with fire the city, and all the spoils thereof."[5]

The problems facing such an appeal are formidable. Assuming for the moment that biblical passages are justifiably regarded as authoritative, it is an easy matter to find many passages, especially in the New Testament, which Christians favor, that speak of loving one's neighbors, forgiving trespasses, turning the other cheek, leaving punishment to God, and so forth. Furthermore, even if the Cathars worshiped other gods, the crusaders murdered thousands of Catholics (remember "Kill them all, God will know his own"), many of whom did not even aid the Cathars but were merely family members of those who did. Nor did the crusaders burn "all the spoils thereof." They burned the owners of the spoils and enriched themselves at their expense, as marauding armies tend to do.

Another attempt at finding an excuse is to claim that the Cathar heresy and the Albigensian Crusade must be understood in their larger theological and historical context. If that is done, the actions of the religious and secular hierarchy will be seen as forces for the good, not evil. We are fortunate in having Southern's justly admired account of the relevant context, and I shall rely on it in what follows.[6]

Southern says about the early Middle Ages that "all agreed that a universal coercive power resided in the church. . . . The purpose of human government was to direct men into a single Christian path. There was no liberalism in the Middle Ages. . . . Everyone thought that coercion should be used as long as it was likely to succeed, and that it should be used to promote the doctrine and discipline of orthodox Christianity. In directing men along this road the church was the sole legitimate source of coercive power" (WSC 21–22). It is, of course, one thing to lay claim to the prerogative of coercion and quite another to have it generally acknowledged. But it was so acknowledged, and we need to understand why powerful monarchs who commanded large forces and great wealth acknowledged it. The reason was that "the church was much more than the source of coercive power. . . . It was the ark of salvation in a sea of destruction. . . . It was membership of the church that gave men a thoroughly intelligible purpose and place in God's universe. So the church was not only *a* state; it was *the* state; it was not only *a* society, it was *the* society. . . . Not only all political activity, but all learning and thought were functions of the church . . . and it turned them into instruments of human well-being in this world. To all this it added the gift of salvation . . . the final and exclusive possession of its members. . . . It was the society of rational and redeemed mankind" (WSC 22). So the church was not one institution among others. It was the framework in which institutions could exist, intellectual life could go on, and salvation could be received. To question the church in the early Middle Ages was to endanger the possibility of civilized life. That is why the prerogatives of the church were acknowledged even by those who had the power to oppose it.

What these prerogatives were was spelled out by Gregory VII, who was pope from 1073 to 1085. We find among them: "the pope can be judged by no one; the Roman church has never erred and never will err till the end of time; the Roman church was founded by Christ alone; the pope alone . . . can revise his own judgements . . . he can depose emperors" (WSC 102). It was recognized, of course, that these amazing claims had to have a basis. Innocent III, who, it will be remembered, launched and directed the Albigensian Crusade, expressed the basis: "We are the successor of the Prince of Apostles [i.e., Peter], but we are not his vicar, nor the vicar of any man or Apostle, but the vicar of Jesus Christ himself" (WSC 105). The popes "were deputies of Christ in all the fullness of His power" (WSC 105), and that was the basis of their claim to absolute authority, coercive power, and indefeasible judgment.

The excuse for the Albigensian Crusade, then, may be said to follow from the historical and theological claims that have just been sketched. The theologically based claim is that the crusade was called for by Innocent III, and he, being pope, could be "judged by no one." He spoke for the church, and he, like other popes, "has never erred and never will err" because he is the vicar of Jesus, who is the son of God and, given the Trinity, God himself. God is omniscient and good, and that is why his vicar could neither err nor do evil. If the crusaders seem to have caused evil, it can only be the result of an imperfect understanding of divine providence.

The historically based claim is that the heresy of Catharism was an attack on the church. The defense of the church and the extirpation of Catharism were justified, quite independently of theological considerations, because they safeguarded civilized life, on which everyone's well-being depended. The alternative was a relapse into barbarism: anarchy and lawlessness. The joint forces of these theological and historical considerations, then, may be offered as the excuse for the Albigensian Crusade.

This attempt at excusing it, however, is a dismal failure. Take the historical considerations first. Let us grant, if only for the sake of argument, the questionable claims that civilized life then depended on the church, that the only alternative to maintaining the church's authority was barbarism, and that Catharism was an attack on the church. There is an enormous gap between granting these dubious claims and excusing what was done. There was no need to murder the Cathars, nor their faithful Catholic supporters, and certainly not the families of the supporters, who often had no idea of what was going on. These people could have been resettled and scattered, or imprisoned, or sent to the galleys, or pressed into fighting forces—as was done to countless criminals and other people regarded as undesirable. If the Cathars had to be murdered because, say, they were keen to martyr themselves, that still left inexcusable the murder of those who sheltered them and, even more inexcusable, the murder of the family members of those who sheltered them. If all these people had to be murdered, there was no need to do it with as great cruelty as it was done. Burning people alive is an extremely painful way of killing them, and many were also tortured and mutilated before they were murdered. Nor should it pass notice that the pope, who could neither err nor be judged, explicitly inflamed the worst passions of the crusaders and instructed them to use cunning and deception, and thus violate the prevailing conventions regarding promise of safe-conduct, mercy to those who surrender, and not punishing the innocent. No reasonable person could believe that such excessive and malevolent actions were required for the defense of civilized life.

The theological considerations adduced by way of excuse may bear a superficial resemblance to reasons, but should not be mistaken for the genuine article. For they merely state some basic beliefs of Catholicism, but do not provide reasons for accepting any of them. *If* the popes are the vicars of Jesus, *if* Jesus is the son of God, *if* the Trinity accurately depicts the relation between father and son, *if* God exists, and *if* God is omniscient and good, then perhaps the popes cannot err or do evil. But unless these hypothetical claims are justified, they provide no excuse whatsoever for the great evil that the crusaders have done.

2.3 Appeal to Faith

It may be said that this attempt to find a morally acceptable excuse is misdirected because it looks for reasons, whereas the excuse for the Albigensian Crusade rests on faith. This brings us to the central concern of this chapter: the relation between evil and faith. In order to proceed, we need to be clear about what is meant by faith. The ordinary sense of the word is so vague as to be virtually useless. Many who appeal to faith use the word in a precise and technical sense, and that is what we need now to understand. For this I turn to the article on faith in the most recent edition of the *Catholic Encyclopedia;* subsequent references are to this source.[7]

Following Aquinas, faith is defined as "the act of intellect assenting to a Divine truth owing to the movement of the will, which is itself moved by the *grace of God.*" Each component of this definition requires explanation. To begin with, faith is an act of intellect, so the stark opposition between faith and reason is mistaken. Faith involves reason, but goes beyond what is vouchsafed by reason. But it goes beyond it in a specific direction: toward truths having to do with God, not other things. There may be attempts to go beyond reason concerning matters other than God, but faith, in its precise and technical sense, has nothing to do with them. Faith must move beyond reason because, as a result of the limitations of the human intellect, many truths having to do with God appear incomprehensible. Faith is "the assent of the intellect to a truth which is beyond its comprehension."

Second, in order to accept these intellectually incomprehensible truths about God, one must make an act of will. One must will to believe that about God which is beyond one's comprehension. But the connection between will and belief is not direct. Not even if a great enough effort is made will belief follow because incomprehension stands in the way. Reason and will can create only receptivity to truths about God, but they are, in themselves, insufficient for accepting these truths. Grace is needed to bridge the remaining gap. Grace brings the intellect from incomprehension to belief by supplementing the will so that incomprehension can be surmounted. Grace does not depend on anything human beings can do, however. It is a "supernatural and an absolutely gratuitous gift." The most one can do is to make oneself ready for it, then "ask and ye shall receive."

Why should one attempt to have faith? Aquinas' answer is: "The disposition of a believer is that of one who accepts another's word for some statement, because it seems fitting or useful to do so. In the same way we believe Divine revelation because the reward of eternal life is promised us for so doing. It is the will which is moved by the prospect of this reward to assent to what is said, even though the intellect is not moved by something which it understands." If what we come to believe is the result of divine revelation, then we have a "form of knowledge which . . . begets absolute certitude in the mind of the recipient." This certainty is warranted, the Vatican Council says, because "we believe that revelation is true, not indeed because the intrinsic truth of the mysteries is clearly seen by the natural light of reason, but because of the authority of *God* Who reveals them, for He can neither deceive nor be deceived."

Let us now return to the basic beliefs listed at the end of the preceding section: God exists, he is omniscient and good, the Trinity describes the relation between Jesus and God, and the popes are the vicars of Jesus. I argued that these beliefs themselves need to be justified if the excuse for the Albigensian Crusade is to be based on them. It may be said now that their justification is faith, which entitles one to hold these beliefs with absolute certainty. Those who doubt them are deficient in intellect or will, or they have not received grace. Doubting thus says something about the doubter, not about the truth of the doubted beliefs. But if faith attests to the truth of these beliefs, and if doubt can cast no aspersion on them, then the Albigensian Crusade must have been good, not evil. For it was directed by the pope, the vicar of Jesus, and thus by the omniscient and good God, who can do no evil.

The question now arises how to reconcile this with torturing, mutilating, and murdering thousands of people, expropriating the property of Cathars and Catholics, burning dying old women, throwing women down wells, blinding people and cutting off their noses and upper lips, putting children and the aged to the sword, and with the hate, deception, and merciless persecution that the pope explicitly called for. There are a number of ways in which the reconciliation may be attempted, but each has unacceptable consequences.

One possible attempt is to say that the goodness of the Albigensian Crusade, contrary to appearances, is just one of those mysteries that are incomprehensible to the human intellect. God ordained the crusade with all that it entailed, so it must have been good. This is unacceptable because Christianity is meant to be a guide to good conduct. But if what seems to be obviously evil must be regarded as good, such as mutilation, torture, and murder, then it fails as a guide because it becomes an incomprehensible mystery what good and evil are. It makes matters even worse that the horrors of the crusade clearly violate explicit moral injunctions laid down in the Bible. In the light of the history of Christianity, it is embarrassing to mention that "Thou shalt not kill" is one of the Ten Commandments,[8] but perhaps the Sermon on the Mount may carry more weight. Jesus says, for instance, "Blessed are those who are persecuted for righteousness' sake"; "I say to you, Do not resist one who is evil"; "forgive men their trespasses"; and "judge not, that you be not judged."[9] If these injunctions apply to the Cathars, then their mutilation, torture, and murder by the crusaders cannot be good. If, on the other hand, the acts of the crusaders are good, then these biblical injunctions cannot hold. In either case, something vouchsafed by faith must be rejected. But then faith cannot be free of doubt and cannot provide even moderate certainty, let alone the absolute one that is claimed for it.

Another attempt to exclude evil from faith is to deny that what guided the pope and the crusaders was genuine faith. If it had been genuine, the actions prompted by it would have been good, but since the actions were evil, the faith must have been spurious. Although those who inspired and committed the horrible acts believed that they were guided by faith, they were mistaken. What they took to be faith was something else, and that is why they inflicted the great evils on the Cathars and others.

This second attempt, unlike the first, has the virtue of psychological plausibility. Human beings often misinterpret their own motives. History, literature, and everyday life provide countless examples in which people take their morally deplorable motives to be morally praiseworthy, proceed to act on them, and end up doing evil, which they do not recognize as such. Their actions are selfish, cruel, or cowardly, but they seem to them to be fair, just, or prudent. This is what may have happened to those involved in the crusades. The papacy was facing numerous challenges during the reign of Innocent III. The Muslims were threatening from Spain, the dispute between the Greek and Roman churches was disrupting Christendom, rulers in Europe were struggling with the church for supremacy in secular matters, and canon law was far from having been systematized. Innocent III sought to assert the authority of the church on every possible occasion. This may have motivated him in launching and directing the Albigensian Crusade. The priests he had put in charge of it may have been similarly motivated, but even if they were not, obedience to the pope would have prompted their actions. The king of France and other secular princes pursued their political aims, to which the financial inducements promised by the pope were important means. And the knights and their retinues who actually did the deeds were moved by fealty to their princes, the invective of their priests, and the prospect of bounty. The crusade was aimed to enhance the power and wealth of the ecclesiastical and secular participants, but what the crusaders told themselves and others was that they were motivated by faith. In all this the unfortunate Cathars were merely the means the crusaders used to achieve their aims. If the crusaders had been motivated by genuine faith, it may be said, they would not have caused great evil. But they did cause it because they sought power and wealth. They, perhaps sincerely, misinterpreted their own motives as faith. It was, however, spurious, not genuine, faith.

No evidence is available that would conclusively prove or disprove this account. If, however, it, or something like it, were true, it would acquit genuine faith from the charge that it may lead to evil. But the acquittal would extract the unacceptable cost of destroying the certainty faith is supposed to yield. For human beings could not be certain whether it is genuine or spurious faith by which they seem to be motivated. The misinterpretation of their own motives is an ever-present danger. They could be entitled to certainty only if they had eliminated that possibility, but given human weakness and fallibility—a Christian might say original sin—the possibility cannot be eliminated. Doubt, therefore, is the appropriate response to all claims of faith, including one's own. The feeling of certainty guarantees nothing, for it may be spurious as well. And when faith calls for torture, mutilation, and murder, doubt ought to replace certainty.

The last attempt to make faith immune to evil I shall consider is to reject the account of faith we have been examining. Faith, then, may be acknowledged to have great importance in the lives of many people, but it is not supposed to have decisive authority or carry certainty. Faith goes beyond beliefs the intellect can support. It involves acts of will by which intellectually unsupported, or insufficiently supported, beliefs may come to be accepted. These beliefs may be about some supernaturally grounded hope that ultimately all manner of things will be well, but the supernatural component is not essential to this understanding of faith, even if it is typically present. The ground of hope may be held to be luck, human perfectibility, the natural goodness of evolution, or the immanent purpose of the universe.

Whatever credibility this kind of faith may have, it is clearly not immune to evil. For appeals to it suffer both from the same liability to misinterpretation as the kind of faith it is intended to replace and from a problem specific to itself. The genuineness of faith is as much open to doubt if it is supposed to yield intellectually unwarranted hope as when it is supposed to yield certainty. Human beings are liable to misinterpret their motives regardless of how faith is understood. They may end up doing evil, while believing it to be good, on one understanding as on another. The difficulty comes not from how faith is understood but from human vice and fallibility that may lead faith astray. The specific problem with this kind of faith is that it is merely one motive among others. Faith, reason, love, loyalty, self-interest, greed, cruelty, and so on may compete and move people in quite different directions. There is nothing in this kind of faith that would make it a more powerful motive than the others. Even if faith were to prompt good rather than evil actions, the actions may not be performed because faith may be overwhelmed by other motives.

It follows from the failure of these attempts to exclude evil from faith that actions prompted by faith can easily turn out to be evil. Faith is therefore morally unacceptable as an excuse for evil actions. It exacerbates the difficulty that, given vice and fallibility, human beings often misinterpret their motives, take for faith what is not, and do evil while believing it to be good. I shall now argue that all kinds of faith are liable to this threat because they go beyond reason.

2.4 The Permanent Threat of Faith

Consider such common human motives as love, duty, habit, guilt, pleasure, fear, promise, commitment, competitiveness, and jealousy. Each is a complex mixture of beliefs, feelings, recollected experiences, and imagined future. Each can go wrong through its constituent elements. The beliefs may be false, the feelings excessive, the recollections mistaken, and the imaginings fantasies. Each prompts actions. It may be better not to heed its promptings, however, not just because one or another of its constituent elements is suspect, but also because the motive may be at variance with one's conception of oneself, the action may be dangerous, immoral, or embarrassing to oneself or others, or there may be a stronger motive that prompts a different or an incompatible action.

People can examine their motives and eliminate these flaws. Those who are reflective do it habitually, others more sporadically. Self-examination is prudent because how well life goes for one to a large extent depends on acting appropriately on unflawed motives. There is, of course, no guarantee that examined motives will be flawless. But examination makes flaws less likely, and unexamined motives often lead to stupid, self-destructive, or immoral actions, which are regretted after the fact.

The vehicle of self-examination is reason. One employs it to scrutinize one's motives for consistency with other motives, effectiveness in leading to desired immediate or long-range goals, conformity to one's values, and likelihood of success in the light of past experiences and present circumstances. If a motive fails these tests, reason provides a powerful impetus against acting on it. The employment of reason is not foolproof, and even when it yields reliable results, they may not be acted on. People often are unreasonable, or less reasonable than self-interest dictates, or reasonable and mistaken. Nevertheless, it is better to be as reasonable as possible about one's motives and actions because the well-being of oneself and others affected by one's actions depends on it.

The permanent threat of faith is that faith, by its very nature, goes beyond reason and thus makes self-examination impossible. For the essence of faith is that it requires an effort of will to accept what to reason appears unacceptable. If what is accepted were not unacceptable to reason, there would be no need to make an effort of will and accept it on faith. Thus there is a crucially important difference between common human motives and faith as a motive. The difference is that common human motives lend themselves to examination by reason, whereas faith does not. Consequently, common human motives can be corrected if they go wrong, but faith cannot be. And faith can go wrong because what is believed to be genuine faith may be spurious, and because when people suppose themselves to be motivated by faith, they may in fact be motivated by something else. The corrosive effects of vice and fallibility cannot be excluded from human motivation, and faith is as liable to them as other motives. In the case of other motives, however, reason can safeguard against this liability, but in the case of faith it cannot because faith would not be faith if it did not go beyond reason. The permanent threat of faith, therefore, is that it may be led astray by vice and fallibility and prompt evil actions. The discussion of the Albigensian Crusade was intended to make this general point concrete.

In order to avoid misunderstanding, I want to emphasize that although the argument has concentrated on Catholic faith, its target is not Catholicism specifically but reliance on faith generally. A long tradition enables defenders of Catholicism to be more articulate about the theological implications of their faith than others tend to be, and that is why the argument focused on them. But the argument is meant to apply to all forms of religious faith, as well as to secular faith, be it political, humanistic, evolutionary, or progressive. The argument is not that faith leads to evil. The argument is that faith may lead to evil and it lacks the resources to avoid its threat. I readily acknowledge that faith may also lead to the good. Nor is the argument that the employment of reason guarantees that evil will be avoided. There is no such guarantee. The argument is that the employment of reason may control one source of evil. Evil also has other sources, and reason can be put to evil uses.

The permanent threat of faith, however, is not merely that it may lead to evil but that it often does. Even a casual survey of history reveals countless occasions when Jews, Catholics, Protestants, and Muslims waged war against other faiths; when they stigmatized, persecuted, forcibly converted people for being heretics, atheists, infidels, witches, possessed by the Devil, or guilty of such abominable sins as extramarital sex, homosexuality, casting a spell, causing a plague, failing to attend church, eating or drinking what is forbidden, or worshiping other than the one true God in other than the one true way. In such wars and for such offenses millions were tortured, mutilated, or murdered. The moral justification offered for inflicting these grievous harms was faith. The simple requirements of ordinary morality were again and again violated in the name of what the faith deemed to be higher. These violations were not aberrations of faith caused by the sleep of reason, but one of the tendencies that result from the very nature of faith.

We may approach this tendency by way of Kierkegaard's reflection on the biblical story in which Abraham feels called upon to sacrifice his son to God. Kierkegaard speaks of the teleological suspension of the ethical. Murder, of course, is ordinarily wrong. But murder in the name of what is higher may be justified. As Kierkegaard puts it about Abraham: "he overstepped the ethical entirely and possessed a higher telos outside of it, in relation to which he suspended the former."[10] This appeal to the higher in order to exempt one's actions from the requirements of ordinary morality is the evil-producing tendency that results from the nature of faith and exacerbates its permanent threat.

Religious and most other forms of faith are committed to the belief that beyond the messy appearances of the observable physical world there is an order that permeates reality. This order is good, and human lives are good to the extent to which they are lived in conformity to it. Some people know the nature and goodness of this order either because it has been revealed to them, or because they have studied some canonical text, or because they possess exceptional insight. Such people are the authorities on how human beings should live. They wield their authority for everyone's benefit because they teach people that it is in their best interest to live in conformity to the order whose nature the authorities know and those subject to them fail to know. Most people, left to their own dim light, do not know where their true interests lie. As a result, they live miserable lives, often without realizing it.

The duty the authorities acquire by their possession of superior knowledge is to make people live as their true interests dictate, that is, to make them live in the way they would live if they knew what the authorities know and they do not. The authorities thus teach when they can and coerce when they must the great mass of humanity in the name of the good. This good is what is higher and to what ordinary morality must be subordinated. For insofar as ordinary morality deviates from the higher, it deviates from the good, and that must be an error. The authorities, of course, are authorities because they know what the higher good requires and what deviates from it.[11]

Individual deviations may be willful or ignorant, but they rarely endanger the faith itself. The organized, systematic deviations of alternative faiths, however, present a fundamental challenge to the faith because they constitute a total, not a piecemeal, rejection of the higher good. And that must be opposed by all the force the authorities can muster. Thus we get the religious wars and persecutions of unbelievers that fill history with outrage after outrage, all committed in the name of the higher good by people who see themselves as benefactors of humanity. And when these people are called to account, they appeal, by way of moral justification, to the supposed knowledge to which they claim to have privileged access and of which critics and doubters are said to be ignorant. But there can be no moral justification for much that defenders of various faiths have done. For a justification can be moral only if it meets a condition, which these attempts fail to do.

Although there are legitimate disagreements about the nature, content, and purpose of morality, no reasonable person can doubt that morality at the very least must protect the minimum conditions of human well-being. There are also legitimate disagreements about what human well-being is or might be, but no reasonable person can deny that there are some minimum requirements in the absence of which well-being is impossible. Among these requirements are protection from physical harms that make it impossible or extremely hard for anyone to function normally, such as murder, mutilation, and torture. There may be disagreements, of course, about borderline cases and gray areas, but there are countless clear cases that leave no room for serious dispute. Murder for fun or profit, torture or mutilation out of curiosity harm their victims. Since morality is committed to protecting the minimum requirements of good lives, it must prohibit simple harms. I shall call this the requirement of elementary decency.[12] It allows justifiable exceptions, so it is not absolute. The infliction of simple harm may be excused, for instance, if it is deserved punishment, self-defense, or the only way of coping with some extreme situation. But claiming an exception must be justified on moral grounds by those who claim it. They must explain why an act that morality ordinarily prohibits is allowed in the particular case at hand. If this condition is met, the infliction of simple harm is excusable. If it is not met, it is inexcusable and evil, and a violation of elementary decency.

The attempts to excuse the simple harms inflicted over the centuries in the name of a higher good fail to meet this condition because they ultimately appeal to faith to justify the violation of elementary decency. But faith could provide what is needed only if it could be shown that it was genuine, not spurious. This, however, cannot be shown because the very nature of faith precludes it. In the first place, there is no public test available that would show the reliability of the knowledge of a higher good that faith is supposed to provide. The vast majority of people, said by the faithful to lack this knowledge, obviously cannot attest to its reliability. Representatives of different faiths who claim to have the knowledge deny that what the others claim to have is knowledge. And those who share the same faith often disagree with each other about what the knowledge they suppose themselves to have really reveals. The persistence of theological disputes about the Trinity, grace, salvation, the reality of Hell, the interpretation of biblical passages, and so forth shows that some who claim to have knowledge of a higher good are mistaken. But there is no way of telling who those are.

It might be said that even if there is no public test by which the reliability of the supposed knowledge of a higher good could be determined, there is the private experience of absolute certainty. Such experiences, however, cannot guarantee their own authenticity. The absolute certainty that people with incompatible faiths have shows that absolute certainty can be misplaced. The certainty with which the Cathars chose to be burned alive was no less absolute than the certainty of the priests who had them burned. Furthermore, loss of faith, conversion, and contrary experiences are standard features of human psychology. They often lead people to doubt what they previously regarded as absolutely certain. Lastly, those who take seriously their own intellectual and moral weaknesses, the dangers of self-deception, and the temptations of seeing themselves as one of the privileged elect will regard their own certainties with suspicion, and if they do not, they should.

To appeal to a higher good as the moral justification for violating the requirements of elementary decency is thus to appeal to a supposed knowledge whose reliability cannot be ascertained and whose claim to being knowledge is open to serious doubt. But this is only half of the case against the simple harms inflicted in the name of a higher good. The other half is the undeniable reality of the suffering of the victims: the mangled bodies of the tortured, mutilated, and murdered; the spilt blood, gore, cries, cut-off limbs, slit throats, hanging entrails of the men, women, and children whose offense is to have held a faith different from their tormentors.' If one combines the uncertainty of the knowledge of a higher good in the name of which these horrors are inflicted with the undeniable experience of the victims' agony, the case against violating the requirements of elementary decency must be seen as overwhelming. The permanent threat of faith is that it leads many people to reject this case.

2.5 Faith and Evil

Evil has causes other than faith, and faith leads not just to evil but also to good, indifferent, or merely bad actions. Nevertheless, when faith is held under certain conditions, it leads to evil. One of these conditions is that the faith is believed to be threatened either from the outside by the incompatible conceptions of the higher good of other faiths or from the inside by disagreements about the higher good that is supposed to be known within the faith. These threats are bound to appear to the faithful as extremely serious for two reasons. One is that they are seen as attacks against the very possibility of human well-being, and thus against morality itself. Since the nature of faith precludes appeal to reason by which disputes about the putative higher good could be settled, the disputes will persist and elicit increasingly shriller responses.

The second reason why the faithful find attacks on their conception of the higher good very serious leads to another condition under which faith tends to prompt evil actions. Faith, religious or secular, is likely to have a central place in how the faithful see themselves, in how they endow the scheme of things and their lives and actions with meaning.

Their whole system of values rests on their faith. Attacks on their faith are thus seen as threats to their identity, to what they most deeply value, to what makes life and their lives meaningful. It would be hard to imagine a more serious attack than this. It is, therefore, bound to engage their strongest feelings and prompt them to rise to a passionate defense of their faith. Attacks on it seem wicked to them, not just ordinary moral failings, because they undermine the very possibility of what makes life worth living. No wonder that their reactions to those they see as the wicked attackers is passionate hatred, which unsurprisingly motivates their excesses and malevolence. But they do not see their actions as excessive and malevolent. They see them as righteous responses to evil. And what makes them misperceive the true moral quality of their actions is the imperviousness of their faith to the moderating influence of reason.

This points to the third condition that makes faith prone to evil. Defenders of the faith are fallible and predisposed to act on such vices as selfishness, greed, cruelty, envy, aggression, and so forth. No one is exempt from these intellectual and moral liabilities, for they are part of the human condition, and thus the condition of the adherents of all faiths. This does not make all beliefs and actions irremediably tainted, but it makes them liable to go wrong in these ways. One task of reason is to prevent that from happening. The attempt is necessary for human well-being, but it may fail, which is one cause of human misery. This use of reason, however, is unavailable to the faithful in the case of beliefs and actions connected with the higher good because the higher good is supposed by them to be beyond reason. The result is that human fallibility and predisposition to vice are left unchecked. In the favorable circumstances created by external and internal threats they are likely to be acted on because the control of reason is removed from their way, and because external and internal threats challenge all faiths and provoke the faithful's responses.

Given these conditions, the joint forces of the supposed knowledge of a higher good on which the possibility of human well-being is believed to depend, threats to the faith, uncontrolled predisposition to vice, and uncorrected fallibility are likely to lead defenders of the besieged faith to evil actions that violate elementary decency. The destruction of the Cathars illustrates why and how this happens. That similar misfortune befell many other persecuted groups is one lesson that emerges from the lamentable history of faiths. It teaches us that the sleep of reason brings forth monsters.

CHAPTER 3

Perilous Dreams

There are political and social fantasists who with fiery eloquence invite a revolutionary overturning of all social orders in the belief that the proudest temple of fair humanity will then at once rise up as though of its own accord. In these perilous dreams there is still an echo of Rousseau's superstition, which believes in a miraculous primeval but as it were *buried* goodness of human nature and ascribes all blame for this burying to the institutions of culture in the form of society, state and education. The experiences of history have taught us, unfortunately, that every such revolution brings about the resurrection of the most savage energies in the shape of . . . dreadfulness and excesses.

—FRIEDRICH NIETZSCHE, *Human, All Too Human*

The preceding chapter dealt with the pitfalls of faith. Given human fallibility and predisposition to vices, we should take great pains to examine our motives, especially when they prompt actions that cause serious harm to others. In other words, we should test our motives by reason. This, of course, is not to say that reason is exempt from fallibility or that vices could not lead to the abuse of reason. The aim of this chapter is to show how reliance on reason can go terribly wrong and lead to evil no less than does reliance on faith.

3.1 Background

Historians customarily distinguish between phases of the 1789 Revolution in France. The last phase, the Terror, ran roughly during 1793–94. It began with the fall of the Gironde and the Jacobins' acquisition of power. By the standards of the Revolution, the Girondin were moderate and the Jacobins radical. But, like everything about the Revolution, this statement needs to be qualified because the Jacobins themselves were divided into moderate, centrist, and radical factions. The moderates were led by Danton, the radicals by Hebert, and the centrists by Robespierre. As the Jacobins were coming into power, the disputes between their factions became polarized. Robespierre's faction eventually prevailed. After an interregnum during which Robespierre shared power with other Jacobins, he became dictator and the Terror started in earnest. It took the form of the arrest, show trial, and execution of thousands of people, including the Girondin, Danton, Hebert, and their followers, who were suspected of opposing—actively or passively, actually or potentially—the policies of Robespierre. The Terror thus consisted in the execution, mostly by guillotine but also by lynching and worse, many thousands of people for no other reason than that they favored or might come to favor policies different from those dictated by Robespierre.

The aim of the Revolution was said by the revolutionaries to be the replacement of the prevailing corrupt absolute monarchy with a regime that secured the ideals of liberty, equality, and fraternity. The revolutionaries were fundamentally divided among themselves about the interpretation of these ideals and about the nature of the regime that would have the best chance of securing them. It had also emerged in the course of the Revolution that the cost of pursuing liberty and equality had to be paid for by the loss of fraternity, so after a while the third member of this secular trinity was dropped from the rhetoric.

The power all revolutionaries sought was the power of legislation. The legislative forum was the Convention, whose members were elected from every department of France. Power over France required control of the Convention. When the Jacobins achieved it, they did so by means of a committee, the Committee of Public Safety. Robespierre acquired power by acquiring control of this committee.

Each revolutionary faction had a constituency that supported it. The Jacobins' constituency was the mob, roaming the streets of Paris, the center of the Revolution. Large parts of France were hardly involved. The revolutionary changes spread from the center to the periphery slowly, unevenly, and many of them were unwelcome. The population of Paris was about 650,000. Most of their lives had gone on during the Revolution much as before. About 5 percent of the population was destitute, maintaining itself by a mixture of crime, prostitution, begging, and odd jobs. These people were the sans-culottes, and they largely composed the mob. The radical Jacobin faction incited them to action whenever political expediency called for it. But even when unincited—having nothing better to do—they formed the crowd that watched the public executions, jeered and abused those about to die, rejoiced at the severed heads, adulated the leaders temporarily in power, and cursed them after they fell. Like flies, they were ever present as the Revolution went on its bloody way. The noise of their enraged, expectant buzzing formed the ghastly background of the slaughter of the innocents. They were the people whom the Jacobins had some claim to be representing.

In 1794 Robespierre lost power and was himself executed. The Terror dragged on for a short while, then petered out, and was eventually replaced by Napoleon, whose victims were in the multiples of hundreds of thousands, including soldiers and civilians from all over Europe and to a lesser extent elsewhere. Thus ended the revolution of liberty, equality, and fraternity. It destroyed much and changed little.

3.2 The Terror

Historical distance and revolutionary rhetoric must not be allowed to obscure the horrible savagery of the Terror. Understanding the evil that was done depends on making it concrete. The descriptions that follow are only a few among many that could be given. After the fall of the Girondin and their "arrest" by the mob the Jacobins incited, the mob was further inflamed by them. This led to the September massacres of 1792. "The bloody work went on for five . . . days and nights. On the morning of the third, the prison of La Force was entered and here took place the murder of the Princesse de Lamballe. . . . The frenzy of the crazed and drunken murderers appears to have reached its highest pitch at La Force. Cannibalism, disembowelment and acts of indescribable ferocity took place here. The Princess . . . refused to swear her hatred of the King and Queen and was duly handed over to the mob. She was dispatched with a pike thrust, her still beating heart was ripped from her body and devoured, her legs and arms were severed from her body and shot through cannon. The horrors that were then perpetrated on her disemboweled torso are indescribable. . . . It has been loosely assumed . . . that most of the other victims were, like herself, aristocrats—an assumption that for some curious reason is often supposed to mitigate these crimes. Very few victims were, in fact, of the former nobility—less than thirty out of the fifteen hundred who were killed."[1]

At this time Robespierre was not yet in full power, but he was one of the most influential persons among the Jacobins and in the Convention. His sympathetic but evenhanded biographer, considering "the degree of Robespierre's responsibility," says that the best evidence indicates that he was guilty "not merely of doing nothing to stop the massacres, not merely of condoning them as an execution of popular justice upon criminals who had escaped the law, but of trying to use them as a cloak for political assassination."[2]

In 1793 Robespierre appointed commissioners to enforce the Jacobin interpretation of the Revolution outside Paris. In the city of Lyon the guillotine was set up, but it was found to be "a messy and inconvenient way of disposing of the political garbage. . . . A number of the condemned, then, were executed in mass shootings. . . . As many as sixty prisoners were tied in a line by ropes and shot at with cannon. Those who were not killed outright by the fire were finished off with sabres, bayonets, and rifles. . . . By the time the killings . . . had finished, one thousand nine hundred and five people had met their end. They included . . . many of the Lyonais notability . . . [and] anyone who could be associated with the capacious category 'the rich,' with 'merchants' or with any tradesmen or manufacturers accused by sans-culottes."[3]

The commissioner in Nantes "supplemented the guillotine with 'vertical deportations.' . . . Holes were punched in the sides of . . . barges. . . . Prisoners were put in with their hands and feet tied and the boats were pushed into the center of the river . . . while victims helplessly watched the water rise about them. . . . Prisoners were stripped of their clothes and belongings . . . young men and women were tied naked together in the boats. Estimates of those who perished in this manner vary greatly, but there were certainly no fewer than two thousand" (Schama 789).

In "the Vendean massacre . . . every atrocity the time could imagine was meted out to the defenseless population. Women were routinely raped, children killed, both mutilated. . . . At Gonnard . . . two hundred old people, along with mothers and children, [were forced] to kneel in front of a large pit they had dug; they were then shot so as to tumble into their grave. . . . Thirty children and two women were buried alive when earth was shoveled onto the pit. . . . The exterminations practiced were . . . the logical outcome of an ideology that progressively dehumanized its adversaries. . . . Robespierre had rejoiced that 'a river of blood would now divide France from its enemies" (Schama 791–92).

In Paris, Robespierre ordered the kangaroo court, known as the Revolutionary Tribunal, to be "as active as crime itself and conclude every case within twenty-four hours." "The victims were shepherded to the courtroom in the morning and, no matter how many of them there might be, their fate was settled by no later than two in the afternoon of that same day. By three o'clock their hair had been cut, their hands bound and they were in the death carts on their way to the scaffold" (Loomis, 325–26). "Between June 10 and July 27, the day Robespierre fell, 1,366 victims perished" (Loomis 328).

"The politicians guillotined one another in order to escape the guillotine themselves, but what of the anonymous hundreds who were sent to
their deaths for no better reason than that they were 'under suspicion'?
. . . Of what possible crime against the state can the seventeen-year-old
hairdresser's apprentice Martin Alleaume have been guilty? Or the
eighty-five-year-old Jacques Bardy? Or Marie Bouchard, an eighteen-year-
old 'domestic servant'? . . . One can only stand perplexed and appalled
before the record of these indiscriminate butcheries that tossed together
nuns, soldiers, ex-nobles, workmen, servant girls and prostitutes, not to
mention the victims without number who belonged to no particular class
or category, but who seem to have been caught like sardines in the
meshes of an invisible net" (Loomis 329). "Yet all who played a role in the
drama . . . believed themselves motivated by patriotic and altruistic
impulses. All . . . were able to value their good intentions more highly
than human life. . . . There is no crime, no murder, no massacre that cannot be justified, provided it be committed in the name of an Ideal"
(Loomis 403).

A historian generally sympathetic to the Revolution notes that "the revolutionary tribunal . . . had become an undiscriminating murder
machine. . . . Imaginary . . . plots and absurd charges were everyday
events."[4] As Robespierre put it: "Let us recognize that there is a conspiracy against public liberty. . . . It derives its strength from a criminal coali-
tion . . . [that] aims at the obstruction of the *patriotes* and the *patrie*. What
is the remedy? To punish the traitors" (Hampson 294). "Robespierre took
the attitude that clemency . . . was a form of sentimental self-indulgence
that would have to be paid for in blood. In view of the desperate situation
. . . a repressive policy was inevitable" (Hampson 230). "There are only
two parties in France: the people and its enemies. We must exterminate
those miserable villains who are eternally conspiring against the rights of
man . . . we must exterminate all our enemies" (Hampson 146). The historian wondering how this came about says, "I think this is where the historian's common-sense approach breaks down; it's simply impossible to
imagine one's self in the climate of hysteria and fear in which they were
working" (Hampson 263).

The result of this climate was the "decree of the 22nd Prairal" drawn up
by Robespierre, but it "expressed in principle the views of the whole
Committee [of Public Safety]," writes the most authoritative English biographer of Robespierre, one who has no doubt about Robespierre's great-
ness (Thompson 2:194). "The Committee was fanatical enough to
approve, and the Convention powerful enough to enforce, as a New
Model of Republican justice . . . a law which denied to prisoners the help
of counsel, made it possible for the court to dispense with witnesses, and

allowed no sentence except acquittal or execution; a law which, at the same time, defined crimes against the state in such wide terms that the slightest indiscretion might bring one within the article of death. To any right-minded or merciful man such procedure must seem a travesty of justice" (Thompson 2:195).

Empowered by this model of republican justice, the Revolutionary Tribunal sent to death 1,258 people in nine weeks, as many as during the preceding fourteen months. "The inescapable fact" about Robespierre is that "under a judicial system which he initiated and helped to direct, . . . a government of which he was, perhaps, the most influential member, perpetrated the worst enormities of the Terror. Whatever reasons of policy or public danger might excuse the normal activities of the Revolutionary Tribunal, no defence is possible for the wholesale massacres . . . in which . . . at an average rate of thirty-six [persons] a day were sent to the guillotine" (Thompson 2:208). Robespierre "became as incapable of distinguishing right from wrong—not to say cruelty from humanity—as a blind man is of distinguishing night from day" (Thompson 2:209–10). Let us now try to understand the frame of mind of the person who was thus incapacitated.

3.3 The Ideologue

Maximilien Robespierre was born in 1758 in the town of Arras, which is about one hundred miles northeast of Paris, not far from the Channel. His father was a feckless lawyer, his mother the daughter of a brewer. She died in childbirth when he was six years old, leaving behind four young children. A few months after her death, his father deserted the children. Robespierre and his brother were raised by their maternal grandparents. At the age of eleven, Robespierre was given a scholarship to the University of Paris. After ten years there, he emerged with a law degree, returned to Arras, and started to practice law. In early 1789, he was elected as a representative of the Third Estate in Arras. He began as a fairly radical democrat, and as the Revolution unfolded, he became more and more radical.

Robespierre never married. He was not known to have had any love affairs. He appears to have had no interest in sex, or in money, food, the arts, nature, or indeed anything but politics. He was about five feet three inches tall, with a slight build and a small head on broad shoulders. He had "nervous spasms which occasionally twisted his neck and shoulders, and showed themselves in the clenching of his hands, the twitching of his features, and the blinking of his eye-lids." His hair was of a light chestnut color. He dressed fashionably and wore glasses, "which he was in the habit of pushing up onto his forehead . . . when he wished to look anyone in the face." "His habitual expression seemed to his friends melancholy, and his enemies arrogant; sometimes he would laugh with the immoderateness of a man who has little sense of humor; sometimes the cold look softened into a smile of ironic and rather alarming sweetness." His voice was of a shrill, rough tone. "His power as a speaker . . . lay less in the manner of his delivery, than in the seriousness of what he had to say, and the deep conviction with which he said it" (Thompson 2:273–74).

This brings us to the central question of what the deep convictions were that dominated Robespierre's frame of mind and motivated his policies and actions. Robespierre made no secret of what his convictions were. He expressed them in several crucial speeches, and records of them, written in his own hand, exist.[5] In his August 1792 speech, Robespierre said that France was living through one of the great events in human history. After an initial period of stumbling, the Revolution of 1789 became in August 1792 "the finest revolution that has ever honoured humanity, indeed the only one with an object worthy of man: to found political societies at last on the immortal principles of equality, justice and reason" (Hampson 158–59).

Two points should be noted. First, the significance of August 1792 is that it marked the establishment of the kangaroo court, the Revolutionary Tribunal, and the beginning of the Terror, as well as the incitement of the mob that led to the previously described September massacres. Second, the ideals of liberty, equality, and fraternity, supposedly justifying the 1789 Revolution, were replaced by Robespierre, without notice or explanation, by equality, justice, and reason. Liberty and fraternity have thus been subordinated to what Robespierre called justice and reason, about which more shortly.

The Revolution was the finest because for the first time in human history "the art of government" aimed not at "deceiving and corrupting man" but at "enlightening them and making them better." The task of the Revolution was "to establish the felicity of perhaps the entire human race." "The French people seems to have out-distanced the rest of the human race by two thousand years" (Hampson 159). But there was a serious obstacle in the way. "Two opposing spirits . . . [are] contending for domination . . . [and] are fighting it out in this great epoch of human history, to determine for ever the destinies of the world. France is the theatre of this terrible combat" (Hampson 158). One is the spirit of republican revolution, the other the spirit of counterrevolution. "The very spirit of the Republic is virtue, in other words love of one's country, that magnanimous devotion that sinks all private interests in the general interest. The enemies of the Republic are the cowardly egoists, the ambitious and the corrupt. You have driven out the kings, but have you driven out those vices that their fatal domination bred within you?" (Hampson 161). The conflicts between the friends and the enemies of the Revolution "are merely the struggle between private interests and the general interest, between cupidity and ambition on the one hand and justice and humanity on the other." The result was that all the political choices of the time were interpreted as choices between morality and immorality, good and evil, virtue and vice. The choices Robespierre favored were of course on the side of the angels, so his opponents could be demonized. "In the system of the French Revolution, whatever is immoral is bad politics, what corrupts is counter-revolutionary" (Hampson 160).

Many people took seriously Robespierre's moralistic demagoguery. Some did because they were afraid of his ever-increasing power, which he used to kill those who disagreed with him. Jacobins accepted it because Robespierre had articulated what they inarticulately believed: a view derived from Rousseau, to which I shall return. Others were overwhelmed by the political changes that were upsetting their lives, by the widespread chaos and uncertainty, by the blood that had already been shed, and they yearned to understand what was going on, what justified it, and what was the aim of it all. Robespierre provided an explanation, a justification, and an aim. Many people accepted them, bombast and implausibility notwithstanding, because it reassured them to have a way of making sense of what they were living through. An explanation taxing their credulity was better than no explanation.

The aim Robespierre had in mind was a society in which "the immortal principles of equality, justice and reason" prevailed. The justification of the massacres was that those killed were the enemies of the republic, counterrevolutionaries who had conspired against the aim whose achievement would "establish the felicity of perhaps the entire human race." And the explanation of the political changes and the bloodshed was that they were required for the achievement of the aim. The pivot on which all turned, therefore, was the triumvirate of equality, justice, and reason. How he understood these principles was spelled out by Robespierre in the Declaration of Rights, which formed the basis of the Constitution of 1793. The following are some extracts from it.

"Article 1. The object of every political association is to safeguard the natural and imprescriptible rights of men." "Article 3. . . . Rights belong equally to all men, whatever their physical and moral differences." "Article 4. Freedom is the right of every man to exercise all his faculties at will. Its rule is justice, its limits are the rights of others, its source is nature, its guarantee is the law." "Article 6. Any law which violates the imprescriptible rights of man is essentially unjust and tyrannical" (Thompson

2:42–43). Thus equality was to be understood as equal protection of rights, including the right to freedom; justice as the system of laws that protected these rights; and reason, presumably, as what enabled people to see how these rights were inherent in or followed from nature. These, then, were the central principles whose implementation was the aim of the Revolution. Let us now see what Robespierre actually said and did.

He said, "We must exterminate all our enemies with the law in our hands" (Hampson 146); "the Declaration of Rights offers no safeguard to conspirators" (Hampson 162); "the suspicions of enlightened patriotism might offer a better guide than formal rules of evidence" (Hampson 163); commenting on an execution, he said, "Even if he had been innocent he had to be condemned if his death could be useful" (Hampson 163); in a letter advising the Revolutionary Tribunal, he wrote, "People are always telling judges to take care to save the innocent; I tell them . . . to beware of saving the guilty" (Hampson 163); following his guidance a decree was passed: "Any person accused of conspiracy who resisted or insulted national justice was [to be] at once deprived of the right to defending himself" (Thompson 2:161); Collot, a commissioner Robespierre personally appointed, expressed succinctly their shared interpretation of the principles enshrined in the declaration: "The rights of man are made, not for counter-revolutionaries, but only for sans-culottes" (Schama 781); and Saint-Just, Robespierre's closest ally, said, "The republic consists in the extermination of everything that opposes it" (Schama 787). Robespierre and his followers did not merely voice these grotesque interpretations of the imprescriptible rights of man; they also acted on their interpretations and compelled others to do likewise. The massacres of the Terror were the consequences.

All in all, justice did not mean the protection of the imprescriptible rights of man, but the legitimation of whatever seemed to Robespierre to advance the cause of the Revolution. Equality did not mean the equal protection of the rights of all citizens, but only the rights of those of whom Robespierre approved. And reason did not mean the impartial and objective evaluation of available evidence, but following Robespierre's dicta wherever they led. Given these interpretations, of course liberty and fraternity were forced out of revolutionary rhetoric.

The inconsistency between the declaration, providing the basis of the constitutional guarantee of equal rights for all citizens, and the actual policies dictated by Robespierre and enforced by his followers was so great and blatant that it required an explanation. This Robespierre provided in a speech in December 1793. "The object of a revolutionary regime is to found a republic; that of a constitutional regime is to carry it on. The first befits a time of war between liberty and its enemies; the second suits a time when freedom is victorious, and at peace with the world." He went on to note that the current regime in France was revolutionary, struggling to become constitutional. But the successful completion of this struggle was threatened, especially by internal enemies. "Under a constitutional regime," he went on, "little is needed but to protect the individual citizen against abuse of power by the government; but under a revolutionary regime the government has to defend itself against all the factions which attack it; and in this fight for life only good citizens deserve public protection, and the punishment of the people's enemies is death" (Thompson 1:127). The revolutionary regime "must be as terrible to the wicked as it is favorable to the good" (Hampson 162). "The Declaration of Rights offers no safeguard to conspirators who have tried to destroy it" (Hampson 162). There was, therefore, no inconsistency between the declaration and the Terror. The declaration guided the constitutional regime, whose establishment was the ultimate aim. The Terror was merely the means to it, forced on the revolutionary regime by its enemies, who prevented the realization of the constitutional regime.

This piece of sophistry was then new, but to those who look back on the twentieth century it is depressingly familiar from the use made of it by numerous murderous regimes. They all claimed that their aim was human well-being, but its achievement, according to them, was threatened by incorrigibly wicked enemies who have disguised their true nature and conspired against the noblest of aims. This threat, they claimed, was so serious and the aim so important as to warrant extreme, albeit temporary, measures. Human well-being depends on identifying its enemies, unmasking their conspiracies, and exterminating them as incorrigible evildoers. To a handful of clear-sighted and courageous heroes of the revolution falls the duty to perform these necessary tasks. They must harden their hearts and do what needs to be done in the interest of the greater good. Once the grave threat is averted, the extreme measures will no longer be necessary, and then human well-being will be within everyone's reach. One of the remarkable features of the ideological frame of mind is that those in its grip actually believe these falsehoods and accept them as justification of their evil actions.

The truth is that their aim of human well-being imposes an arbitrary vision on countless unwilling recipients who have questioned and rejected it in favor of other visions, or in favor of no vision at all but rather of allowing individuals and societies to decide for themselves what their well-being might be and how they might pursue it. The distinction between revolutionary and constitutional regimes is just an excuse for violating the simple requirements of morality. The distinction does not reflect actual political realities, but indicates the revolutionaries' sense of urgency that leads them to trample on elementary decency. Their supposed enemies are often people whose only offense is reluctance to outrage reason and morality. The so-called emergency is created by the ideologues' impatience and intolerance, not by mythical conspirators bent on sabotaging human well-being. The conspiracies they are forever unmasking usually reflect their resentments and suspicions, often of rival revolutionary factions, not plots by those they single out for maltreatment. And, to return to the case at hand, even if all the falsehoods Robespierre had believed were true, they would not have begun to justify the murder of children, aged people, distant relatives of the accused, and those killed on the basis of the flimsiest unsubstantiated suspicion. Nor would they justify the excesses and malevolence involved in disemboweling, lynching, mutilating, burying alive, drowning, and hacking to pieces their unfortunate victims. None of this, however, had the slightest effect on the utter certainty with which Robespierre held his convictions and imposed his aim. We need now to understand the assumptions on which his convictions and certainty rested.

3.4 Justification by Ideology

An ideology is a coherent world view used to understand the prevailing political conditions and to suggest ways of improving them. Typical ideologies have five interdependent constituents. The first is a general view about the nature of reality. It may be derived from science, religion, history, or some combination of these and other approaches to discovering and organizing facts into a system. It is an attempt to form an objective, disinterested, dispassionate perspective, one that God might have, if there were a God. Its result is a metaphysical outlook, the view of the world *sub specie aeternitatis*. The second is a view about the nature of human beings and how their well-being is affected by the nature of reality. It is an anthropocentric outlook whose chief interest is in how human beings fit into the scheme of things. It yields a perspective *sub specie humanitatis*. The third is a system of values upon whose realization human well-being is taken to depend. It is in accordance with it that facts are evaluated, their relative importance is judged, and particular evaluations and judgments are justified or criticized. The fourth is an explanation of why the actual state of affairs falls short of what they might be if people in general were guided by the right system of values. It explains why there is so much human misery. The fifth is a set of policies intended to close, or at least to reduce, the gap between how things are and how they ought to be. It is a program for decreasing human misery and increasing human well-being. An ideology combines these constituents into a coherent whole whose parts reciprocally reinforce one another.

Moderately well educated and reasonable people ought to know that in the course of history many different and often incompatible ideologies have been held; that all the great religions, metaphysical systems, large-scale poetic or prophetic visions, and enduring cultures were animated by one or more ideologies; and that all ideologies are essentially speculative interpretations that go beyond undeniable facts and simple truths. These interpretations are fallible, involve hypotheses about matters that transcend the existing state of knowledge, and are especially prone to wishful, self-deceiving, anxious, or self-serving thinking and to unchecked flights of fantasy and imagination. Reasonable people, therefore, ought to regard ideologies, including their own, with robust skepticism and demand of them conformity to uncontroversial standards of reason.

These standards require that ideologies should be logically consistent; capable of explaining indisputable and relevant facts; responsive to new evidence and serious criticism; and willing to treat the success or failure of policies derived from them as confirming or disconfirming evidence. These are minimum standards, and although more than one ideology can meet them, not all of them will. The standards, therefore, can be used to show that some ideologies are unreasonable. This may not deter their adherents from holding them, but it ought to deter reasonable people from regarding them as acceptable guides to human well-being.

The source of Robespierre's deepest convictions and of the certainty with which he held them was his unquestioning commitment to an ideology he had largely derived from Rousseau. I shall leave aside how faithfully Robespierre followed Rousseau and how much Rousseau's ideas can be blamed for the Terror. The salient point is the content of Robespierre's ideology, which certainly owed a great deal to Rousseau, whom he regarded as "the tutor of the human race" (Hampson 184).

To begin with his metaphysical outlook, Robespierre rejected the materialism prevalent among the philosophes, and he never wavered from the conviction that there were spiritual values that were eternal verities. These values are expressed in universal, unalterable, and imprescriptible principles. The judgments of individuals ought to conform to these principles, which are moral, and apply to everyone, regardless of whether individuals recognize or abide by them. They are closely connected with God and Providence; unfortunately, Robespierre is not known to have offered a systematic account of how he understood them. He made clear, though, that he did not accept the Christian view. His idea of God was probably deistic, but he also held that God providentially interferes with human affairs (Cobban 137).

Robespierre believed that politics was an application of morality and that a good government was based on moral principles. He thought that moral principles were inherent in human nature. Uncorrupted human beings intuitively recognize and abide by them. He did not think that this makes individual human beings morally good, but he thought that individuals taken together to form a people are morally good (Cobban 137–39).

Good government, he believed, depends on there being a single sovereign will that is the source of power. This sovereign will was above all constitutional bodies, for it was the lawmaker, the source and the interpreter of justice. Thus, "the end of politics is the embodiment of morality in government, the people are good, the people's will must therefore be sovereign" (Cobban 140). In Robespierre's ideology, "the sovereignty of the people was equated with the sovereignty of the legislative assembly; . . . the sovereignty of the legislature constituted . . . the rule of law; where the rule of law prevailed . . . political liberty existed; finally, political liberty . . . was the same as liberty for the individual member of the community" (Cobban 144).

We have encountered earlier Robespierre's highly influential Declaration of Rights. In a major speech about it, he began: "Man is born for happiness and freedom, yet everywhere he is unhappy and enslaved." This, of course, is a virtual quotation of the opening sentence of Rousseau's *Social Contract*. He goes on to say that "the object of society is the preservation of his [man's] rights, and the perfecting of his nature" (Thompson 1:247). The question is how this ideal can be made real. Robespierre's answer is that it must be accomplished by legislation that expresses, as Rousseau had thought, the general will of the people. When this is done, "the law is based on the public interest, the people itself is its support, and its sanction is that of all citizens, who made it, and to whom it belongs," and then "the laws . . . are in harmony with the principles of justice, and with the general will" (Thompson 1:50).

But why should it be supposed that the general will expresses the principles of justice that protect people's rights? Because, Robespierre writes in an article paraphrasing Rousseau's *Emile*, "man is good when he comes from the hands of nature . . . if he is corrupted, this aberration must therefore be imputed to bad social institutions" (Hampson 175). There is a problem, however, because bad social institutions have corrupted people. Their actual will is not what it would be if they were in their uncorrupted, naturally good state. The actual will of the people, expressed for instance in an election, must be distinguished, therefore, from the general will. But then who could know what the general will is?

Robespierre answers: "There do exist pure and sensitive souls . . . a tender, but imperious and irresistible passion . . . a profound horror of tyranny, a compassionate zeal for the oppressed . . . a love of humanity still more holy and sublime, without which a revolution is no more that the destruction of a lesser by a greater crime. There do exist a generous ambition to found on earth the first republic . . . an enlightened egoism, which finds pleasure in the quiet of a pure conscience, and in the ravishing spectacle of public happiness . . . burning in hearts; I can feel it in my own" (Thompson 2:47). The plain message when the bombast is peeled away is Robespierre's belief that the people, having been corrupted, cannot be trusted to know what is good for them, but he, Robespierre, can be because he is uncorrupted, and that the great crimes for which he is responsible are justified because he has committed them with a pure conscience for the sake of what he knows is the public happiness. This is his justification for the Terror he unleashed and the basis of the certainty with which he held his convictions.

Robespierre's convictions, certainty, and the supposed justification of his actions derive from his ideology, whose constituents form a coherent whole. Its coherence enabled him always to know and say where he stood on particular political issues and why. This made him formidable, a forceful and persuasive speaker, and it created the impression that he was a highly principled man. The appearance, however, was deceptive. The coherence of the constituents provided no reason whatsoever for accepting the constituents in the first place. The coherence of his ideology was the coherence of fairy tales. But, unlike fairy tales, his ideology was malignant. He used it to unleash and to justify the horrors of the Terror. It is crucial to understanding Robespierre's frame of mind to recognize that his ideology had no basis in reason. Robespierre "nowhere provided an adequate theoretic justification" (Cobban 139); "these rights of man—upon what do they rest? Robespierre . . . does not arrive at them by reasoning" (Thompson 2:47).

The basis of his deep convictions was thus not reason but a strong feeling he allowed to grow into a passion and become the guide of his life. He did not ask whether he should nurture it, whether it was an appropriate reaction to the facts, whether it was too strong, or whether he should be guided by it. He made no effort to make it conform to the requirements of reason and morality because he recognized their requirements only insofar as they conformed to his passion. His passion became his standard of reason, morality, and truth. The aim of his politics was to make the world fit his passion, and he did not even try to make his passion fit the world. The predictable result was that his uncontrolled passion blinded him to the simple requirements of reason and morality and led him to cause the lynching, disemboweling, beheading, drowning, and burying alive of thousands of people simply because he suspected that they might disagree with his passionately held views. And as if this had not been bad enough, he made it worse by self-righteously proclaiming that his vicious actions were virtuous and that he was the champion of reason and morality. This made him not merely evil but odious as well.

3.5 Ideology and Evil

Consider now the following defense of Robespierre. If evil is understood as serious, excessive, malevolent, and morally inexcusable harm caused by human beings to other human beings, then Robespierre's actions were evil. He himself, however, was not evil because he did not believe that the serious harm he caused was morally inexcusable. His ideology led him to believe that his actions were morally justified. If he had believed that his actions were evil, he would not have done them. As it was, he sincerely believed that he was acting reasonably and morally. He should not, therefore, be blamed for what he did. It was not his fault that his sincere beliefs turned out to be false. He acted in good faith, people can do no more than that, so even though his actions were evil, he should be excused.

The assumption underlying this defense is that people should not be held responsible for evil actions if they sincerely believe that their actions are not evil. This assumption is false, and the defense of Robespierre that rests on it is untenable. If the assumption were true, it would have the absurd consequence of exempting from responsibility SS concentration camp guards, if they were sincere Nazis; KGB torturers, provided they were committed Communists; Islamic terrorists, if they were truly fanatical; rapists, if they were really convinced that women liked it; and so forth. Responsibility for such evil actions is not weakened but strengthened by the reprehensible beliefs of the evildoers. One wants to say about them that they ought not hold beliefs—sincerely or otherwise—from which evil actions follow. And this is just what is right to say in response to the attempt to deny that Robespierre was evil. If his ideology led him to do evil, he should not have held it. That he held it sincerely makes him more, not less, culpable.

Doubts, however, may persist. Many people do not choose the ideology they hold, but accept it as a result of indoctrination. It is too much to demand of people to resist indoctrination if it is persistent and sophisticated and they have no reasonable alternatives. The first thing to say in response to this doubt is that it concedes that the assumption underlying

Robespierre's defense is false. For, contrary to the assumption, sincere belief in an evil ideology does not exempt people from responsibility for their evil actions. A plausible claim for exemption requires that they should believe their ideology as a result of indoctrination they could not withstand. If they had a choice, they are properly held responsible for accepting the ideology that prompts evil actions.

It must be said next that Robespierre chose his ideology. There is no evidence of indoctrination in his case. He constructed his ideology from his readings, education, and early political experience. He was acquainted with several alternatives to what he garnered from Rousseau. He read Fenelon, Guicciardini, Francis Bacon, and Pope (Thompson 1:180). He was familiar with the outlooks of monarchists and of moderates such as Mirabeau and the Girondin. His education acquainted him with Christianity. He participated in the debates of the Convention about adopting the model of English constitutional monarchy. The American Revolution was well known to politicians in France. And he practiced law for several years and was thus trained to sift through and evaluate evidence and the interpretations of facts. He had the opportunity, the ability, and the training to think critically about his ideology, yet he did not. He ought to have done so, but he failed, so he is responsible for the great evil his ideology led him to cause.

He did not realize what he was doing because his passion blinded him to the fact that his actions violated elementary requirements of reason and morality. It made him see himself as a romantic hero battling against great odds, opposed by evil enemies, striving "to establish the felicity of perhaps the entire human race" (Hampson 159). It propelled his relentless, merciless quest for power, in the course of which he arranged for the extermination of thousands of people. It made him regard politics as war between good and evil, himself as the authority on the good, and others who did not agree with him as evil and deserving extermination. Instead of controlling his passion, he allowed it to control him.

One can only speculate about the source of his passion. Perhaps he was a sadist and his ideology served to disguise it from himself and others. Perhaps power gave him the only pleasure he was able to enjoy. Perhaps he began by loathing himself and he found self-esteem by championing his ideology. Perhaps he felt that God had chosen him to make the world just. As his biographer says, "Philosophy cannot explain this: it can only turn away from a state of mind that ought not to have existed, or hand it over to the practitioners of mental pathology" (Thompson 1:148).

There is, however, one further observation that helps illuminate Robespierre's frame of mind. It was crude, misshapen, yearning for certainty rather than understanding. When he succeeded in concocting an ideology from the flotsam of Rousseau's ideas and other bits and pieces of experiences and information, he held on to it with fanatical dedication. For the ideology helped him to explain many things; it provided him with a perspective for evaluating the political scene and thus answered a need Robespierre keenly felt. This is readily understandable; the need is felt by many people. Crudity enters because Robespierre made it much too easy for himself to satisfy it. He did not ask whether his ideology fit the facts; he did not stand back from it and compare it with other ideologies; he did not ask how it appeared from the perspective of other ideologies; he did not wonder what reasons others had for rejecting it. He was hell-bent on protecting what he had and excluding doubt. And with that came the exclusion of other possibilities in life. His frame of mind was misshapen because the ideology he settled on was not the result of a critical comparison of various ideologies and commitment to the one he had reason to find the most plausible. He settled on the one that came to hand, and he held on to it passionately in the face of challenges. He did not ask whether his ideology was true or, at least, reasonable. He judged what was true or reasonable by the yardstick of his ideology.

Having a crude mind does not make people evil. They may be harmless cranks, dogmatic fools, or overbearing bores. Much depends on the object of their crudity and how passionately they are committed to it. If the object is an ideology, an overall guide to life and action, especially political action, and their commitment to it is their ruling passion in life, then the threat of evil is much more serious. But it is still just a threat. For a passionately held ideology may not prompt evil actions. It is possible to build into ideologies safeguards protecting the requirements of reason and morality. It must be said, however, that ideologies do not have a reassuring historical record on this point. Nazism, Communism, various kinds of fundamentalism and terrorism and racism demonstrate how easily ideologies lead to inhumanity. Still, not even evil ideologies lead necessarily to evil actions. Ideologues must have the opportunity to act in accordance with their beliefs. Ideologies, having a central political dimension, require that the opportunity be political. Such opportunities are created by the combination of generally felt deep resentment about the burden people must bear, weak or weakening government, and no prospect of quick and substantial improvement. Lenin in Zurich and Hitler in the immediate aftermath of the war were just nuisances. Lenin in Kerensky's Russia and Hitler in Weimar Germany used the opportunity to transform themselves from nuisances into evildoers.

The conclusion, therefore, is not the simple-minded claim that ideology causes evil. It is the much more complicated claim that evil has many causes, ideologies are one of them, but only if political opportunity favors them, if there are ideologues with passionate commitment and crude minds, and if the ideology fails to protect the requirements of reason and morality. It was the joint presence of these conditions that made Robespierre the evildoer he was.

A Fatal Fusion

The deeper he went into his story, the clearer emerged the picture of the fatal fusion between his own character and the sequence of events.

—GITTA SERENY, *Into That Darkness*

The leaders of the Albigensian Crusade and Robespierre were both fanatics, but of quite different kinds. The crusaders were religious fanatics who relied on their unquestioned faith. Robespierre was an ideological fanatic who relied on what he mistook as reason. The first were indifferent to reason, the second abused it. In this chapter I shall consider an evildoer who was not a fanatic at all. He was an ordinary person with ordinary vices whose circumstances gave full scope to the exercise of his vices, and he far surpassed as an evildoer both the crusaders and Robespierre.

4.1 Inferno

The Nazis had two kinds of concentration camps: one for forced labor, the other for extermination. There was a chance of survival in the former, but virtually none in the latter. The most conservative estimate is that about two million people were murdered in the extermination camps, and about eighty survived. There were four extermination camps, all in German-occupied Poland: Chelmno, Belsec, Sobibor, and Treblinka. The first was established in late 1941, the last three in early 1942; all were obliterated by the Germans close to the end of 1943. The buildings were destroyed, the earth was plowed, crops were planted, and farms were established on the soil rendered fertile by the corpses and ashes of the dead.

Franz Stangl was the *Kommandant* of Treblinka almost from the beginning of the exterminations until the camp was closed down. After the war he escaped to Syria; from there he went to Brazil, where he lived until 1968, when he was extradited to what then was West Germany. He was tried, convicted for complicity in the murder of nine hundred thousand people, and sentenced to life imprisonment. He died in jail in 1971, apparently from a heart attack. Between his conviction and death he was extensively interviewed by Gitta Sereny, a journalist who was then and remains today a widely respected and knowledgeable expert on the horrors of Nazi Germany. She speaks German as a native, which is the language in which the interviews took place. She made it clear to Stangl that she wanted to understand his character, motivation, and feelings about what he had done, and that she would write about it. Stangl agreed, and this was the basis on which the interviews, with only the two of them present, proceeded. Sereny apparently was the only person to whom Stangl ever talked in any detail about Treblinka, what preceded it, and how he viewed it in retrospect.

Sereny is the author of several influential books. One of them, *Into That Darkness*,[1] is directly concerned with Stangl. It contains her interviews with him, the results of her investigations checking the veracity of what Stangl told her, and her reflections on Stangl and what he said. Another book, *The Healing Wound*,[2] has a long essay on Stangl and several others dealing with what she calls the German trauma, which is the title of the English edition of this book. Both books have been favorably received, and there is a consensus among historians and still living witnesses to those terrible times and events that her account is reliable.

Sereny explains the purpose of the interviews as follows: "It was essential before it was too late, I felt, to penetrate the personality of at least one of the people who had been intimately associated with this total evil. If it could be achieved, an evaluation of such a person's background, his childhood, and eventually his adult motivation and reactions, *as he saw them,* rather than as we wished or prejudged them to be, might teach us to understand better to what extent evil in human beings is created by their genes, and to what extent by their society and environment" (D 9–10). This is partly also my own purpose, but I mean to go further than Sereny has done both in seeking to understand the cause of evil in Stangl's character and actions and in answering the question how it is reasonable for us to see Stangl, regardless of how he saw himself. I rely on Sereny's account of the facts but interpret them differently.

Here is Stangl's description of what he found as he was taking command of the already functioning extermination camp at Treblinka. "I drove there with an SS driver. We could smell it kilometers away. The road ran alongside the railway tracks. As we got nearer Treblinka but still perhaps fifteen, twenty minutes' drive away, we began to see corpses next to the rails, first just two or three, then more and as we drove into what was Treblinka station there were hundreds of them—just lying there—they'd obviously been there for days, in the heat. In the station was a train full of Jews, some dead, some still alive . . . it looked as if it had been there for days. . . . Treblinka that day was the most awful thing I saw all during the Third Reich. . . . It was Dante's *Inferno*. . . . Dante come to life. When I got out of the car on the *Sortierungsplatz* [Sorting Square] I stepped knee-deep into money: I did not know which way to turn, where to go. I waded in paper notes, currency, precious stones, jewellery and clothes. They were everywhere, strewn all over the square. The smell was indescribable: the hundreds, no, the thousands of bodies everywhere, putrefying, decomposing. Across the square in the woods, just a few hundred yards away on the other side of the barbed-wire fence, there were tents and open fires with groups of Ukrainian guards and girls—whores from Warsaw I found out later—weaving drunk, dancing, singing, playing music . . . there was shooting everywhere. . . . I went straight back to Warsaw and told Globocnik [the SS general in charge of all the extermination camps] that it was impossible: no order such as he had given me could be carried out in that place. 'It is the end of the world,' I said to him and told him about the thousands of rotting corpses. He said, 'It's supposed to be the end of the world for them.' . . . I told him that I was prepared to see that all material [the valuables] as of now would be safely delivered to his office. . . . All I was doing was to confirm to him that I would be carrying out this *assignment* as a police officer under his command" (W 117–19). Stangl put an end to this disorder. He organized the extermination and made sure it would proceed efficiently. As an SS man assigned to Treblinka said: "Stangl did improve things . . . all he did was look after the death camp, the burning and all that; there everything had to run just so because the whole camp organization depended on it. I think what he really cared about was to have the place run like clockwork" (D 202).

The routine was as follows. The transports arrived at Treblinka in the early morning. "When the first train arrived," relates the Polish station master, "we would hear it from far away. Not because of the noise of the train, but because of the cries of the people, and the shooting. . . . The train was very full—incredibly full it seemed. It was a hot day but . . . the difference in temperature between inside the cars and out was obviously such that a kind of fog came out and surrounded the train. There were chalked figures on each car—you know the Germans with their methodical ways—that is why I know exactly how many people were killed at Treblinka. The figures on each car varied between 150 and 180. . . . We began to note down the figures that very first day, and we never stopped for a year, until it was over. . . . We had been told that the track to the camp could only take twenty cars at a time. One train usually had at least twenty cars, and sometimes in the weeks and months to come, three trains would arrive together. So everything except twenty cars would just stay in our station until they finished with each lot of twenty" (D 151–52).

One of the eighty survivors describes what happened to him: "They put us on a freight train, a hundred or a hundred and fifty in each car; so many that we had to stand up one against another. There were no windows, no sanitary facilities, there was no light, no air. People urinated, defecated and vomited. A few, the weakest, died standing up and had to stay standing up—there was no room to do anything else with them. . . . When the door of our car was pushed open, all we could think of was to get out into the air. What I saw first was two guards with whips—later we found out they were Ukrainian SS. They immediately began to shout, 'Raus, raus [Out, out],' and hit out blindly at those who stood in front. . . . It was all perfectly planned to get us out of the car with no delay. They only opened three cars at a time—that was part of the system. . . . The hurry, the noise, the fear and confusion were indescribable. . . . About twenty meters away, across the 'square,' I saw a line of SS officers and they were shooting. I especially noticed Stangl because he wore a white jacket—it stuck out. . . . The purpose was to get us all to run in one direction; through a gate and a kind of corridor into yet another square" (D 122).

At this square, men and women were first separated and then ordered into "the undressing barracks where the victims stripped, left their clothes, had their hair cut off if they were women [for use as mattress stuffing], and were internally searched for valuables" (D 165). "One of the SS men . . . told us in a chatty sort of tone that we were going into a disinfection bath and afterwards would be assigned work. Clothes, he said, could be left in a heap on the floor, and we'd find them later" (D 176). From the undressing barracks, people entered "'the Road to Heaven' [as the SS called it]. This . . . was a path ten feet wide with tenfoot fences of barbed wire on each side . . . through which the naked prisoners, in rows of five, had to run the hundred meters up the hill to the 'baths'—the gas chambers—and where, when as happened frequently, the gassing mechanism broke down, they had to stand waiting their turn for hours at a time" (D 165).

Stangl says, "I'd be working in my office—there was a great deal of paper work—till about 11 [A.M.]. Then I made my next round, starting up at the *Totenlager* [the gas chamber]. By that time they were well ahead with the work up there." Sereny explains: "He meant that by this time the 5,000 to 6,000 people who had arrived that morning were dead: the 'work' was the disposal of the bodies which took most of the rest of the day and during some months continued during the night." Stangl continues: "By that time of the morning everything was pretty much finished in the lower camp. A transport was normally dealt with in two or three hours. At 12 I had lunch—we usually had meat, potatoes, some fresh vegetables such as cauliflowers—we grew them ourselves quite soon—and after lunch I had about half an hour's rest. Then another round and more work in the office" (D 170).

The last step was the disposal of the bodies. "Out of every transport they kept fifty strong men and boys and made them clean up after a transport had been killed. The corpses weren't burned then—they were buried in lime pits. And when they had finished cleaning up, they too were killed. This happened every day in the beginning. It was only later that semi-permanent Kommandos were formed who did this work for weeks, months and—a few of them—throughout the whole existence of the camp" (D 126–27).

This, then, was the system Stangl organized and whose efficient functioning he supervised for about seventeen months, during which time about nine hundred thousand people were murdered at Treblinka. Sereny reports, "The SS general in charge of the extermination of the Jews in the four death camps in Poland, Odilo Globocnik, had asked Himmler in January 1944 to award Stangl an Iron Cross, describing him as 'the best camp Kommandant in Poland'" (D 11–12).

4.2 The Man

Who was this man, Stangl, in white clothes supervising the daily murder of thousands of people, enjoying his lunch of meat and potatoes with homegrown fresh vegetables, and having a quiet nap between herding naked men, women, and children into the gas chambers and disposing of their corpses? What manner of man would preside over this hell on earth and organize its smooth functioning? Franz Stangl was born in a small town in Austria in 1908. His father was then a night watchman, but his heart was in his past service as a soldier in an elite regiment. He was a petty tyrant who imposed what he regarded as military discipline on his family. He often beat both his much younger wife and their children. He died when Stangl was eight years old, lamented by no one. Stangl's mother then married a widower who had two children. He was a kind man, a good stepfather, and Stangl became inseparable from one of his stepbrothers who was his age. He went to school, and he learned to play the zither so well that he later earned quite a bit of money by giving lessons. He left school at fifteen and apprenticed for three years in a textile mill. He then passed the required exams and at eighteen became the youngest master weaver in Austria. He soon had many people working under him. He earned good money, but he gave much of it to his parents. After five years at this work, he realized that he had achieved all he could in the textile mill. He then applied to join the police. He sat for a difficult exam, passed, and in 1931, at the age of twenty-three, was told to report to the police for basic training. After two years, he became a rookie. He did very well and was sent for further training to the police academy. In 1935 he was transferred to the political division of the police, where he worked as an investigator, wearing civilian clothes, charged with detecting antigovernment activities. To have achieved all this by the age of twenty-seven was spectacular success.

His personal life was also going well. In 1935 he married the woman to whom he had been long engaged. They had a close marriage, and their devotion to each other did not falter through the many years and tumultuous events in Austria, Germany, Syria, Brazil, and then Germany again. He loved his wife, cared deeply for her opinion, and she reciprocated. They eventually had two children, whom he loved and who loved him. Theirs was an exemplary family, the psychological mainstay of his life, and he was always loyal and protective of them, who, in turn, remained loyal to him throughout his life. His wife was a devout Catholic, but he himself, although nominally Catholic, had no deep religious commitment and went to church only rarely. Apart from his family, he also had close friendships with other men, first in the police and later in the SS.

In 1938 came the *Anschluss,* the incorporation of Austria into Germany. Even before it, Stangl had sympathized with the Nazi Party in Austria and with what the Nazis were doing in Germany. After the *Anschluss,* members of the Austrian police had to demonstrate their loyalty to the Nazi cause in numerous ways. Those who failed lost their jobs, many were maltreated, and some were sent to concentration camps. Stangl knew this, of course, and he was among those who had satisfied the Nazis by, among other things, renouncing his Catholic allegiance. In 1939 the political branch of what used to be the Austrian police and to which Stangl belonged was incorporated into the Gestapo. Stangl was given the rank of *Kriminalassistent,* which was less than what he thought he deserved, and after his vigorous protest he was raised to the rank of

Kriminalbeamter. In 1940 he was told to report for duty as the police super-intendent of a special institute, where the highly secret euthanasia pro-gram was run by the Nazis. It involved, at first, the murder of people deemed to be incurably insane or having extremely low intelligence; later political prisoners were added.

When Stangl understood what the program was about, he was at first reluctant to accept the position. It was then explained to him that the actual murders were done by the medical staff, the victims were in a vege-tative state, the selection process required the certification of several physicians, programs like this were legal in America and Russia, they were kept secret in Austria and Germany only to spare the sensitivity of the general population, and his role would merely be to uphold law and order. It was also explained to him that with the position came promo-tion, the alternative to accepting it involved a much worse position and no promotion, and he was reminded of the fate of those whose loyalty was in question. Stangl then accepted the position and reported to duty. He soon found out that what he was told about the program and the safe-guards were all lies, but he stayed on. He did not tell his wife what his new job involved. And he claimed not to know that the people murdered included political prisoners who were transferred from concentration camps. The murders were done by gas.

In 1942 the euthanasia program was discontinued, and Stangl was told to go to Berlin, where he received the order to proceed to Poland and report to SS Polizeiführer (Chief of Police) Globocnik. He was to organ-ize the construction of what he was told was a supply camp at Sobibor, which, then unknown to Stangl, was to be one of several extermination camps. He discovered, however, that the camp had a gas chamber. He recognized it as such because it was identical to the one used in the euthanasia program. Stangl then knew that he was not constructing a supply camp. At this time, he was ordered to Belsec, an already function-ing extermination camp, and he came face to face with the full horror of what was done there. Stangl told his superior at Belsec that he was not up to such an assignment. The superior replied that he would convey this to the headquarters and that Stangl should return to Sobibor. Stangl heard nothing further and continued the construction at Sobibor. When it was finished, it began to function as an extermination camp under Stangl's command. During the first two months of its existence about one hun-dred thousand people were murdered. He was then summoned to the headquarters, and in the same sinister and ambiguous manner as before in the euthanasia program, he was given by Globocnik the new assign-ment of commanding Treblinka. The prospect of promotion and other rewards for his loyalty and efficient service were dangled before him and threats for disloyalty were implied. None of this was said plainly, but it was intimated in a way that was at once deniable and yet menacing. Globocnik took no note of his previous request for another assignment. Stangl then accepted the job of being *Kommandant* at Treblinka.

As this was going on, Stangl's wife and children came to visit him. She had no idea what Stangl's assignment was, but she soon found out from a drunken SS man. She was horrified and confronted her husband. She cried, ranted, begged, and argued to convince Stangl that he should get out of it. But Stangl said it was impossible and assured her that his activities were purely administrative. After much persuasion she believed him. It was at this point that he received the order to go to Treblinka. He made sure that his family returned to Austria and responded to Globocnik "to confirm to him that I would be carrying out this *assignment* as a police officer under his command" (D 163).

Sereny then asks Stangl the pivotal question: "You . . . had acknowledged . . . that what was being committed was a crime. How could you, in all conscience . . . take any part in this crime?" Stangl's reply is: "It was a matter of survival—always of survival. What I had to do, while I continued my efforts to get out, was to limit my actions to what I—in my conscience—could answer for. At police training school they taught us . . . that the definition of a crime must meet four requirements: there has to be a subject, an object, an action and intent. If any of these four elements are missing, then we are not dealing with a punishable offence. . . . The 'subject' was the government, the 'object' the Jews, and the 'action' the gassings. . . . I could tell myself that for me the fourth element, 'intent' . . . was missing" (D 164).

This is a crucial exchange, and I shall return to it shortly. For the moment, however, let us note that part of the significance of Stangl's reply is that it contains the explanation of what he told himself in Treblinka as he supervised the murders and what made it psychologically possible for him to preside over the extermination of nine hundred thousand people: he acted under necessity, against his will, without intent. What his actions actually involved we have already seen.

In late 1943 Treblinka was closed down. Serious effort was made to remove all traces of its existence. Stangl was reassigned to the comparatively innocuous task of antipartisan activity in Trieste, Yugoslavia, and Italy. He did this from 1944 to the end of the war. After the war he was briefly interned by the American forces. He was released, made his way to Rome, and from there, with the help of the escape route the Vatican had arranged for many fleeing Nazis, he went to Syria. He got a job first in a textile mill in Damascus and later as a mechanical engineer, on the strength of some correspondence courses he had taken years before in

Austria. He did well, earned an excellent salary, and got his family to join him. They saved enough to make it possible to leave for Brazil in 1951. Once there, he quickly learned Portuguese, found a job as a weaver, but was soon promoted to a planning position. From there he went to work for the Brazilian Volkswagen works. He and his family became moderately prosperous; their children grew up and married; and Stangl and his wife lived a peaceful and contented life until 1968, when he was arrested by the Brazilian police and extradited to West Germany.

4.3 His Responsibility and Choices

Let us now consider the question of Stangl's responsibility. If it were denied that this man is responsible for his actions, it is hard to see how anybody could ever be held responsible for anything. But Stangl did deny it. We need now to understand how Stangl thought about his responsibility, and whether there was more to his thinking than a craven attempt to obfuscate his guilt. This brings us to the passage to which I promised to return. Here it is again: Sereny asks, "You . . . had acknowledged . . . that what was being committed was a crime. How could you, in all conscience . . . take any part in this crime?" Stangl's reply is, "It was a matter of survival—always of survival. What I had to do, while I continued to get out, was to limit my actions to what I—in my conscience—could answer for. At police training school they taught us . . . that the definition of a crime must meet four requirements: there has to be a subject, an object, an action and intent. If any of these four elements are missing, then we are not dealing with a punishable offence. . . . The 'subject' was the government, the 'object' the Jews, and the 'action' the gassings. . . . I could tell myself that for me the fourth element, 'intent' . . . was missing" (D 164).

What Stangl says cries out for dissent. The "subject" could hardly be the government since that is an abstract entity incapable of action; it must be individuals, like Stangl, who perhaps acted on behalf of the Nazi government. The "object" was not just the Jews but also the insane, Gypsies, homosexuals, anti-Nazis, prisoners of war, and so forth. The "action" was not just gassing but also the excess and malevolence shown by the transports, the deception, the humiliation, the separation of families, the whipping, and so forth that preceded the gassing. The crime in question was not just a legal but also a moral matter, and the two often diverge. Let us, however, ignore these matters and concentrate on what Stangl says about "intent."

Stangl claims that the absence of intent prevents his actions—which even he conceded were evil—from reflecting on him and making him an evil person. Intent involves understanding and choice, but much depends on how they are interpreted. Understanding is of the relevant facts and their moral significance. If I did not and could not be expected to know that the glass of wine I gave you was poisoned, then I could not have had the intent to kill you, at any rate not in that way. Again, if I did not know and had no reason to believe that the moral significance of giving a ride to a man who asked me is that I was helping a terrorist get away, then I could not have had the intent to help him. Lack of either kind of understanding may or may not be excusable. If normal adults could normally be expected to have the understanding I lack, then either I must point at some special circumstance to explain my lack of it or my ignorance does not excuse me from responsibility. If I am in shock, that is one thing; if I am inattentive because I think only of myself, that is quite another. People, therefore, may be responsible even for actions they have not fully understood if they should have had the understanding they lacked. As we have seen, however, Stangl had the required understanding; he knew the relevant facts and the moral significance of what he was doing, even though he worked hard to protect himself from what he understood. If he is to be excused from responsibility, it must be on account of his lack of choice.

The simple view of choice is that it consists in selecting one from at least two alternative courses of action. This, however, is too simple. If I hand over my wallet at gunpoint, I can be said to have made the choice to lose it rather than my life. But my choice was hardly genuine because the alternatives among which I had to choose were forced on me. I did not choose to lose my wallet, and it would be crazy to hold me responsible for it. Moreover, if even forced choices are accepted as genuine, then the absurdity would follow that just about anything done is chosen. If I sneeze, then, on this view, I have made a choice because I could have shot myself instead. Adopting this view would trivialize the moral significance of choice. Choice is important when selecting an alternative that reflects my character, values, or judgment. This leaves plenty of room for insignificant choices, such as the flavor of the ice cream I eat. Important choices, then, may be said to reflect considered preferences rather than responses forced on one, and that is why they are taken to matter for responsibility and morality. It makes no substantive difference whether we reserve the name "choice" exclusively for important ones or whether we distinguish between forced and trivial choices, on the one hand, and important ones, on the other. From the moral point of view important choices matter, and that is what I will mean by *choice* from now on.

In Sereny's interviews with Stangl, choice is a frequently recurring topic. Stangl denies again and again that he had a choice, and again and again Sereny presses him on that point. Stangl says he could not have acted differently, that his alternatives were forced on him, and so he had no choice, and Sereny questions him by citing possible alternatives. Stangl says that "it wasn't a question of 'getting out': if it had only been as simple as that! . . . We heard every day of this one and that one being arrested, sent to concentration camp, shot. . . . What it had already become . . . was a question of survival" (D 35); "Don't you see? He [Globocnik] had me just where he wanted me. . . . Can you imagine what would have happened to me if I had returned there [to Austria] under these circumstances? No, he had me flat: I was a prisoner" (D 134); "It was a matter of survival—always of survival" (D 164); "My conscience is clear about what I did, myself. . . . I have never intentionally hurt anyone" (D 364). As against this, Sereny presents several cases of people in the SS and among the staff of concentration camps who had opted out (D 51–52, 97; W 262–65) without anything dire happening to them. It goes against the grain to admit, but a much stronger case can be made on Stangl's than on Sereny's side.

The central weakness of Sereny's case is that the fact that some people could opt out does not show that Stangl could. The "could" in question expresses a psychological possibility: there were some admirable people who had the moral strength to refuse to take part in the murders and were courageous enough to face the attendant risks. But Stangl was not one of them. He lacked the moral strength and the courage that made it possible for others to act admirably. Given Stangl's character, it was psychologically impossible for him to opt out. And, it should be remembered, what stopped him was not just fear but also ambition. His career depended on doing as he was told. This, of course, makes him a deplorable person. The present point, however, is not that, but that given his character—his ambition and lack of moral strength—he had no choice. His character was his destiny. He was a mass murderer, but since he did not choose to be one, he should not be held responsible for it.

This defense of Stangl is outrageous, and something is obviously very wrong with it. It is crucial, however, to be clear about what that is. It may be said against it that it is absurd to deny Stangl's responsibility on the grounds that his deplorable character left him no choice in his circumstances but to become a mass murderer, for he ought not to have had that character. The trouble with this is that Stangl did not choose his character either; he did not choose to be ambitious and to lack moral strength. These traits were in his nature, among his potentialities, and his upbringing and circumstances fostered his ambition and weakened such moral strength as he may have had. His character was deplorable, but if choice were necessary for responsibility, he was not responsible for his character. Stangl's defense thus survives this objection.

A more considered objection may be that Stangl was able to make choices and it is right to hold him responsible. This objection, however, ignores that the choices Stangl made were forced. His choices were made in circumstances analogous to the choice between dying and handing over one's wallet to an armed robber. As he saw it, his choice was between destroying the life his successful career made possible for his family and himself and becoming a mass murderer. He chose the latter. But his choice was between alternatives that were forced on him. If it had not been for his circumstances, which included being manipulated by his superiors, he would have pursued his career and would not have had to face mass murder as a possible option. The forced choices he made were unavoidable responses in untoward circumstances, and they do not express his preferences. It would be wrong, therefore, to hold him responsible for them.

Are we to conclude, then, that this person—the best camp *Kommandant* in Poland, who supervised the murder of nine hundred thousand people while sporting white clothes and having a decent lunch followed by a cozy nap, this person who grew vegetables and kept himself fastidiously clean in the midst of carnage—was not responsible for what he was and did? Of course he was responsible. But holding him to it depends on rejecting the assumption that responsibility is only for unforced choices. This is not to deny that choice is often relevant to responsibility. It is to deny that without choice there can be no responsibility. Well, then, what makes it reasonable to hold people responsible for actions they have not chosen? The following would: their actions are evil; they are not isolated episodes in their lives but parts of a recurrent pattern of conduct; they are predictable expressions of their character; and the people could understand the moral significance of their actions. In short, it is reasonable to hold evildoers responsible even for unchosen evil actions if they regularly and characteristically perform them and have the capacity to understand what they are doing.

People like this are evil, and part of the purpose of morality is to protect others from them. To say that they are responsible is to say that they are appropriate subjects of the moral judgment that no one ought to act as these evildoers do; they are dangerous and harmful; they are to be feared and condemned; they should be held up as examples to avoid; children should be taught not to become like them; and society should be arranged so as to prevent them from harming the rest.

The reasonable ascription of responsibility depends on several factors. Choice is one, but there are others: the consequences of evil actions; the severity and scope of the harm that has been done; the excess and malevolence involved in the actions; the overall character and history of the evildoers; the extent to which the evildoers understand the relevant facts and the moral significance of their actions; the generally held moral beliefs in their context; as well as the state of the surrounding society, whether it is stable or chaotic, prosperous or impoverished, orthodox or permissive; and so forth. It is a bad mistake and a disservice to morality to focus on one of these factors and insist on its being *the* condition of responsibility. Responsibility depends on some combination of these factors. In particular contexts some of these factors are more important than others; in other contexts the reverse is true. The respective importance of these factors shifts. In any context, good reasons can and should be given for regarding some factors more important than the others, but these reasons themselves vary with contexts. Sometimes the harm done is so great to so many victims that it dwarfs the importance of the evildoers' past actions. At other times, although the actions cause harm to fewer people, they show such excess and malevolence as to merit the most severe condemnation. On yet other occasions, responsibility is diminished because although the evildoer's actions were chosen, the choices reflected prevailing mistaken moral beliefs.

Stangl's denial of his responsibility rests on the assumption I am rejecting. Choice is not the pivot on which responsibility turns, not because the pivot is something else, but because there is no pivot. The point is not that consequences, or character, or the prevailing moral beliefs are more important than choice, but that the lack of choice does not preclude the assignment of responsibility. The insistence that it does deprives morality of the resources to respond adequately to such horrendous evil as Stangl had done. Perhaps he did not choose it, but his character was such that in the circumstances of Nazi Germany he became a mass murderer. It is reasonable to hold him responsible for his actions, even though without the fatal fusion of his character and circumstances, he might not have done what he did.

4.4 His Character

If we did not know that Stangl was one of the worst mass murderers in history, we could not infer it from the other known facts of his life. His dominant traits were intelligence, hard work, respect for established authority, love of his family, and, above all, ambition. The crucial link between his character and the horrendous evil he had done was his ambition. That he was ambitious is clear from his life and from what other people said about him. According to Frau Stangl's sister, Stangl was an illegal Nazi before the *Anschluss* because "if he hadn't been, he wouldn't have got on so fast. And that's what they wanted, both of them—to get on" (D 33–34). His wife was aware of his "wild ambition," and she said "I am very proud of him" because "he was constantly being promoted, praised and decorated for this and that achievement" (D 45). He strove to rise wherever he was. He was not just a master weaver, but the youngest one in the country; his advancement in the Austrian police had been exceptionally fast; he was not merely a Gestapo officer, but one selected for the most secret euthanasia program; he was not just a camp *Kommandant*, but the best one in Poland; in Syria, where he began as a simple weaver, he soon rose to a supervisory position; in Brazil, in no time at all, he went from a virtually penniless immigrant to a planning position in the Volkswagen works and to a comfortable middle-class life. When Sereny asked him: "Would it not have been possible for you . . . to do your work a little less 'superbly'?" he replied, "I had to do as well as I could. That is how I am" (D 229). And that, at any rate, was true: ambition was in his nature; it is what drove him.

Ambition can take many different forms. Stangl's took the form of rising through the various hierarchies he had encountered: as a weaver, policeman, SS officer, mechanical engineer, and planner. He realized his ambition because he was fastidious, methodical, efficient, hardworking, and obedient to those above him in the hierarchy. He brought the same skills and drive to do well to whatever he happened to be doing. This in itself is neither good nor bad. What makes it one or the other depends on the task at hand and the circumstances. Stangl seized the opportunities his circumstances afforded, and that is how he got from lowly beginnings to an ever-rising status. The motivating force of ambition was an enduring pattern in his life, but the circumstances in which he could act on it were, from the moral point of view, vastly different. One wants to say to Stangl: you ought to have curbed your ambition in the circumstances you found in the extermination camps, you ought not to have let it drive you to mass murder. We need to understand why Stangl did not restrain his ambition.

There can be no doubt that Stangl knew that what he was doing in Treblinka was horribly wrong. That is why he lied to his wife about the extent of his involvement and made efforts, at least at the beginning, to relinquish his assignment. That is why he admitted to Sereny that he had been "on the road to catastrophe" (D 29); why he was horrified of his first experiences of the exterminations in Belsec and Treblinka; why he said to Sereny, "My guilt is that I am still here." "Still here?" she asked, and Stangl replied, "I should have died. That was my guilt," but Sereny presses him for clarity, "Do you mean you should have . . . had the courage to die?" and Stangl responds, "You can put it like that" (D 364–65), and again, "I should have killed myself in 1938" (D 39). That is why he says in reply to

Sereny's question, "What was the worst place in the camp for you?" "The undressing barracks . . . I avoided it from my innermost being; I couldn't confront them; I couldn't lie to them; I avoided at any price talking to those who were about to die: I couldn't stand it" (D 203). That is why he had to hide his feelings: "if I had made public what I felt . . . it would have made no difference. Not an iota. It would have all gone on just the same" (D 231). And that is why he agreed with Sereny that "you . . . had acknowledged to yoursel[f] that what was being committed here [at Treblinka] was a crime" (D 163).

Stangl was thus driven by ambition to actions he knew were evil. How could he have done what he regarded as so wrong as to make suicide preferable? The answer is that he had erected a protective shield between his actions and himself. This enabled him to prevent the knowledge of the nature of his actions and his feelings about them to affect his motivation to perform those actions, as well as to deny that his actions reflected on him. He acknowledged that he performed his actions, but he denied that he was responsible for them.

It is understandable that people tried to protect themselves from the horror that was a constant presence in the extermination camps. One way was to desensitize themselves, to prevent their feelings from focusing on the outrage and suffering they had been routinely witnessing. This was just what Stangl had done. He, of course, had to protect himself from the horror that he himself had a major share in causing. He did it partly by teaching himself not to think of those he murdered as human. He says, "I think it started the day I first saw the *Totenlager* in Treblinka. I remember . . . the pits full of blue-black corpses. It had nothing to do with humanity—it couldn't have; it was a mass—a mass of rotting flesh . . . that started me thinking of them as cargo" (D 201). Sereny asks him, "There were many children, did they ever make you think of your children, of how you would feel in the position of those parents?" and Stangl replies, "No, I can't say I ever thought that way. You see I rarely saw them as individuals. It was always a huge mass. I sometimes stood on the wall and saw them in the tube [the path to the gas chamber]. But—how can I explain it—they were naked, packed together, running, being driven by whips like . . ." "the sentence trailed off," Sereny says (D 201). Something else Stangl says, however, makes obvious how the sentence should be completed. "When I was on a trip once, years later in Brazil, my train stopped next to a slaughterhouse. The cattle in the pens, hearing the noise of the train, trotted up to the fence and stared at the train. They were very close to my window, one crowding the other, looking at me through that fence. I thought then, 'Look at this; this reminds me of Poland; that's just how the people looked, trustingly. . . . Those big eyes . . . which looked at me . . . not knowing that in no time at all they'd all be dead. . . . Cargo. . . . They were cargo" (D 201).

Part of Stangl's self-protection, then, was to deny the humanity of his victims. Another part emerges from his response to Sereny's question, "Would it be true to say that you got used to the liquidations?" He replies, "To tell the truth one did become used to it. . . . It was months before I could look one of them in the eye. I repressed it all by trying to create a special place: gardens, new barracks, new kitchens, new everything. . . . There were hundreds of ways to take one's mind off it; I used them all . . . of course, thoughts came. But I forced them away. I made myself concentrate on work, work and again work" (D 200).

There were, then, three stratagems that together constituted Stangl's self-protection: denying the humanity of his victims; desensitizing himself to the horror by seeing it as mere routine; and inventing other tasks on which his attention could focus. Just how successful he was can perhaps be gauged from a grotesque feature of his behavior, which was commented on by numerous witnesses. The SS uniform worn by all the guards was field gray, but Stangl wore white riding clothes. Sereny says, "It was when he tried to explain this to me that I became aware for the first time of how he had lived—and was still living when we spoke—on two levels of consciousness, and conscience." Stangl's explanation was that "when I came to Poland I had very few clothes . . . one day, in a small town not far away, I found a weaving mill. . . . They were making nice linen—off-white. I asked whether they'd sell me some. And that is how I got the white material; I had a jacket made right away and a little later jodhpurs and a coat." To Sereny's question, "But even so, how could you go into the camp in this get-up?" Stangl replies, "The roads were bad, riding was the best means of transport." Sereny tries again, "Yes, but to attend the unloading of these people who were about to die, in white riding clothes . . . ?" "It was hot," Stangl said (D 117–18). He was genuinely unaware of the glaringly obvious symbolic significance of his clothes because his psychic distance from the horror was so successfully established that the inappropriateness of his clothing to the circumstances simply did not occur to him. As far as he was aware, there were no circumstances to which his clothing would be inappropriate. The weather was hot, that is why he wore white.

On one level, Stangl knew perfectly well that he was engaged in mass murder, and he had strong feelings about it. But he taught himself to disregard his knowledge and feelings by refusing to see his victims as human, by desensitizing himself through routine, and by diverting his attention to the make-work he had invented. He thus succeeded in making himself operate on another level where he could prevent his knowledge and feelings from influencing his actions. He could preside over the horror because he did not let himself see it as horror.

The facts so helpfully assembled by Sereny, then, suggest the following interpretation of Stangl's mass murder. His superiors manipulated him into becoming an extermination camp *Kommandant* by a sinister combination of implied rewards and threats. But he could be manipulated only because ambition and lack of moral strength led him to crave the rewards and succumb to the threats. He knew what he was doing and felt badly about it, but he systematically falsified his knowledge and feelings and thus prevented them from affecting his actions. If he had not been ambitious, he could not have been manipulated into performing so well at increasingly evil tasks. If his circumstances had not been those of Nazified Austria and Germany, his ambition would have taken a different form. It was the fatal fusion of his character and circumstances that made him a mass murderer.

4.5 Ambition and Evil

Ambition in itself is neither good nor bad. It is natural for people to want to do well in life, rise in the world, and enjoy the rewards of money, status, and recognition. For some people ambition is merely one motive among others; for others it becomes a ruling passion and dominates their lives and activities. Stangl was one of the latter. His will, intellect, and energy were always clearly focused. He was quick to find out in each of the many and very different contexts in which he found himself what he had to do to excel, and he did what led to it without questioning the requirements or indeed his drive. He was invariably successful. Such people are perhaps not particularly likable, but there need be nothing morally objectionable about their activities. Ambition, therefore, is not intrinsically bad, but it is intrinsically dangerous to be ruled by it. For if it dominates people's lives, then it tends to override moral scruples that curb the conduct of those who are less ambitious. And if those driven by ambition are given the opportunity to rise by doing well at evil enterprises, there will be little that restrains them. They silence such moral qualms as they may have, and do what they have to do in order to excel. This is what happened to Stangl, and this is what he did.

A clue to how totally he was driven by ambition is that the moral qualms he had to silence in himself were provoked by his daily supervision over horrors that must be exceptionally rare in history. Yet he managed to come to terms with what he was doing; his stratagems worked;

and his ambition led him to become the best extermination camp *Kommandant* in Poland. So strong was his ambition, and so successful was he in desensitizing himself to the carnage, that if he had not been extradited, tried, and sentenced for life, if Sereny had not put to him the questions he had not himself asked, then he would have lived out his life in Brazil without giving much thought to the nine hundred thousand people he had murdered.

What made this psychological feat possible was his total identification with the ambition that drove him. Until the interviews, there was no gap between himself and his ambition into which reflection, doubt, self-questioning could enter. As the dancer is inseparable from the dance, so Stangl was inseparable from his ambition. And his identification was strengthened by all the important influences on him: by the wife he loved, by the superiors he respected, obeyed, and feared, by the political systems under which he lived, and by the status and comforts he enjoyed. It is understandable why he did what he did, but to understand is not to excuse or to forgive. It is to see evil for what it is and condemn evildoers for what they are.

CHAPTER 5

The Revenge of Ruined Pride

Envy, that does with misery reside,
The joy and the revenge of ruin'd pride.

—JOHN DRYDEN, "To His Sacred Majesty"

It may be said that the evil inflicted on the Cathars and the victims of the French Revolution and Nazism had a political dimension. The evildoers acted as representatives of a public authority. They did what they did because they had the vices they had, but it was their political situation and position that gave scope to their vices and led to the spectacular and horrifying evil they caused. This chapter is about an evildoer in whose crimes politics plays virtually no role. The evil he caused was personal. Religion or ideology had no part in it. He had no faith; he did not abuse reason more than many other people; and ambition was not an important part of his motivation.

5.1 The Crimes and the Criminal

There were five corpses: two women and three men. A young man, outside the house, was shot four times. He was lucky. A woman inside was stabbed sixteen times on the chest and back. The wounds were deep, penetrating the heart, lungs, and liver, causing massive hemorrhage. She was eight months pregnant. The other woman was stabbed twenty-eight times. She was found in the garden, just outside the house, where she attempted to flee after the first stabs. She was pursued and received the final stabs that ended her life, her white nightgown dyed red by the blood she lost. One of the men fought. He was struck over the head thirteen times, shot twice, and stabbed fifty-one times. The last man was shot, stabbed seven times, and bled to death. He had a rope tied around his neck. The rope was thrown over a rafter and its other end was tied around the pregnant woman's neck. The rope forced both to stand. The murderers used a towel immersed in the pregnant woman's blood to write various words on the walls. The following night the murderers broke into a house, tied up a man, and killed him with twelve knife stabs and fourteen punctures inflicted with a double-tined fork. They left the knife in his throat. There was also a woman tied up in one of the bedrooms. She had been stabbed forty-one times on her back, buttocks, jaw, and hand. In this case too, their blood was used to leave words on the walls.

The murders were committed in Los Angeles in the summer of 1969, and the words written in blood were "pig," "death to pigs," and the misspelled "healter skelter." These crimes were the infamous Tate-LaBianca murders, and the murderers were Charles Manson and his so-called Family.[1] Much has been written about Manson and the crimes. Most of it is divided between the hasty, though understandable, opinion that he was the Devil incarnate and the depraved opinion of countercultural revolutionaries that he was a hero. Both views are mistaken. Manson was certainly an evil man, but his larger-than-life stature was an artifact of the moral chaos of the 1960s and early 1970s. He was demonized by those who feared the disintegration of society and glorified by subversives who yearned for some meaning in their lives beyond drug-induced hallucinations, unlimited sexual opportunities, and perfervid condemnation of the society in which they lived as parasites.

Manson's crimes were horrible, but unfortunately not extraordinary or rare. The cruel and bloody murders of innocent people are frequent, as anyone may learn from the media. Manson is an unexceptional specimen of a type of evildoer whose characteristic vice, given the opportunity, will lead to evil actions. Holding the man, the vice, and the actions in horrified awe is an obstacle to mounting an effective defense against them. A precondition of such a defense is understanding the vice that motivated Manson and his actions.

Manson was released from jail in 1967, after having completed seven years of a ten-year sentence. He was thirty-two and had spent seventeen of those years in some form of detention. When not in an institution he was a burglar, a car thief, a pimp, an armed robber, and a rapist of both sexes. These are crimes he admits to having committed (MW 21–74), and many of them are part of his official criminal record (HS 136–46).

Manson was born in 1934, the illegitimate son of a sixteen-year-old woman. His mother was a petty criminal, in and out of jail, living with various men, and an occasional prostitute. When she was in jail, Manson was cared for by her family. At the age of eight, however, his mother formally declared herself unable to look after him, and thus began his many years in institutions. His record in all them was uniformly bad. He was described as "dangerous," "not [to] be trusted," having "homosexual and assaultive tendencies," "safe only under supervision," "unpredictable . . . requir[ing] supervision both at work and in quarters," and "criminally sophisticated" (HS 139–40). He escaped whenever he could, but he was always caught. As a result of his escapes and record, he was transferred to increasingly more severe institutions until he ended up in the Federal Reformatory at Chillicothe, Ohio. During his time there he was often badly beaten and raped. In 1954, at the age of nineteen, he was released. He had had no education and was virtually illiterate.

In 1955 he got married, had a child, worked at various low-paying jobs, beat his wife, and stole cars, at which he was caught, and was sent to jail for three years. His wife stopped visiting him after a while, moved elsewhere with their child, and filed for divorce, and that was the last contact Manson had with either. He was paroled in 1957, resumed his career as a car thief, began pimping, and in 1959 was caught stealing a check. His parole was revoked, he was resentenced, and he began a jail term that came to an end in 1967.

During this last jail term Manson improved his primitive reading and writing skills, became a Scientology enthusiast, and most important, discovered music. He learned to play the guitar and spent much time practicing, playing, and composing. He said: "I was serious about the music trip and felt I had my head turned in the right direction. I felt I had come a long way. . . . However, I had not outgrown my desire to impress, especially when I had my guitar in hand and was singing in front of a group. I felt confident and positive when I entertained. . . . I became obsessed with music. I enjoyed playing the music of recording stars, but even more, I enjoyed writing and composing songs of my own" (MW 73).

After his release in 1967 he made his way, guitar in hand, to Haight-Ashbury in San Francisco. There the easy availability of sex and drugs, the lack of curiosity about his past, the welcoming acceptance of himself and his music were very appealing to him. He fit right in with the crowd of students, runaways, war protesters, drug pushers and addicts, even though he was about ten years older than most. As he put it: "People were like the music, very fast. And all seemed willing. Pretty little girls were running around every place with no panties or bras and asking for love. Grass and hallucinatory drugs were being handed to you on the streets. It was a different world than I had ever been in and one that I believed was too good to be true. It was a convict's dream and after being locked up for seven solid years . . . I joined it and the generation that lived it" (MW 81). He moved into the apartment of a young woman, the first member of what was soon to grow into his Family. He earned some money by a little guitar playing and singing, drug pushing, and theft.

As Manson was living in the congenial setting of Haight-Ashbury, his reputation as a sage spread among those pretty little girls running around without bras and panties. He had sex with as many as he could. This did no harm to his emerging status as a guru, but he did not leave it at that. He developed several lines of patter calculated to appeal to the gullible young surrounding him. One was the corruption of the system and the need to create an island where innocence, purity, and above all love can flourish unsullied. Another was doing one's own thing, acting on one's desires, and realizing that being oneself was good and inhibitions, conventions, and limits were bad. A third line actually showed some ingenuity. He told the girls that they had a problem with their fathers, which many of them, being runaways, not surprisingly did have. He then told them that he was their father, would teach them love, and that they should make love to him imagining that he was their father. This was not without verisimilitude because many of the girls were fourteen, fifteen, sixteen years old and he could have been their father. All this was accompanied with his guitar playing and singing. As he put it: "I had the answers for all the hang-ups and frustrations of these kids fleeing their homes. . . . Be your own person, love yourself, but let go of your ego. Don't be influenced by material things. Nothing is wrong if it feels good and satisfies you. . . . Love is for everyone, to be shared" (MW 103). The combination worked, and he maintained this posture until the very end.

A posture, however, it was. "I've got a thousand faces. . . . And in my life, I've played every one of those faces" (MW 229). Here is an example (from years later) of Manson playing some of his faces. It is related by the author of *Manson in His Own Words,* who interviewed him for hundreds of hours in prison. "I brought with me the young woman . . . who wanted to interview him for a local newspaper. . . . [She] was in her late twenties, neither a beauty nor homely, but by the time Manson had talked to her for a while, she must have believed she was the most attractive woman on earth. . . . When he spoke to her, he was polite, courteous and complimentary. His normal profanity and prison slang had disappeared, and in fact, he was more articulate than I would have believed possible. Very soon he was holding her hand and caressing the skin of her bare arm while she listened intently to every word he said. He stood up and began massaging the back of the interviewer's neck and shoulders. She closed her eyes and smiled appreciatively. Then, continuing the conversation, he casually reached across the table and picked up the cord of the tape recorder we were using. He looked at me and winked. Suddenly and menacingly, he wrapped the cord around the woman's neck. . . . Manson applied some pressure on the cord and in an intimidating voice said, 'Whatta yaw think . . . should I take this little bitch's life?' . . . Just as I was contemplating a rescue effort, he laughed and loosened the cord, saying, 'See bitch, you never want to trust a stranger'" (MW 229–30).

Resuming the chronological account, congenial as Manson had found San Francisco, he left it for Los Angeles because he realized that the recording industry was centered there and he imagined himself worthy of fame and fortune as a musician. He took with him some of the girls, and they set up residence on a derelict ranch at the northern edge of Los Angeles. He worked hard and successfully at making contacts with ex-cons, drug dealers, motorcycle gangs, ranch hands, producers of porno-graphic films, and most important, people in the recording industry. What he had to offer them were girls—pretty, nubile, willing girls. For the ranch quickly became a place to which young girls could come as they rebelled against their family, school, and middle-class existence. After a few months, the Family had about twenty core members and about another twenty with more fluid allegiances. A few of the core members were young men, but most were young girls, who were regular users of various hallucinogenic drugs, sexually hyperactive, all loving Manson, the sage, the unquestioned father of the Family. The girls willingly had sex with all the people approved by Manson. The Family's living expenses were covered by various means: stolen cars that were dismantled at the ranch and sold in parts, the distribution of drugs, pornographic films that Manson made using the girls, and whatever the girls could steal from their families and strangers.

Manson continued to beguile the girls with the patter about the rotten system, the island of love the ranch had become, and the beauty of the girls expressing their authentic selves, and he now added the idea of being Jesus Christ. He did not quite come out and say so, but he hinted darkly that he had lived before, two thousand years ago, and had died on the cross. The girls swallowed all this and were totally dominated by him. "Manson said that each person should be independent, but the whole Family was dependent on him. He said that he couldn't tell anyone else what to do, that they should 'do what your love tells you,' but he also told them, 'I am your love,' and his wants became theirs" (HS 225). They did what he told them to do, and they lived in the southern California sum-mer heat, often nude, hallucinating in a drug-induced haze, having sex with all comers, and competing to please Manson, their imagined father. Here is how the prosecutor describes the first Family members he talked to: "I was immediately struck by their expressions. They seemed to radiate contentment. I'd seen others like this—true believers, religious fanatics—

yet I was shocked and impressed. Nothing seemed to faze them. They smiled almost continually, no matter what was said. For them all questions had been answered. There was no need to search any more, because they had found the truth. And their truth was 'Charlie is love'" (HS 132).

But loving Charlie was just another of his faces. He thought that "women had only two purposes in life . . . to serve men and to give birth to children," and that "women were only as good as their men. They were only a reflection of their men," but he needed them because "it was only through women . . . that [he] could attract the men," whom he wanted in the Family because "men represented power, strength" (HS 225). Or, as he put it in an interview in 1981, when he was asked what he thought of women: "Oh, I like them, yeh, they're nice, they're put together well and everything, and they're soft and spongy—long as they kept their mouths shut and do what they're supposed to do."[2] He was a "sophisticated con man" who knew exactly how to manipulate the girls: "You can convince anybody of anything if you just push it at them all the time" (HS 483).

For Manson, however, all this was a sideshow. His real interest was to succeed in the world of music. The girls, the sex, the drugs, the stolen cars, his being a sage were just means to what he wanted more than anything: success as a recording artist. In this he failed completely. He was an amateur enthusiast, and all professionals quickly recognized him as such. He pleaded with them, offered girls and drugs as bribes, threatened them—all to no avail. He had thought that in music he had finally found something in life that made it worth living, something that pleased him, that he was good at, that he could be respected for, and he came up against the unanimously adverse judgment of the people on whom his success depended. In August 1969 the murders took place.

At the lengthy trial, Manson pleaded not guilty, but after it was over and the sentences had been passed, he readily admitted his guilt. He was an active participant in the second murders, but not in the first. He acknowledged, however, that he planned and directed both, specified that the killings should be bloody so as to cause outrage, supplied the weapons and the ropes, chose the victims and the times, ordered the writings on the walls, and dominated the participating members of the Family. He sent them off to the first murders, it is to him that the murderers returned after the mayhem, and it was he who after hearing their account went to the scene to remove the fingerprints and weapons that were left behind by his frenzied followers. They all received sentences of death. But shortly thereafter the death penalty was abolished in California and their sentences were commuted to life imprisonment. This made them eligible for parole in about ten years. Manson is still in prison.

5.2 The Vice

This description of Manson's life and actions is from the outside. It tells the facts, but not how Manson felt about himself and the world, and what motivated him. Nor does it explain the nature of the murders. Why were they committed just then? Why were those victims chosen? Why was there so much savagery? Why were the victims stabbed dozens of times? What was the significance of the words written in blood at both crimes? The answers to these questions and the key to Manson's feelings and motives are to be found in envy.

This may seem implausible at first because to modern sensibility envy does not appear to be a serious enough vice to warrant the moral condemnation Manson's crimes deserve. Behind this doubt is the simplistic view that envy is to want what someone else has. And one's immediate next thought is that since everyone has such feelings at some time or another, it cannot be all that bad. Envy, however, is a far more serious vice than this simplistic view implies. There is a deep truth in the biblical murder of Abel by the envious Cain. Christian theologians were not exaggerating in regarding envy as one of the deadly sins. Milton was not wrong to say that Satan was led by envy to become what he was. The malignity of Shakespeare's envious Iago, perhaps the most evil character in all his plays, was not just a poet's fancy. The envy portrayed by Dostoevsky in his underground man and by Melville's Claggart in *Billy Budd* point to one of the most destructive vices to which human beings are prone. And Nietzsche's analysis of the form of envy he calls *ressentiment* is a profound treatment of this prevalent and deplorable human tendency.[3]

Showing that Manson was indeed motivated by envy requires a two-stage argument. The first must explain why envy tends to be ruinous for both its subject and object. The second must provide reasons for thinking that envy motivated Manson's crimes. The best available definition of envy provides a good starting point for the first stage of the argument: "Envy is an emotion that is essentially both selfish and malevolent. It is aimed at persons, and implies dislike of one who possesses what the envious man himself covets or desires, and a wish to harm him. Graspingness for self and ill-will lie at the basis of it. There is in it also a consciousness of inferiority to the person envied, and a chafing under this consciousness. He who got what I envy is felt by me to have the advantage of me, and I resent it. . . . As signifying in the envious man a want that is ungratified, and as pointing to a sense of impotence inasmuch as he lacks the sense of power which possession of the desired object would give him, envy is in itself a painful emotion, although it is associated with pleasure when misfortune is seen to befall the object of it."[4]

All but one of the essential elements of envy are noted in this definition. The missing one is the recognition that the objects of envy fall at various points on a continuum that ranges from envying some material possession to envying the life a person lives. I may envy you specifically for the car you have, or far more generally for being happy, successful, or respected. The more general the object, the less assuageable is the envy of it. I can buy or steal a car like yours, and then the cause of my envy disappears. But it is much more difficult to live the life I envy you for having. For an enviable life depends on being a certain kind of person, as well as on receiving appropriate acknowledgment for it. The first is a matter of talents, skills, and admirable characteristics; the second is the good fortune of being respected for these excellences. If the object of my envy is your life, then my envy may just persist or grow in strength since my deficiencies or the contingencies of fortune may make it impossible for me to become what I envy you for being. The simplistic view of envy comes from thinking of its object as some material possession. A deeper view recognizes the serious moral danger of unassuageable envy.

At the root of this danger is the comparison essential to envy between the envier and the envied. The comparison is drawn by the envier, and it yields the result that the envied person has a considerable advantage the envier lacks. It is built into envy that the envied is much better and the envier is much worse off in some respect that matters to the envier. I will not envy your collection of CDs, or promotion to general, or popularity as a film star, if I am tone-deaf, or a pacifist, or dedicated to solitude. Envy occurs when I mind the respect in which I am so much worse off than you. But there is a respect in which people unavoidably mind the unfavorable comparison between themselves and others: in succeeding at the kind of life they want for themselves. When they see that they are failing and others are succeeding at this all-important endeavor, then the very existence of the successful others becomes a reproach to the failures.

There are several possible reactions to this reproach. One is admiration and the attempt to emulate the successful ones. Others are to make an effort to ignore the unfavorable comparison by retreating into a private fantasy life, or to deceive oneself, or to cultivate an ironic detachment and smile condescendingly at the futility of human endeavors. Yet another is to ask why the others are succeeding when one is failing. This question may be prompted by self-conscious inquisitiveness or by strong dissatisfaction and unfavorable circumstances that force the comparison on one. It has two possible answers. The first attributes failure to one's deficiency and the others' success to their excellence. The second blames it on one's bad and the others' good fortune. In either case, the envier's already bad feelings are bound to get worse.

If the unfavorable comparison is acknowledged to result from one's deficiency, then one's pride, understood as self-esteem or self-respect, is ruined. For one has proved to be deficient at the most important endeavor of living the kind of life one wants. This is not a temporary setback, but an irremediable failure, since the remedy could come only from the self that has been shown incapable of producing it. If the unfavorable comparison is attributed to luck, then one will conclude that the others do not deserve success and one does not deserve failure. A natural reaction to this is resentment.

It is also natural, however, to want to avoid acknowledging one's deficiency, for it is painful and there is a kind of finality about it. Ruined pride cannot be easily rebuilt, but since luck is fickle, there is always hope that one's bad luck and the others' good luck will change. So the predisposition to protect one's psychic well-being naturally prompts people to safeguard their pride and direct their resentment outward rather than inward, toward the injustice of the world and the undeserved success of others rather than toward their own deficiency. Nevertheless, one's fear of being proved deficient cannot be entirely laid to rest. It will linger in the background, not letting one dismiss the suspicion that one's deficiency is at least partly to be blamed for one's failure. It may be said, then, that this fear is the recessive and the resentment the dominant strain in envy.

Consider now the psychological state of envious people. They know that their lives are going badly, and they are miserable on account of it. Their misery is increased because their circumstances make it unavoidable for them to witness the flourishing lives of others. It exacerbates matters that these other lives flourish because they are succeeding in just those respects in which the enviers want to succeed but fail. They behold the spectacle of the satisfaction the successful take in their lives, and they feel frustration and disappointment about their own lives. They have to explain to themselves why they come off so badly by comparison. Blaming themselves would increase their misery because it would add injury to their pride to their already great frustrations. So they blame the world for being duped by the pretended excellences of the successful and for failing to recognize the true merits they themselves possess. The choice between explaining their failure by the corruption of the world and by their own deficiency, however, is not a true choice, for all their hopes, fears, and resentments depend on the first explanation being true and the second false. They credit themselves with seeing through the prevailing corrupt system of evaluation and the phony claims of excellence of those who are favored by the system, and so they cultivate cynicism as a bulwark that protects them from having to acknowledge their own deficiency.

Cynicism not only explains their failure; it also directs their resentment away from themselves and toward the system and those who benefit from it. This resentment tends to grow into hatred because of two exacerbating conditions. One is their feeling of impotence; the other is their chafing under the impersonality and corruption of a system that takes no notice of their pains, efforts, improvements, of how much success would mean to them, and of how much failure matters. Both conditions have an element of truth to them, but the significance of these truths is systematically misinterpreted by enviers.

It is true that the enviers are impotent in the face of their failure. It is also often true that their repeated attempts to succeed have led nowhere. The cause of their impotence, however, is not the unfairness of the system, but their reluctance to face their own deficiency. If they faced it, they would no longer be impotent because they might do something to succeed, namely, make themselves less deficient. Instead of resenting the system, they might try to develop whatever talents, skills, or characteristics are needed for success. But the formidable obstacle to this course of action is that they would first have to admit their own deficiency and thus deepen the injury to their pride. It is much easier to nurture their resentment, protect what is left of their pride, and continue to disguise from themselves the true cause of their failure.

There is truth also to the enviers' claim that most public human endeavors are conducted in the framework of some system or another, and these systems are impersonal and hardly ever free of corruption. They have to be impersonal because they are designed and maintained to encourage achievement and enforce the rules that determine what may or may not be done in pursuing it. It is the performance that matters, not how hard or easy it was for the performers or how important would success or failure be in their lives. The individuality of the performers is thus a matter of indifference from the point of view of the system. This makes failure even more bitter for those who have done much to improve, who have staked a lot on success, and for whom failure is calamitous.

Add to this that all human systems are imperfect and possess varying degrees of corruption. When enviers blame the corrupt system for their failure, they can usually cite evidence showing that some corruption exists. There is no doubt that corruption is always deplorable, even if it is ubiquitous. But the enviers relish rather than deplore the corruption because it legitimizes their resentment. If they could not blame the corrupt system for their failure, they would have to blame themselves, which would be far worse. So they nourish their resentment, encourage its growth into hatred, and congratulate themselves for their keen moral sense and championship of justice.

This is how envy combines misery of failure, resentment of success, fear of deficiency, cynicism about achievement, rage over impotence, and self-righteous indignation. If the hatred it fuels is strong enough, if the opportunity presents itself, if the risk seems worth taking, then envy may result in spectacularly excessive and malevolent evil actions that appear to others as incomprehensible senseless violence, motiveless malignity, or crazed inhumanity, but they are the understandable revenge of the enviers' ruined pride.

5.3   The Motive

Thus we come to the second stage of the argument. It must show, not just claim, that Manson was motivated by envy to commit his crimes. We may begin by noting a turning point in Manson's life: his discovery of music. He was in the second year of what was to be a seven-year prison term. He was twenty-seven. Reflecting on this time at the age of fifty-one, in prison almost twenty years after the murders, knowing that he will never be released, he says to his interviewer, who came as close to a friend as Manson ever had, "I was doing hard time. . . . My life, my mind, was being mutilated by concrete and steel. . . . I was depressed, and I wasn't just sick of jails—I was fed up with being the individual prisons had made of me. . . . I was taking an honest look at myself: I didn't like my life or the outlook of my future. . . . The answer was . . . [to] improve my mind and habits so that I could overcome my weaknesses and resist temptations. I wanted to develop character and stop being a fool" (MW 67–68). And he goes on: "I saw myself as I really was: an immature, mixed-up person with nothing but a mouth going for him. I was without direction or a proper goal in life . . . the flippant little fool" (MW. 73) It was at this point that "I became obsessed with music. . . . I felt confident and positive when I entertained. . . . Music . . . helped me to overcome my other hang-ups . . . I had become very happy and content . . . I was accepted, even appreciated as an individual" (MW 73–74). This time in jail was a significant period in Manson's life.

Looking back at his preceding twenty-seven years, he says, "Rejection, more than love and acceptance, has been a part of my life since birth. . . . I realize I am only what I've always been, 'a half-assed nothing'" (MW 26). "My ego has been crushed. . . . With all my experience of people turning their backs on me, I should have known better than to trust anyone but myself. Still, I had hoped—and was again rejected" (MW 64). And the voice of ruined pride goes on, "I never went to school, so I never growed up to read and write too good, so I have stayed in jail and I have stayed stupid. . . . You broke me years ago. . . . My life has never been important to anyone" (HS 389–91). It is easy to see, given this dismal view of himself, the importance music had acquired in his life. For the first time Manson found something that satisfied him and was appreciated by others. He thought that his pride might be reclaimed through music. But this was a tentative thought because he was full of apprehension on account of his deficiencies.

As the time of his release approached, "thoughts of leaving brought back the feelings of inferiority I had studied so hard to master" (MW 74). "I had dreams and plans, but as I was being processed for release, I knew the dreams would never be realized and the plans were nothing more than wishful thinking. . . . I told the officer who was signing me out, "You know what, man, I don't want to leave! I don't have a home out there! Why don't you just take me back inside? . . . My plea was ignored" (MW 77–78). Before our hearts are broken by this piteous whining, we should remember that they come from the man who "got a thousand faces" (MW 229); who beat his wife, prostituted his lovers, raped men and women when he could; who was a robber, a pimp, and a tightly wound coil of violence; who twisted the cord around his naive visitor's neck; "whose abuse and neglect from early childhood on doesn't explain it all," as his sympathetic interviewer notes, "for others with an equally unhappy past have managed to escape" (MW 232); and who was responsible for the horrible Tate-LaBianca murders.

Manson, then, was released from prison, full of fears on account of his deficiencies, hoping to rebuild his life around music, and he made his way, after a few months of abandon to sex and drugs in Haight-Ashbury, to Los Angeles, the center of the music business. He had in tow a number of young girls, the beginning of his Family. His new life got under way on the ranch he found, the Family was growing, he had a home base for disassembling stolen cars, dealing in drugs, and producing pornographic films, and he set out to realize the hopes centered on becoming a successful musician. He got to the fringes of the recording industry by providing girls, drugs, and the frisson it gave to musicians and businessmen to rub up against an ex-con. But he got no further than the fringes, for he met one disappointment after another, and as he was rebuffed, so his resentment grew.

A producer of television shows who was also a record company executive listened to Manson's playing and singing and "had been unimpressed," saying a plain "no" to Manson's hopes (HS 155). Another gave "Manson fifty dollars, all the money he had in his pocket, because 'I felt sorry for these people' . . . As for Manson's talent, he 'wasn't impressed enough to allot the time necessary' to prepare and record him'" (HS

185). A widely recorded professional musician, quite sympathetic to Manson, said: "Charlie never had a musical bone in his body" (HS 251). A folk-song expert thought that Manson was "a moderately talented amateur" (HS 214). Seeking a more receptive audience, Manson went to Big Sur and played at the Esalen Institute. He said that he "played his guitar for a bunch of people who were supposed to be the top people there, and they rejected his music. Some people pretended that they were asleep . . . and some just got up and walked out" (HS 275). With all these rejections "my back was against the wall," said Manson, and he threatened a pivotal person who could really have helped him realize his musical hopes: "the guy turned the tables on me by saying, 'You know what Manson, you're a flakey nothing . . . we owe you nothing. And because of your attitude, nothing is what you get. Now get out of my office, and if you want to keep playing tough guy, I'm going to make a phone call, and it's *adios* Manson.'" Then, Manson says, "I left his office with some shit on my face, and a very disgusted feeling in my stomach" (MW 184).

All this meant the collapse of his hope of rebuilding his life around music. He says: "My dream of the last ten years had gone the way of any dream when you wake up. Back to reality. I was the same grubby nothing whose mother dumped him on the State." He was "feeling down and sorry for myself," but "the self-pity was pretty well shadowed by hate and contempt. Hate for the world that denied. Contempt for people who can't see or understand" (MW 185). He saw people in authority as corrupt. "I could not see enough honest faces in the world to pattern myself after. . . . Those who have money and success abuse every law written and get away with it" (MW 63). He understood "how corrupt the system was" (MW 72). He hated "a society that spoke lies and denied their children something or someone to respect" (MW 144). "I have screamed about the injustice of the system" (MW 224). He was full of "bitterness and contempt" and with "the feeling of power . . . coupled with hatred" (MW 200–201). "I became devoid of caring emotion" (MW 202). His view was "fuck this world and everyone in it" (MW 203).

All the elements of envy as Manson's motive are now in place. His pride was ruined twice over: first by the combination of his unfortunate childhood, the maltreatment and punishment he received in various institutions, and the failure of his marriage, other relationships, and criminal projects; and second by the rejection of his musical aspirations. Comparing himself with others who had succeeded in just those ways in which he had tried and failed, he could not deny the substantial differences in their respective positions. But he could and did deny that either he or they deserved what they got. He thought that the differences were unjust, the results of the dishonesty and corruption of the successful and their refusal to recognize his merits. He also realized his impotence in the face of this supposed conspiracy of injustice. His lifelong resentment steadily grew and finally rigidified into violent implacable hatred of all those who benefited from the injustice of the world and who rendered him powerless to change anything. The final assault on his pride came with the realization that the hope he had for his music was doomed. The meaning he had managed to give his life disintegrated, he lost his purpose, the denial of his deficiency was becoming unsustainable, his rage mounted, and it erupted in the spectacular Tate-LaBianca murders, which revenged his ruined pride.

Envy explains both Manson's depraved motive for the murders and the horrible savagery with which they were done. The murders followed shortly after Manson realized that he would not succeed in music. The first victims were chosen because they happened to be present in the house of the music executive who humiliatingly ejected him on a previous occasion; and the second victims because they were rich, successful, and lived in an exclusive neighborhood full of such people. The multiple stab wounds, the blood, and the savagery expressed Manson's violence and hatred. And the significance of the words written in blood on the walls was that "pig" meant the establishment that was Manson's target, "death to pigs" is what he was dealing out, and the misspelled "healter skelter" meant, in Manson's private vocabulary, the chaos that he hoped to unloose on the world.

5.4 The Judgment

It is important, but not easy, to arrive at a balanced judgment of Manson in particular and envy in general. There can be no reasonable doubt that the Tate-LaBianca murders were evil acts. They caused serious, excessive, malevolent, and inexcusable harm to innocent people, and that is what is meant by an act being evil. But what about Manson himself, the agent of those acts? The murder of innocent people is always morally unjustifiable, regardless of whether it serves a purpose, such as bringing about a revolution or revenging a wrong. But even if there were some goal important enough to justify the murder of the innocent as a means to its achievement, it still would not justify the excesses and the malevolence of the Tate-LaBianca murders. Yet it would be wrong to conclude from this that Manson did evil for its own sake. His actions were evil, but he had his utterly misguided moral reasons for performing them. These reasons came from Manson's private morality, which he substituted for the real thing. According to it, right and wrong were determined by how he felt about them. His reasons were bad, but he believed—albeit wrongly—that they were good. He believed that his private morality justified him in having and expressing hatred of his victims because they were corrupt, unjust, and against him, and thus they deserved the horrible deaths he inflicted on them. Manson may have been justified in hating those who maltreated him, but his victims were not among those who had. And much of his hatred was really resentment of his own inferiority and rage over his deficiencies and misfortunes. Nor did he have any way of knowing or any reason for suspecting that his victims were corrupt and unjust. Some of them were affluent and successful, but these pleasant things may be achieved honestly. Manson's belief that they were not was groundless. Manson, therefore, had conspicuously bad reasons for the spectacular evil he caused. He was an evil person regardless of what he believed.

It might now be said, in a spirit of misguided reluctance to assign blame, that although Manson was an evil person, he was a product of his society. The implication is that if blame is to be assigned, it should fall not on Manson but on the society that produced him. Although this view is widespread, it is untenable. We are all subject to the good and bad influences of our society. The same influences, however, affect different people differently, partly because they have different characters and different histories of action. Some influences on Manson were undoubtedly bad, but not all who were subject to them became criminals, even fewer turned into murderers, and of those not many are known to have committed crimes as horrible as the Tate-LaBianca murders. People are not helpless, passive recipients of social influences. They can control their reactions and refuse to act on them. And even very bad influences can be counteracted by reason, will, emotion, or imagination, as well as by good influences. Manson was receptive to bad social influences and resistant to good ones. Social influences, therefore, should no more be blamed for making Manson into an evil person than the influences of the ambient climate or the prevailing religions. It was up to Manson to make what he could of the influences on him, and he is properly blamed for becoming an evil person whose ruling vice was envy and whose malevolent motive led him to commit savagely excessive acts of murder.

This brings us to the disputed judgment of the significance of envy in contemporary life. Does Manson's envy exemplify a widespread form of evil, or is it merely an individual aberration that perhaps explains Manson's actions but little else? I believe that envy is a serious moral threat that cannot be eliminated from moral life and a major contributor to the prevalence of evil. Manson is an extreme example of what happens when the possibility that threatens is realized. His actions were unusual only in their extremity, but not in being motivated by envy. Unfortunately, disputes about the seriousness of the threat of envy have become politicized. This makes a balanced judgment much more difficult.

One of the several pivotal points on which thinkers on the right and the left differ is equality. Those on the right believe that egalitarianism is unjust and motivated by envy.[5] Those on the left believe that equality is a requirement of justice and in an egalitarian society envy would wither away.[6] This is not the place to discuss the respective merits of these views. It is sufficient for present purposes to note that both assume the simplistic view that takes material possessions to be the objects of envy. Leftists advocate the equalization of material possessions, rightists oppose it, and both appeal to justice to support their views. As we have seen, however, envy is much more complex and has much deeper sources than wanting some material object that someone else has. The sources of envy are the recognized excellences and deficiencies of human beings, the tendency to compare oneself and one's life with other people and their lives, pride in coming out well in these comparisons, and resentment if one does not. These sources of envy lie deep in human nature. It is, therefore, a mistake to attribute envy merely to differences in material possessions or to suppose that their redistribution would eliminate envy. If people did not envy material possessions, they would envy something else. The threat of envy results from human differences, not from the surface manifestations of those differences.

The reason why the threat of envy cannot be eliminated from moral life is that differences in such excellences as talents, skills, and admirable characteristics will persist as long as there are human beings; people will go on taking pride in their excellences; and they will continue to feel badly about their deficiencies. These attitudes are not only unavoidable but also reasonable. For everyone wants to live a good life, and having some excellences is necessary for it. It is natural to feel badly if one is shown to be deficient in this requirement. The ineliminable threat of envy comes from the natural tendency to direct this bad feeling outward as resentment of others rather than inward as spur to self-improvement. It is natural because turning it inward causes further injury to one's pride. Although natural, the tendency is also unreasonable because it precludes the self-improvement required for a better life. Saving one's pride by cultivating resentment of others is easier than recognizing one's deficiencies and need for improvement. This is why envy will continue to make a significant contribution to the prevalence of evil.

5.5 Envy and Evil

Envy is a vice because, if circumstances encourage or permit, it tends to motivate evil actions. Given the psychological makeup of ordinary human beings, who are neither angels nor devils, they value their pride and resent injury to it. Such injury is frequent because comparisons routinely prompt the adverse conclusion that someone else is undeservedly better off than oneself. People rarely admit that they deserve to be worse off in some important respect than others because it would injure their pride and thus make them even worse off. Envy, therefore, is an understandable vice, and its elimination is unlikely.

One implication of this view of envy is that the influential idea of the Enlightenment that human beings are naturally good and they do evil only because social influences corrupt them is mistaken. As we have seen, envy is a natural expression of human psychology, not a corruption of it. Some virtues and vices are alike in being developments of basic human propensities. Virtues, therefore, are not signs of psychological health, and vices are not symptoms of psychological malfunction.

From the moral point of view, of course, virtues are good and vices bad, but psychology and morality may motivate different actions. It would be comforting if this were otherwise; if virtues were natural and vices unnatural; if human beings were basically good and caused evil only as a result of interrupted development. The understanding of envy we have reached shows, however, that this comforting view is false. This does not mean that human beings are basically bad or that vices are natural and virtues are not. It means that human beings are psychologically complex and morally ambivalent. It also means that the Enlightenment dream of human perfectibility should be recognized for what it is: a dream.

Another implication of the view of envy we have arrived at is that the manipulation of social influences is likely to affect only the expression of envy, not envy itself. For whether envy is felt and whether it motivates actions depend on how people respond to the injury of their pride, not on the state of the society in which they live. Envy is a matter of psychology, not of sociology or politics. Altering the sociological or political circumstances in which envy is felt will not, therefore, affect whether it is felt. Social and political changes can certainly make the expression of envy in evil actions more or less likely. There is everything to be said in favor of making appropriate changes. But these changes can only ameliorate the effects of envy and will leave its causes untouched.

The idea, therefore, that reforming society will reform the people who live in it is as much a dream as human perfectibility. If reform consists in the redistribution of wealth, then people will envy other people's beauty, sex life, children, taste, style, eloquence, learning, physical fitness, and so forth. If reform aims at the improvement of moral education, it may bring about increased knowledge of what ought and ought not to be done. As experience and introspection amply show, however, people routinely act contrary to what they know are requirements of morality. Moreover, advocates of particular reforms are often concerned with imposing, in the name of morality, their political agenda on others who hold reasonable but contrary moral and political views. Proposed reforms often suffer from the very ills they aim to cure. This is hardly surprising since the reformers are members of the society whose members, they claim, stand in need of reform. None of this is meant to oppose genuine reform. It is meant to express reasonable doubt that reform will alter the existing balance of good and evil actions. It is more likely to change the ways in which good and evil are done and leave their balance roughly where it was. Is there, then, nothing that can be done about the vice of envy itself? Of course there is. The best hope is to concentrate on oneself and do what one can not to be envious. Success in this endeavor, however, depends on having considerable self-knowledge and self-control. These are admirable character traits, but their development is as difficult now as it has ever been.

CHAPTER 6

Wickedness in High Places

For we wrestle not against flesh and blood, but
against principalities, against powers, against the
rulers of the darkness of this world, against
spiritual wickedness in high places.

—PAUL, EPISTLE TO THE EPHESIANS

The evildoers discussed in this chapter were moderately well
educated. They knew some history, and the atrocities of the Nazis were
very much in their minds as they committed their own atrocities. They
were self-conscious and reflective. This is one way in which they differ
from the preceding cases. But there is also another difference. The crusaders, Robespierre, and Stangl tried to remain aloof from the evil they
caused. They went about their ghastly task with as little personal involvement as possible. For Manson, of course, it was personal, not political,
and he was anything but aloof. The evildoers of this chapter combined
political and personal motivation for their actions. For them, the political
was personal. Politics formed an important part of their psyche, and they
defined themselves, as well as their victims, in political terms.

6.1 What Was Done

In 1976 the military forces of Argentina staged a coup, seized
power, appointed a junta that remained in power until 1983, and waged
what has been called "the dirty war." The name reflects the facts that the
junta ignored the rules and practices of conventional war, its targets were
Argentinean civilians suspected of being or supporting urban guerrillas,

83

and it proceeded outside the law to kidnap, torture, imprison, and murder many thousands of people. Low estimates put the murders between eleven thousand and fifteen thousand. The number of suspects kidnapped, tortured, and imprisoned is known to be much higher through the testimony of survivors.

The dirty war was conducted by the officers of the Argentinean army, navy, and air force, with the approval and active cooperation of junior and noncommissioned career officers in each of the three branches. All in all, about seven hundred military personnel were involved. They operated 340 detention centers.[1] Their activities were divided into detention (i.e., kidnapping), interrogation (i.e., torture), and elimination (i.e., murder). The personnel were rotated so that most of the seven hundred were involved in each activity.[2] The police cooperated with the military by active assistance or by declaring "free zones" in which the dirty war could be waged without their interference. As for the judiciary, "the military dictatorship dismissed all high-ranking judges and required lower-ranking magistrates to swear their loyalty to the new government" (Osiel 13).

The horrors of the dirty war are catalogued in mind-numbing detail in a volume entitled *Nunca Más* ("never again").[3] The volume is the report of the Argentine National Commission, set up after the fall of the junta. It is based on the commission's investigation and the testimony of survivors. The following is a description, one of many in the volume, of how the kidnapping routinely proceeded. "My husband . . . was kidnapped. . . . A group of men in civilian clothes knocked him unconscious, forced him into a private car without number plates, and drove him off to an unknown destination. . . . When I returned home, I was captured at the door by these people, who were holding my mother as a hostage 'in case I didn't turn up.' They blindfolded me and tied my hands. I was taken to a place I haven't been able to identify, where I was subjected to all kinds of physical and moral torture, while they put me through an incoherent interrogation" (Report 17).

The kind of torture to which thousands of people were subjected is described by one who had endured it. "For days they applied electric shocks to my gums, nipples, genitals, abdomen and ears. . . . They then began to beat me systematically and rhythmically with wooden sticks on my back, the backs of my thighs, my calves and the soles of my feet. At first the pain was dreadful. Then it became unbearable. . . . This continued for several days, alternating the two tortures. Sometimes they did both at the same time. . . . In between torture sessions they left me hanging by my arms from hooks fixed in the wall of the cell where they had thrown me. . . . On two or three occasions they also burnt me with a metal instrument . . . not like a cigarette, which gets squashed, but something more like a red-hot nail. . . . One day they put me face down on the torture table, tied me up . . . and began to strip the skin from the soles of my feet. I imagine, although I didn't see it because I was blindfolded, that they were doing it with a razor blade or a scalpel. I could feel them pulling as if they were trying to separate the skin at the edge of the wound with a pair of pincers. . . . I'm not sure when, they took me off to the 'operating theatre.' There they tied me up and began to torture my testicles. . . . I'd never experienced such pain. It was as though they were pulling out all my insides . . . as though my throat, brain, stomach and testicles were linked by a nylon thread which they were pulling on, while at the same time crushing everything" (Report 23–24).

When the victims were not being tortured, "treatment consisted of keeping the prisoners hooded . . . sitting, without talking or moving. . . . We were made to sit on the floor with nothing to lean against from the moment we got up at six in the morning until eight in the evening . . . we spent fourteen hours a day in that position. We couldn't utter a word, or even turn our heads. . . . A companion ceased to be included on the interrogators' list and was forgotten. Six months went by. . . . This man had been sitting there, hooded, without speaking or moving, for six months, awaiting death" (Report 59).

These descriptions, I must stress, are of the typical experiences of thousands of people; they are not exceptional treatments meted out in special cases. Of course, the descriptions are the testimonies of survivors. Thousands did not have the option to testify because they were murdered after having been first kidnapped and then tortured and imprisoned for months on end. The following account of how the murders were routinely done comes from one of the murderers who many years later felt conscience-stricken and told the truth. He was Adolfo Francisco Scilingo, a lieutenant commander in the navy. He gave the account to a journalist, who tape-recorded it with his consent and later published it (Verbitsky).

"It was called the flight. . . . I went to the basement, where the ones who were going to fly were. . . . They were informed that they were going to be transferred to the south and would be given a vaccination— I mean a dose of something to knock them out, a sedative. . . . Then they were put on a navy truck. . . . We went to the military airport . . . and there learned that it was . . . a Skyvan belonging to the coast guard which was going to make the flight. . . . They put me in charge of the first flight. . . . The subversives were carried out like zombies and loaded onto the airplane" (Verbitsky 21–22). At this point Scilingo became disturbed, interrupted his account, and continued it on a later occasion. "You asked me what happened in the airplanes. Once the plane had taken off, the doctor on board gave them a second dose of an extremely

powerful tranquilizer. It put them into deep sleep. . . . In their unconscious state, the prisoners were stripped, and when the commander of
the airplane gave the order [many miles from land over the ocean] . . .
the hatch was opened and they were thrown out, naked, one by one"
(Verbitsky 48–49). The interviewer asks: "How many people do you calculate were killed in this way? Between fifteen and twenty per
Wednesday. For how long? Two years. Two years, a hundred
Wednesdays, from fifteen hundred to two thousand people. Yes"
(Verbitsky 51). This was the navy's method of murder, and only one of
several methods. The army did it differently. Taken together they
account for the estimate of eleven thousand to fifteen thousand murders.

6.2 Why It Was Done

The dirty war was evil, and the people who waged it are responsible for horrendous atrocities. But the evil was not done in a vacuum.
Accounts of it that begin with the coup in 1976 and go on to describe the
resulting cruelty and the suffering are symptoms of moralistic self-indulgence that hinders understanding and reasonable response.[4] It has been
well said that "it would be wrong to minimize the disruptive effects of left-
wing terrorism on Argentine society in the late 1960s and early 1970s, as
many scholars are inclined to do. . . . There was very much a real 'war'
between the guerrillas and the military and . . . the guerrillas were not in
retreat by the time of the 1976 coup. . . . Military officers had become one
of the guerilla's principal targets. Family members of several officers were
murdered in such attacks" (Osiel 12).

During this time the cold war was at its height. Cuba was actively
attempting to subvert South America, and leftist guerilla groups were
trained and financed by Cuba and the Soviet Union. There were several
leftist guerilla groups operating, but "the Montoneros were the most
steadfast" of them.[5] The casualty figures accepted by the Argentinean
legal expert, Carlos Santiago Nino, who was assigned the responsibility
after the fall of the junta to devise the legal response to the dirty war, were
as follows: "200 political deaths during 1974, 860 during 1975, and 149 in
the three months prior to the 1976 coup. . . . Between May 1973 and
March 1976, the 1,358 terrorist-related deaths involved 445 subversives,
180 policeman, 66 members of the military, and 677 civilians" (Nino 15).

An Argentinean opponent of the junta who unequivocally condemned
the dirty war observed that "there were many anti-intellectual intellectuals,
eager to plunge into revolutionary praxis, who fomented the idolization of

violence to which many young persons proved suicidally receptive. . . . Any argument against violence was viewed as a betrayal of some grandiose cause. . . . The guerrillas certainly contributed greatly to the brutality of the 1976 coup" (Osiel 15). It is apparent that "the guerrillas expressly sought to provoke a coup, reasoning that state repression would in turn elicit popular support for armed struggle. By the early 1970s, then, large segments of public opinion had come to endorse or indulge routine use of extra-legal means in political life, on both left and right, an attitude that was to prevail for the ensuing decade" (Osiel 15).

The coup of 1976 and the subsequent dirty war were responses to this state of affairs. None of this excuses or lessens the evil that was done by the military, but it helps illuminate why it was done. The junta and the officers waged the dirty war as a conscious response to the guerrillas, and they supposed—wrongly—that the savagery of their response was justified by the real threat the guerrillas presented to the stability of Argentina.[6] As General Videla, a member of the junta, said in a radio address one day after the coup: "The armed forces have assumed the direction of the state in fulfillment of an obligation from which they cannot back away. They do so only after calm meditation about the irreparable consequences to the destiny of the nation that would be caused by the adoption of a different stance. This decision is aimed at ending misrule, corruption, and the scourge of subversion."[7]

The views expressed in this speech were not just propaganda. High- and low-ranking officers alike really believed that they had an obligation to defend the nation from the threat of subversion. A retired admiral was asked in an interview, "Why was it necessary to torture?" He responded, "We had to fight like they fight. . . . I've vomited more than once after seeing horrible things. We are condemnable. We've killed people without trials that we know were guerrillas. . . . But we did it so others didn't suffer more. As a good Christian I have problems of conscience. . . . If you want to combat subversion, you get down in the mud and get dirty. . . . We must condemn torture. The day we stop condemning torture—although we tortured— . . . is the day we stop being human beings" (Rosenberg 125–26).

This admiral merely witnessed what was done, but here is an officer speaking who actually did it: "It was a war against an armed guerilla organization. . . . This is very important. If you don't look at it as a war, it makes no sense. We had to fight in the enemy's camp. If the enemy was in civilian clothes that was where we had to go. . . . The guerrillas were fanatics. They lived for war. We had to do the same. . . . The prisoner would be tied down, and I'd have to interrogate him. I felt destroyed. When you think about the 'enemy,' it's depersonalized. But it isn't that way. . . . You

have to get used to it. At first, I'll be honest, it was hard to accustom ourselves to put up with torture. We're like everyone else. The person who
likes war is crazy. We all would have preferred to fight in uniform. . . . The
last thing we wanted to do was interrogate. . . . In the first phase of the war
everyone who was captured was executed. . . . We knew that if we put
them into courts, they would ask for all the guarantees of the system they
were attacking. . . . Let's say that ten thousand guerrillas disappeared. If
we hadn't done it, how many more people would have died at the hand of
the guerrillas? . . . It's a barbarity, but that's what war is. . . . I really feel
that any armed forces with a decent level of culture and human feeling
would do the same as we did" (Rosenberg 128–31).

Another officer, an active participant in the dirty war, said at the conclusion of his trial: "A soldier always follows orders; but an officer is a gen-
tleman as well as a soldier, and if he always takes refuge in due obedience,
he would be betraying the confidence the nation places in him when it
entrusts him with its most precious things: the care of its land and traditions and the blood of its children. . . . I feel free in my professional conscience. . . . I might have made some small mistakes, but in the big things
I don't repent anything" (Rosenberg 134–35 and Osiel 27).

Virtually the same view is expressed by Scilingo, who did repent. He
said: "We were all convinced it was the best thing that could be done for
the country." "All of us were convinced that we were involved in a different kind of war, for which we were not prepared, and that we were using
the means we had at hand, that the enemy continually had good information and we had to deny them that information." "We were totally convinced of what we were doing. The way we had internalized it, with the
situation we were living through in this country, it would be a total lie if I
told you that I wouldn't do it again under the same conditions. I would be
a hypocrite. . . . It was something you had to do. . . . No one liked to do it,
it wasn't a pleasant thing. But it was done, and it was understood that this
was the best way" (Verbitsky 25, 29–30, 23–24).

If the horrors involved in the kidnapping, torture, imprisonment,
and murder of thousands of people are put side by side with the sincere, passionately held beliefs of the officers in the necessity of the
dirty war against subversives who threatened the nation they were obli-
gated to protect, then an obvious question arises. How could the officers believe that what they were doing was morally justified? What is
the frame of mind that could make it seem obligatory to murder more
than ten thousand people in response to the murder of about one
thousand; to torture people for months on end, not to extract information, but to punish them; to throw thousands of drugged and naked
people out of airplanes?

6.3 Failed Justification

We may begin to understand the dirty warriors' frame of mind by seeing why their own justification of their actions is indefensible. They regarded themselves as acting under the moral necessity to protect their moral vision of the Argentinean state. That vision combined "traditional Catholicism, fierce nationalism, and intense xenophobia merged into the ideal of an organic society free of political dissent, cultural experimentation, class conflict, religious diversity, or secular doubt" (Osiel 11). They believed that subversives were threatening this ideal and that they, as the military, had a sworn duty to protect it. They were supported in this belief by the archbishop of Argentina, who said in a public statement that "the Church thinks that the circumstances at this time demand that the armed forces run the government. . . . In accepting this responsibility, the armed forces are carrying out their duty" (Osiel 210–11 n. 9). They would have preferred to carry out their duty by legal means, but that was no longer possible because the subversion permeated the judiciary. Extralegal methods were thus forced on them, and that is why it became morally necessary for them to kidnap, torture, imprison, and murder the subversives. It was the subversives who waged an unconventional war, and the defenders of the good of Argentina had no choice but to react in the same way. They were forced to do what they recognized was normally immoral, but they were justified because the alternatives would have resulted in a far worse outcome.

This attempt to provide a moral justification for what was done is an obvious failure. Consider first who were thought to be appropriate targets of extralegal actions. The president of the junta stated that the target "is not just someone with a gun or a bomb, but also someone who spreads ideas that are contrary to Western civilization." He defined subversion as consisting of "any concealed or open, invidious . . . action that attempts to change or destroy a people's moral criteria and way of life, for the purpose of seizing power or imposing . . . a new way of life based on a different ordering of human values" (Osiel 12). And another member of the junta said: "We cannot allow a minuscule minority to continue perturbing the minds of our youth, inculcating ideas completely alien to our sense of nationality. . . . All that is subversion" (Osiel 174 n. 6). This way of thinking about subversion makes it possible to regard anyone who disagrees with the dirty warriors' vision of a good society as a morally justified target of kidnapping, torture, imprisonment, and murder.

This possibility in fact became actual practice. The victims included countless people whose subversion consisted in being friends, neighbors, or family members of those who were merely suspected of falling under the intolerably vague notion of subversion. The advantage of vagueness was that it gave the dirty warriors a virtually free hand to kidnap, torture, imprison, and murder whomever they pleased. Their kidnappings, for instance, were riddled with mistaken identities, arbitrariness, personal likes and dislikes, the accidental presence or absence of their intended victims or of their acquaintances, and so forth. No reasonable person could believe that such actions were justified by moral necessity.

The moral justification proffered rests on obfuscation about subversion. If subversion is understood as broadly as the dirty warriors meant it to be, then the subversives included large numbers of law-abiding Argentineans merely because they held religious, political, or moral views different from those of the dirty warriors. Such people were not guerrillas, fanatics, or communists; they had waged no conventional or unconventional war; they were subversive only in the sense that they disagreed with ultramontane Catholicism. Even if there were a moral justification of the kidnapping, torture, imprisonment, and murder of guerrillas, there could be none for treating these non-guerrillas in the same way.

Any plausibility that the junta's moral justification may have derives from a narrow interpretation in which subversives were those who engaged in guerilla activity. But the actions of the dirty warriors were directed against subversives in the broad sense in which both guerrillas and non-guerrillas were regarded as subversives. For the moral justification of their actions, however, the dirty warriors appealed to subversion in the narrow sense. By this stratagem they claimed to be morally justified in inflicting grievous harm on guerrillas and non-guerrillas alike. But their so-called moral justification was indefensible because in their actions they ignored the crucial distinction on which the justification of their actions rested.

Furthermore, the assumption that the treatment of the guerrillas themselves was justified because there was no alternative to it is patently false. Perhaps there was no alternative to taking extralegal action against them; perhaps it was morally necessary to render them harmless; perhaps in a few instances even torture was justified in order to extract information that made it possible to stop guerrillas at large from continuing their campaign of murder. But this cannot be used to justify the systematic use of torture as a method of punishment. Nor can the justification of imprisonment be used to justify keeping the prisoners hooded, manacled, and sitting motionless fourteen hours a day for many months as they were awaiting execution. There were also obvious alternatives to murder. The guerrillas could have been exiled; or, if that were thought to be too lenient, they could have been imprisoned in remote places, which abound in Argentina. It is outrageous to claim that moral necessity dictated drugging and denuding them in preparation for throwing them out of an airplane.

The dirty warriors were neither stupid nor deranged. The conspicuous failure of this attempt at moral justification could not have been hidden from them. Yet they undoubtedly believed that they had morality on their side. Their frame of mind, therefore, could not have been accurately reflected by this indefensible justification. They must have had a different ground for believing in the moral justification of what they were doing. Understanding how they could have done the evil they did, while believing themselves to be morally justified, requires looking elsewhere for understanding their frame of mind.

It has been suggested that the actions of the dirty warriors and their belief that their actions were morally justified should be explained in terms of their obedience to orders (e.g., Osiel). They were career military officers, trained and sworn to obey their superiors, it was their duty to do so, and in doing what they did, they followed orders. War, as many of them said, is a terrible thing requiring soldiers to do what is normally immoral. But the war was forced on them and their actions were morally justified because they were responses to aggression and the fulfillment of their military obligation.

It presents a very serious problem for this attempt to understand the dirty warriors' frame of mind that the orders they followed may have been illegal. Their duty was to follow only legal orders. The difficulty is to determine whether their orders were indeed illegal; if they were, whether the dirty warriors could have been expected to know that; and if they did know, whether it was a realistic possibility in their circumstances to refuse to obey them.

Much has been written about the supposed obligation to obey orders. It was at the center of both the Nuremberg trials of the Nazi leaders and the trial of Adolf Eichmann in Israel. The difficulty was deepened by Hannah Arendt's book about the Eichmann trial and the controversy it created.[8] And it was deepened yet further by the Milgram experiments, which seemed to show that many ordinary people will do what an authority tells them to do even if it is normally immoral.[9] The whole problem and its bearing on the responsibility of the dirty warriors has been well discussed by the legal scholars Carlos Santiago Nino and Mark Osiel in their respective books (see notes 1 and 5). It is characteristic of the complexities of the issues that they have reached incompatible conclusions.

Reasonable and morally committed people can disagree whether an order is legal if it conforms to existing laws or whether it is also required that the existing laws should be morally acceptable. It is difficult to judge how much officers can be expected to worry about the legality of the orders they receive, often by radio or telephone, in the middle of a conventional or unconventional action, when they face the enemy and physical danger, have to act quickly and decisively, must calculate what the enemy might do and what the likely casualties of their troops might be. It is no less difficult to know how far officers ought to go in refusing to obey an order whose legality they doubt. Should they risk being shot for mutiny? Should they take their own doubts seriously when they know that they see only a small part of the situation while their order came from a superior who has a more complete picture? When is it reasonable that officers should act contrary to many years of training in which obeying orders was drilled into them?

These are difficult and complex questions, but fortunately there is no need to try to answer them. For I believe there are three strong reasons for rejecting this approach to understanding the dirty warriors' frame of mind. First, when the legality of the order is the focus, the questions are interpreted as questions of law. And while they are that, they are also questions of morality. These are different questions because legally permissible actions may be immoral, and morally permissible actions may be illegal. One can recognize that historical and contingent influences have shaped the laws of Argentina and ask about the morality of the dirty warriors' actions independently of their legality. The pivotal question about explaining evil concerns the frame of mind that made it possible for the dirty warriors to perform evil actions and believe that they were morally justified. This is a moral question. The question of the legal standing of their evil actions is no doubt important, but answering it will not help to understand what leads people to perform evil actions.

The second reason for rejecting this approach is that the explanation that they obeyed orders falls far short of explaining the dirty warriors' frame of mind. For it does not explain why they obeyed orders to begin with and why they supposed that obeying orders constitutes a moral justification of any action, but especially of an evil one. Explaining a frame of mind requires more than being able to say accurately that it led to certain actions. It requires also an explanation of why it led specifically to those actions, and in the present case, it requires the explanation as well of why the obedient but normally immoral actions were believed to be morally justified.

The third reason for not following this approach is that it is mistaken about obedience. The superiors of the dirty warriors told them what to do and they did it. But this is not enough for ascribing obedience to them. Obedience involves submission. Those who obey subordinate their will to a command. They do what someone else wants them to do, not what they would do in the absence of the command. They follow someone else's will, not their own. The first displaces the second. If it did not, they would not have to be commanded to do it; they would do it on their own accord. If one lover tells another: make love to me, and he does, he is not obeying an order. Obedience, therefore, requires that there be a difference between what subjects are commanded to do and what they would do if it were not for the command.

In the dirty war there was no difference between the motivations of the junta and the officers: they wanted to do the same things. The officers' actions expressed their own will, but it was also the will of their superiors. There was no question of obedience because the officers did what they wanted to do, namely, put an end to the subversion. Their superiors did not so much as command as direct their actions. If the officers were like racehorses raring to go, then their superiors were jockeys spurring them on. And this, I believe, is the clue to the right approach to explaining their frame of mind.

6.4 Condemnation

To be a military officer in Argentina was a life-shaping commitment. It was to enter into a form of life with its distinctive customs, rules, limits, and possibilities. It had a code of its own, its standards of excellence and deficiency, its heroes and traitors. It defined the requirements of honor, set duties and responsibilities, and maintained a hierarchical organization in which rising depended on excellence as measured by the group's values and ideals. It also provided a good livelihood, high social status in the larger society, and psychological security through an ethos of solidarity, camaraderie, and dedication to a common purpose. It inculcated an ideal of personal honor that involved being protectors of the nation, warriors ready to risk their lives for the common good, dedicated and competent professionals who knew how to do what had to be done, and an island of integrity and efficiency in a corrupt world. In the course of their training, officers internalized the code, values, and ideals of the group. Their training taught them skills, but it was far more important that it formed their ideal of honor. Their deepest aspiration became to live up to this ideal and to be true to it as officers. Being an officer was thus inseparable from their character and frame of mind.

A childhood friend describes a naval officer, one of the most notorious dirty warriors, thus: "When Alfredo Astiz, Jr. was growing up, his classmates called him Brother Sailor because he talked only about the sea. When he went into the navy officers school after high school, it was as if following a predestined course. . . . The fathers are naval officers . . . the sons then go to navy school . . . children go to navy schools in navy buses, their families attend mass with navy priests in navy churches, they spend their weekends at navy clubs, they get well at navy hospitals or are buried in navy cemeteries. A sailor who says something stupid is derided: 'Don't be a civilian.' The only opinion heard and read are navy opinions. The same people own the radio, TV, and newspaper. . . . Daughters of navy families marry young officers. . . . And the boys go into the navy, where, beginning at fifteen, they sniff the heady breezes of prestige and majesty" (Rosenberg 103–4).

As a result of their total immersion into this background, officers came to share an ideal of honor and a frame of mind. They were trained to see and evaluate the world in the same way. Their commitment to the same code, values, and ideals ensured that they would respond to what they saw in similar ways. Once they were truly immersed in their form of life, the role of orders was not to make them do this or that, but to coordinate and direct what they were first trained and then spontaneously wanted to do. When they acted in their military capacity, they were not obeying orders, but did what they saw as their plain duty, as the right thing to do.

This takes us part of the way toward explaining the dirty warriors' frame of mind, but more is required. For it may be said in response to this account that the military in many other countries forms groups not essentially different from the one in Argentina, but they have not been led by their frame of mind to wage dirty war when threatened by subversion. What was it, then, about the frame of mind of the Argentinean military that resulted in such an evil outcome?

Argentina was highly politicized. Politics, of course, is present in all large societies, but in a politicized one it is a dominant presence. When this happens it becomes very difficult, if not impossible, for people to live their lives without paying close attention to the prevailing political issues and conflicts. Their livelihood, security, plans for the future, hopes and fears for themselves and their children to a large extent depend on the outcome of the struggle between contending political forces. This is how it has been in Argentina ever since 1810, when it became independent of Spain. But politics there took a particular form.[10]

The political forces contending for power were not parties or classes but groups. The military was one of them. Others were the Catholic church, the oligarchy of large landowners, citified professionals, capitalists, and labor unions. These groups competed for power, formed temporary and shifting alliances, pursued what they took to be their own interests, and did what they could to prevent the other groups from achieving hegemony. They were much more than interest groups. It is true that each had what might be called a lay constituency whose interests they represented, but at the core of each group there was a dedicated cadre—militant officers, ultramontane priests, virtually feudal landlords, Marxist professors, greedy owners of large manufacturing firms, Peronist union officials—whose self-image, frame of mind, character, values, and ideals were as much defined by membership in their group as were those of the officers who waged the dirty war.

The cadres of each group participated in their characteristic but very different ways of life, internalized the group's ethos, had a vision of what Argentina ought to be, and were at best mildly disapproving, but more often hostile, to the form of life, ethos, and vision of other groups. The struggle for power among these groups was thus not primarily economic but moral. The politics of Argentina was a state of permanent conflict in which the opposing groups saw one another in moral terms as good or evil. The clash between moral visions, the dedication of the cadre of each group to its own moral outlook, made compromise appear as betrayal, the balancing of competing visions as the victory of expediency over integrity, and the toleration of moral outlooks different from their own as unprincipled.

Complicated as is this struggle of each against the rest, accuracy requires the recognition of additional complexities. First, the groups were not homogeneous. Each was an alliance of several subgroups with partly overlapping and partly differing ethos. The military, for instance, comprised the navy, the army, and the air force. There were differences among them, not so serious as to prevent them from joining for the common purpose of defeating subversion, but serious enough to make the ways in which they waged the dirty war markedly different. Second, in each group there was a moderate and a radical faction. The moderates hoped to avoid violence, while radicals encouraged polarization, even if it risked violent confrontation, hoping that their vision, being the one true and the good, would emerge victorious. When emergencies were not pressing, the moderates had the upper hand; when times were bad, the radicals carried more weight. Third, the groups had to respond to external influences on Argentina, not just to conditions internal to it. Communism, coups and revolutions in neighboring countries, the world economy, international tensions, and so forth had seriously affected conditions in Argentina. The groups had ties with foreign powers who influenced their policies through financial and/or moral support, in often conflicting ways, and this, of course, exacerbated the already considerable tension between them.

As a result of politicization Argentina sank from being the world's seventh largest economy in the 1930s to insolvency. Although rich in natural resources, having a highly skilled labor force, and capable of self-sufficiency, its disastrous economic policies, serving the short-term interests of the group temporarily in power, caused hyperinflation, which impoverished its middle class and drove working people to desperation. It destroyed law and order as the state lurched from coup to coup. Many, enabled by their wealth, talent, or skill to leave, left, thus making the future of those who remained even bleaker. It created an atmosphere of cynicism and distrust, compelling individuals to see each other in political terms, thus poisoning friendships, love affairs, and relations between neighbors, colleagues, teachers and students. Everything became politicized; nothing was firm and secure; calculation replaced trust.

The politicization of Argentina had a formative influence on the frame of mind of its elite. The distinction between "us" and "them" became central. It was an essentially moral and political, not an economic or class, distinction. "We" had morality on our side, "our" vision of what Argentina ought to be was true, the conduct of "our" group was virtuous, while "they" were immoral, "their" vision was corrupt, and what "they" did was vicious. The cadre's frame of mind in each group thus had a dual aspect: benign toward those in the group, hostile toward those in other groups. The first were treated kindly, given the benefit of the doubt, and their transgressions minimized. The second merited hostility and suspicion, and their transgressions were taken as evidence confirming their status as vicious enemies.

Corresponding to these two aspects of the prevalent frame of mind were two aspects of the activities of the groups: defensive and aggressive. The defensive one was deeper and more important, even though the aggressive one was usually more visible and dramatic. For what the defensive one ultimately protected was the most important possession of the members of the group: their ideal of honor. Their livelihood, security, status, prestige, the future of Argentina mattered, of course, but what mattered much more was their image of themselves as moral agents dedicated to the pursuit of their vision of the good in a world hostile to it. This is what they were really about, what gave meaning and purpose to their lives, the unifying element of their form of life, and the justification of their actions. The root of their aggressive activities was that other groups threatened their honor by casting doubt on their vision of the good. The very existence of a group committed to another vision would have been a threat, but of course, other groups did more than just exist. They too acted both defensively and aggressively. Each group, therefore, regarded at least some of the others as permanent threats to what was most important in life. No wonder, then, that when provoked by aggression, urged by their radical faction, having the means and the opportunity, they acted with excess and malevolence to eradicate the group that threatened their deepest values.

This was the immediate cause of the dirty war. The provoking aggression was subversion by the temporarily cooperating radical factions of Peronist trade unions and Marxist professionals. The military's own radical faction staged the coup of 1976 and controlled the junta. The means were their arms, facilities, and training. The opportunity was the general yearning in Argentina for law and order. And kidnapping, torture, imprisonment, and murder were the forms their excesses and malevolence took. But the more remote and deeper cause of the dirty war was the frame of mind that was the result of the politics of Argentina: politics that led people to see political disagreements as attacks on their honor; replaced individuality with group membership; pitted groups against one another; made toleration, compromise, and moderation impossible; and saw political arrangements in terms of good vs. evil, us vs. them. This politicized frame of mind made Argentina into a society where, as the epigraph says, the rulers of the darkness of this world held power, and wickedness flourished in high places.

6.5 Honor and Evil

We now have an answer to the question posed earlier of how the dirty warriors could believe that what they were doing was morally justified. The answer is that their frame of mind prevented them from seeing that what they were doing was evil. So, on the one hand, there are the actions—kidnapping, torture, imprisonment, and murder—which were incontestably evil because they caused serious, excessive, malevolent, and inexcusable harm to thousands of people. And, on the other hand, there are the evildoers, who acknowledged causing serious harm to many but believed that their actions were justified, and thus not evil. We have seen that their beliefs were mistaken and also that the mistake was the result of their frame of mind, which was itself a product of the politicization of Argentina. The dirty warriors were evildoers, but they sincerely believed that what they were doing was morally right.

This explanation of how the dirty warriors could have done the evil they did is general. It shows how political conditions influenced their frame of mind, and how their frame of mind led them to ignore or misdescribe relevant facts. This is not to say, however, that the dirty warriors had identical frames of mind. The political conditions in Argentina, their honor as military officers, and their long years of training and immersion in the military form of life were major and formative influences on them. But they were subject also to other influences, which differed from person to person. They were individuals with different personalities, character traits, and strengths and weaknesses. These differing influences also affected their frame of mind and shaped their ideal of honor. They were all dirty warriors and did great evil, but the individual differences among them shaped their subsequent attitudes to what they did. Some of them soon stopped thinking about the whole business; others left the military because they could not silence their belatedly awakened consciences; yet others became devoutly religious; there were those who distracted themselves with wine, women, and song; and a few repented.

In the light of all this, what is their responsibility? If we accept that they sincerely believed during the dirty war that their actions were justified, we may still wonder whether it was reasonable for them to hold that belief sincerely. We may want to say that they ought to have been more reasonable, that they ought not have held their beliefs, not even if they were sincere. But the response to this is surely that their frame of mind stood in the way of their realization that their beliefs were mistaken. As it stands, this response is much too abstract. We need to consider the concrete details of a typical situation in which a dirty warrior performed evil actions, mistakenly believed that they were morally right, and his frame of mind prevented him from questioning his belief.

Imagine, then, a man on the sixth consecutive day of torturing a woman who lies naked, stretched out on a table, her wrists and ankles fastened to hooks, so she can hardly move. He attaches electrodes to her nipples and vagina, pulls a lever, and administers electric shocks that make the woman convulse, scream, and beg him to stop. But he does not stop then, and not for several days coming, because his sense of duty compels him to go on. He is not pressing her for information, for she has long ago told all she could, which amounted to very little. She is merely suspected of being a subversive on the basis of having been seen in the company of someone who was also a suspected subversive. Hers is merely one of thousands of such cases, dozens of which were handled as routine matters by this man. This, then, is the dirty warrior whose frame of mind prevents him from doubting the moral rightness of what he is doing.

Let us think about what such a frame of mind would have to be. The man has in front of him the woman he is torturing. Her agony is palpable and undeniable. The man thinks, however, that causing it is morally right because his vision of what Argentina ought to be is threatened by subversives. Of these two considerations the second carries much more weight for him, so he sees the threat to his vision as justifying his torturing the woman. But how could he believe that in view of the facts known to him, namely, that there is only the most tenuous reason for thinking that the woman is a subversive, the torture no longer does anything (and it is doubtful that it ever did) to defeat the subversion, and, in any case, the woman will soon be thrown out of an airplane by himself or one of his fellow dirty warriors? The only way he could believe that torturing the woman is morally justified is by refusing to take into account facts known to him and having obvious bearing on the truth of his belief. But his refusal makes holding the mistaken belief his fault. He holds it because he ignores facts incompatible with his belief. He ought not hold the belief. But he does hold it, so he is responsible for the evil actions motivated by it.

It may be said against this that holding him responsible rests on a failure to appreciate the psychological mechanism that leads him to ignore pertinent facts. He does not ignore them willfully. He is blinded to them by the overwhelming importance of maintaining his honor. The facts threaten by showing that his honor as a man selflessly dedicated to the pursuit of the good is lost. Acknowledging that would lead to loss of meaning and purpose in his life, convict him of betraying his deepest value, and bring about his psychological disintegration. Being blind to the facts is as little his doing as fainting is the doing of his victims. Just as fainting is a physiological defense against extreme pain, so blindness is a psychological defense against threatening facts. People should not be held responsible for either.

What must surely be said about this attempted defense of the dirty warrior is that if his honor leads him to ignore that he is torturing people without a morally acceptable reason, then there is something terribly wrong with his honor. Honor that results in patterns of such evil actions is depraved. What makes it so is not that it is deliberately formed, but that it leads, in the case at hand, to torturing innocent people. Generally speaking, the reasonable judgment about the dirty warriors is that since their actions formed characteristic patterns and caused serious, excessive, malevolent, and inexcusable harm to thousands of people, their actions were evil; since their evil actions faithfully reflected their honor, their honor was depraved; and since their honor largely made them the people they were, they were evil people.

There are good reasons for trying to understand how and why they became evil. We have seen that the politicization of Argentina had a great deal to do with it. But it would be a bad mistake to suppose that to understand is to excuse. The nature of evil is not altered by understanding its cause. In normal circumstances the responsibility of evildoers does not dissolve by understanding how or why they came to do evil. Responsibility is for the evil done, not for the causes that led to the doing of it.

This is not to say that people who are insane, have low intelligence, or are otherwise incapacitated should not be exempted from responsibility for their evil actions. They should be. But normal people in normal circumstances are responsible for the readily foreseeable consequences of their actions. There is no reason to suppose that the dirty warriors were in any way hampered in this respect. They knew perfectly well what was likely to happen to the people they kidnapped; they knew the suffering caused by the torture and imprisonment they inflicted on them; and they knew that many of their victims would be murdered, often personally by themselves. These were readily foreseeable consequences of their actions. The dirty warriors are, therefore, responsible for the evil actions that caused them.

CHAPTER 7

Disenchantment with Ordinary Life

The normal process of life contains moments . . . in which radical evil gets its innings and takes its solid turn. . . .
Disenchantment with ordinary life [follows] and . . . the whole
range of habitual values may . . . come to appear ghastly mockery.

—WILLIAM JAMES, *The Varieties of Religious Experience*

All the evildoers I have discussed so far went about their
deplorable labors with grim determination. With the possible exception
of Manson, they did not enjoy what they did. They saw evil as something
they had to do. Any satisfaction they may have had was derived from their
success in achieving their ends, but not from the means they employed.
The evildoer in this chapter differs from them because he enjoys doing
evil. He finds a welcome relief from an otherwise mundane life. Doing
evil makes him feel fully alive, and he relishes the danger and risks he is
taking. Evildoing often requires talent, strength, and self-reliance, and
evildoers often enjoy engagement in what they are good at, just as much
as other people.

7.1 The Psychopath

John Allen provides a rare and revealing account of his life,
deeds, and how he regards them in his autobiography, *Assault with a
Deadly Weapon*.[1] The book is based on many hours of his tape-recorded
recollections, follow-up questions posed by his editors, and his tape-
recorded answers. As the foreword says: "John Allen . . . worked the
streets and alleys of Washington, D.C., . . . over a period of more than

twenty-five years." What he did was to "cultivate fear and willingly use violence in the service of two separable but common values—his material
interest and his sense of personal honor and respect" (xv). Allen was
born in 1942, and he tape-recorded his autobiography in 1975. His criminal record includes theft, rape, assault, armed robbery, and holdup; and,
as he says, he was at various times also a mugger, a pimp running five
prostitutes, and a wholesale drug dealer.

Here are some examples of what he did. He and a friend broke into a
junkyard. "So we looking for what we gonna take, and we destroy a few
things—naturally we *always* gotta *destroy* something. Just imagine two
young dudes in a junk shop who can do *anything* they want. They can
take anything. . . . They can break up what they want. I think I was kind
of proud of myself for breaking into that junk shop—succeeding" (13).
Or, "there was an apartment area . . . not too far from my neighborhood. . . . People . . . we felt that they were better off than us. . . . We
housebreak their property, or we beat somebody up and rob them"
(32). Or, "this particular day after my argument with the boss of the
gang, I go home and find the gun . . . and went back to our little hide-
out. I asked the boss, say 'You going to straighten it up or what?' And he
said, 'No.' And I knew that I couldn't beat him straight up fighting. So I
shot him. . . . So automatically everybody else looked upon me as being
the boss. . . . I think that's kind of what I wanted all the time anyway"
(42). At another time, "we going across the playground and somebody
threw a couple of bricks. . . . I turned around and started firing, and
everybody started splitting. I fired at Rock and hit him in the side. He
turned round and round. B.K. said, 'You didn't have to do that.' I fired
again and hit B.K. in the arm, and he turned and ran. . . . Rock was still
turning round and round, and then he took off. I fired at him again,
and this time I got him in the leg and he hit the ground, crying. . . . I
was standing over him, and if it don't be for Snap, I would have killed
him. I was that mad" (64).

Thinking about this life of his and of the things he did, he says, "I know
how to steal. I know how to be hard on the broads. I know how to stick
somebody up better than anything. I know how to take a small amount of
narcotics and eventually work it way up and make me some money.
Fencing property or credit cards, I know how to do all that. But society
says all that's wrong. . . . I was getting what I wanted out of street life, and
I was doing better than what I thought I would actually do" (53–54). And
he goes on, "It was really something, but it was a lot of fun. I know one
thing: out of all the things I've done—and I done more bad than good—
I done some cruel things, I done some unnecessary things, but I am not
really sorry for maybe three things I done my whole life. 'Cause I like to

have fun in my life" (57). "And when I am hurt, I strike out. Always. There's no other way for me to get relief but to strike out. Then, when I do strike out, I am relieved" (96). And he says, "Sometimes in my lifestyle, the way I live, people got to be hurt, so you accept that as part of your business, part of your life" (232).

Allen's account makes clear that he knew that his life involved habitual evil actions. He was indifferent to morality and to the suffering of his victims. He chose his life because he wanted thrills. He did not care about the price others had to pay so that he could have them. His actions expressed the kind of person he was, and he knowingly and intentionally cultivated being and acting that way. People often do evil because they hate, envy, fear, are jealous of, or are provoked by their victims. Allen was motivated differently because the identity of his victims was immaterial to his actions. His evildoing was impersonal. His feelings were directed not toward those he shot, beat up, or robbed, but toward the thrills he sought by means of his crimes. Nor were his crimes motivated by need for money. He derived no profit from many of them; his violence far exceeded what was necessary for robbery; and when he had money, he squandered it. His life and actions need to be understood by what was going on inside him rather than by his circumstances. Why did he want thrills so much and why was it evil—rather than sex, wealth, power, music, sport, and so on— that thrilled him?

John Allen was a psychopath. The *Diagnostic Manual* of the American Psychiatric Association describes psychopaths under the heading of antisocial personality disorder (APD). "The essential feature of APD is a pervasive pattern of disregard for, and violation of, the rights of others. . . . This pattern has also been referred to as psychopathy, sociopathy. . . . Individuals with APD fail to conform to social norms . . . are frequently deceitful and manipulative in order to gain personal profit or pleasure . . . repeatedly lie, use an alias, con others, or malinger . . . tend to be irritable and aggressive and may repeatedly get into physical fights or commit physical assault . . . display a reckless disregard for the safety of themselves or others . . . tend to be consistently and extremely irresponsible . . . may be indifferent to, or provide a superficial rationalization for, having hurt, mistreated, or stolen from someone . . . may blame the victims for being foolish, helpless, or deserving their fate . . . fail to . . . make amends for their behavior . . . believe that everyone is out to 'help number one' and that one should stop at nothing to avoid being pushed around . . . lack empathy and tend to be callous, cynical, and contemptuous of the feelings, rights, and sufferings of others . . . have an inflated and arrogant self-appraisal . . . be excessively opinionated, self-assured, or cocky." The *Diagnostic Manual* goes on to note that "individuals with this disorder may also experience dysphoria [restlessness] including . . . inability to tolerate boredom."[2]

This is a useful description of a state of mind, but it must be treated with caution. It is easy to read the *Diagnostic Manual* as describing a disease. Psychopaths may be said to be diseased in an extended sense of that term, but characterizing them in that way tends to mislead. They are diseased in that there is something wrong with them, but not in the sense of being mentally ill. They are not delusional, their intelligence is not impaired, they know what they are doing, they are in control of their actions, they plan, and they act accordingly. What is wrong with them is that they regularly violate normal moral restraints. But their violations are intentional, so they are properly held responsible for them. The problem with them is not mental illness but criminality.

The connection between crime and boredom has been noted not just by the *Diagnostic Manual* but also by the anthropologist Robert Edgerton, who formulated the admittedly speculative hypothesis that "certain aspects of human nature . . . may well predispose humans toward violence. . . . Man's intolerance for boredom . . . could compel humans to seek new experience, variety, with rule violation a likely outcome."[3] But the most influential view connecting psychopaths to boredom is that of the psychiatrist Hervey Cleckley, whose book on psychopaths is derived from extensive forensic clinical experience. He says: "The psychopath is likely to be bored. . . . He will seek . . . more than the ordinary person to relieve the tedium of his unrewarding existence. . . . Few, if any, of the scruples that in the ordinary man might oppose and control . . . impulses seem to influence him. . . . The psychopath finds it hard to understand why [others] continually criticize, reproach, quarrel with, and interfere with him. . . . It is not necessary to assume great cruelty or conscious hatred in him commensurate with the degree of suffering he deals out to others. . . . The psychopath looks as if he were reacting to what is trivial by showing that he just doesn't give a damn. . . . He may be prompted by simple tedium to acts of folly or crime. . . . The emptiness or superficiality of life without major goals or deep loyalties, or real love, would leave a person . . . so bored that he would eventually turn to hazardous, self-damaging, outlandish, antisocial, and even self-destructive exploits in order to find something fresh and stimulating in which to apply his relatively useless and unchallenged energies and talents."[4]

John Allen fits this description. He recorded the thoughts cited earlier at the age of thirty-three. He was then a paraplegic, permanently confined to a wheelchair as a result of having been shot in the spine during an unsuccessful robbery. Prior to this, he spent all told fourteen years in various jails. He had no money. He lived in the poverty-stricken neighborhood and circumstances into which he was born. And what did he think of his life then? He says, "I still like the notoriety, the excitement, the danger" (223). "What I really miss," he says at a different place, is "the excitement of sticking up and the planning and getting away with it—whether it come out to be a car chase or just plain old-fashioned foot race outrunning the police—knowing all the little alleys and shortcuts to go through" (102). But now "I get tremendously bored. Sometimes I stay in the house two, three weeks, doing nothing but looking out the window. . . . Ever since I've been talking [into the tape-recorder] I've been telling about myself—my life and how exciting it was, that I am sorry for nothing that happened or something I did" (226). Shortly after these recordings were made, he was once again arrested—confined to a wheelchair as he was—for armed robbery.

John Allen chose the life he lived because he was motivated, on the one hand, by the vices of cruelty, aggressiveness, and self-centeredness and, on the other hand, by his desire to seek thrills in order to avoid boredom. It was the coincidence of his vices and boredom that led to evil being the means whereby he was thrilled. Someone without the vices might have found less malignant thrills, and someone without boredom might have accepted moral restraints on his vices for the sake of pursuing other interests. The thrill of evil and the threat of boredom were jointly strong enough motives to make John Allen indifferent to the suffering he inflicted on his victims and to feel no regrets or guilt about his chosen life and actions.

I want now to follow up this connection between boredom and evil because it will lead to understanding something important about both evil and morality. The form of evil connected with boredom is one among others. I do not claim that boredom is the root of all evil or that boredom must lead to evil. Nevertheless, understanding boredom helps to clarify why many people find evil thrilling and why they actively seek it in violation of what they recognize as moral requirements.

7.2 Boredom

Everyone is bored sometimes because everyone has to put up with boring experiences. Long trips, waiting in reception rooms, routine and monotonous chores, the often-heard stories of a relative or a guest, most political speeches, the ailments of casual acquaintances, social realist novels, aleatoric music, and so forth are boring and trivial. They may irritate, but they do not present a serious threat, especially since one can withdraw from continued exposure to them. Trivial boredom is episodic and voluntary, and its cause is the experienced object. Boredom, however, may be chronic, involuntary, and resulting from one's attitude rather than from the object of the attitude. In chronic boredom everything is boring, not because one is exposed to boring objects, but because one is bored regardless of what object comes to one's attention. The threat comes from chronic, not trivial, boredom, and that is what I will mean by boredom from now on.

The threat of boredom has been recognized by a wide array of reflective people. There cannot be many things about which Russell and Heidegger agree, but the first says, "Boredom as a factor in human behavior has received, in my opinion, for less attention than it deserves. It has been, I believe, one of the great motive powers throughout the historical epoch, and is so at the present day more than ever,"[5] and the second comments, albeit with unfortunate mixed metaphors, that "this profound boredom, drifting hither and thither in the abysses of existence like a mute fog, drowns all things, all men and oneself along them. . . . All things, and we with them, sink into a kind of indifference. . . . There is nothing to hold onto."[6] In one of the few full-length books on boredom, Sean Desmond Healy writes: "There would at first glance seem to be no good reason for supposing that boredom . . . should have steadily and continuously increased in modern times. . . . And yet the records of man's thought and experience indicate otherwise . . . boredom has a history and has gradually emerged from near obscurity to center stage."[7] Anthropologist Ralph Linton claims that "it seems probable that the human capacity for being bored, rather than man's social or natural needs, lies at the root of man's cultural advance."[8] Psychologist Karl Scheibe holds that "boredom . . . is the paramount motivational issue of our times."[9] According to sociologist O. E. Klapp, "a strange cloud hangs over modern life. At first it was not noticed; now it is thicker than ever. It embarrasses claims that the quality of life is getting better. . . . It is thickest in cities where there are the most varieties, pleasure, and opportunities. Like smog, it spreads to all sorts of places it is not supposed to be. . . . The most common name for this cloud is boredom."[10] The literary historian Reinhard Kuhn observes that "in the twentieth century ennui is not one theme among others; it is the dominant theme, and, like a persistent obsession, it intrudes upon the work of most contemporary writers."[11] In his formidably learned cultural history, reflecting on our age, Jacques Barzun says: "Whether sports events or soap opera or rock concert, entertainment in its main 20C forms was seated and passive. The amount supplied was unexampled. . . . It became people's chief object in life, because for the millions work had lost its power to satisfy the spirit. Yielding no finished object, taking place only abstractly on paper and in words over a wire, it starved the feeling of accomplishment. It was drudgery without reward, boredom unrelieved. . . . After a time, estimated a little over a century, the western mind was set upon by a blight: it was boredom."[12]

The threat of boredom has, of course, existed before modern times. The author of Ecclesiastes asks: "What does man gain by all the toil at which he toils under the sun?" and answers: "A generation goes, and a generation comes, but the earth remains forever. . . . All things are full of weariness; a man cannot utter it. . . . What has been is what will be, and what has been done is what will be done; and there is nothing new under the sun. . . . All is vanity and a striving after wind. What is crooked cannot be made straight, and what is lacking cannot be numbered. . . . In much wisdom is much vexation, and he who increases knowledge increases sorrow. . . . The fate of the sons of men and the fate of beasts is the same; as one dies, so dies the other. . . . The dead who are already dead [are] more fortunate than the living who are still alive; but better than both is he who has not yet been."[13]

In the Christian tradition, boredom was called *acedia* and held to be one of the cardinal sins. As Kuhn writes in a monumental study of its history: "*Acedia* (or accidie) [is] a word derived from the Greek . . . signifying lack of interest . . . a condition of the soul characterized by torpor, dryness, and indifference culminating in a disgust. . . . Unlike the other capital sins, acedia may bring about a crisis in which man becomes aware of his actual condition. . . . The dangers inherent in this state of affairs are immense, for it can lead to the greatest evils and culminate in the total despair that assures its victim of eternal damnation. . . . Acedia is especially pernicious because it opens the way for all other vices. . . . Its victim . . . [is] alienated from his fellow men, feels himself misunderstood. He holds his peers and superiors in contempt and considers himself as being better than they."[14]

Acedia is standardly translated as boredom or ennui. They are synonyms, differing only in etymology. I shall continue to speak of boredom and proceed to consider why it is more prevalent in our times than before, why its threat is serious, and then return to the connection between boredom and evil.

7.3 Prevalence

In order to understand why boredom is prevalent now, consider Johan Huizinga's wonderful description of ordinary life at the close of the Middle Ages—a life from which boredom is conspicuously absent. "The contrast between suffering and joy, between adversity and happiness, appeared more striking. All experience had yet to the minds of men the directness and absoluteness of the pleasure and pain of child-life. Every event, every action, was still embodied in expressive and solemn forms, which raised them to the dignity of a ritual. For it was not merely the great facts of birth, marriage and death which, by the sacredness of the sacrament, were raised to the rank of mysteries; incidents of less importance, like a journey, a task, a visit, were equally attended by a thousand formalities. . . . Calamities and indigence were more afflicting than at present; it was more difficult to guard against them, and to find solace. Illness and health presented a more striking contrast; the cold and darkness of winter were real evils. . . . We, at the present day, can hardly understand the keenness with which a fur coat, a good fire on the hearth, a soft bed, a glass of wine, were formerly enjoyed. . . . All things in life were of a proud or cruel publicity. . . . Executions and other public acts of justice, hawking, marriages and funerals, were all announced by cries and processions, songs and music. . . . All things presenting themselves to the mind in violent contrasts and impressive forms, lent a tone of excitement and passion to everyday life and tended to produce perpetual oscillation between despair and distracted joy, between cruelty and pious tenderness which characterize life in the Middle Ages."[15]

The vast majority lived close to the edge because life expectancy was short, infant mortality high, medical care unavailable, anesthesia unknown, literacy rare, travel exceptional, and social mobility virtually impossible; there were no stores, engines, electricity, welfare programs, or newspapers; most people lived and died in the village and the house in which they were born; families had to satisfy their own needs or perish; there was no appeal from the rule of the local authority; crop failure meant starvation; flood, fire, drought, war, pestilence caused irreversible damage; hygiene, contraception, schooling, crop rotation, emigration, or the questioning of accepted beliefs were possibilities realizable only in the distant future. There was much to fear from these and other adversities, but there was also much to hope from the promise the church held out of a better life after the present one. Everyone knew what was right and wrong, good and bad, what was a sin, and where salvation lay. There was a shared ideal sanctified by the church and reaffirmed by its local representatives. People's beliefs, emotions, and motives were thus focused on the hardships they feared and needed to overcome and on the ideal they unquestioningly accepted and which gave them hope of a better future life. They were thus fully engaged with their fears and hopes and with what they believed and felt they had to do about them. Their lives had no room into which boredom could fit.

Our lives are different in many ways, but two of them are important for understanding the contemporary prevalence of boredom. One is that for us comfort has replaced medieval hardships. We no longer have to struggle to obtain the basic necessities of life. Great improvements in technology, medicine, education, agriculture, communication, and mobility have freed us from living as close to the edge as the predecessors of whom Huizinga writes. To be sure, we have to earn a living and cope with adversities, but the work we do and the adversities we face are much less demanding than before, and the consequences of failure are much less dire. Comfort loosens the hold necessity has on our lives, and it gives us leisure, which we can use at our discretion.

Another important difference is that the authoritative world view of the Middle Ages, which provided the unquestioningly accepted ideal that gave hope and solace, no longer carries conviction for us. Countless people have no religious beliefs; others have them, but hold them so weakly that they rarely affect how they live and act; and even seriously committed religious believers are bound to recognize that many reasonable and decent people do not share their beliefs without being noticeably worse off. There no longer is for us an ideal whose authority and inspiration we generally recognize. All ideals are questioned, and this weakens the hope and solace they may provide. The unified world view of the Middle Ages has collapsed. People are freer than ever before to choose what they believe and how they live their lives.

These two characteristic conditions of contemporary life—greatly increased comfort and freedom—raise questions about the meaning and purpose of our lives that only the privileged few faced before: what should we do with our comfortable lives, how should we fill our leisure time, and to what ideals should we choose to aspire? The fact is that the use to which countless people put their freedom is to ignore the questions. They content themselves with the comforts they have, and they are discouraged by their uncertainty from asking the questions about where the answers may be found. Ignoring the questions, however, has the price of having no direction in their lives, no goals beyond securing continued comfort. They have enough to live by, but little to live for. Instinct and training ensure that they carry on, but the reason for doing so is missing. They are without a sense of what is important beyond the basic necessities. They feel empty, dissatisfied, and they seek distractions that would divert their attention from these bad feelings and give them some way of filling their comfortable and empty lives. Boredom is a symptom of this unsatisfactory mode of existence. And since that mode is characteristic of contemporary life, boredom has become more prevalent for us than it has been before.

Boredom is a serious threat because it fills the vacuum created by the loss of meaning and purpose in one's life. This is a state of mind in which one has nothing to live for. Everything seems pointless and indifferent; nothing seems to matter. Facts are acknowledged, but none has more significance than any other. The distinction previously drawn between important and unimportant matters becomes untenable because the standard appealed to is no longer recognized as such. Earlier beliefs and commitments are remembered, but they cease to carry any conviction. All evaluations appear arbitrary because the ground on which they were based has disappeared. Others who are not similarly afflicted seem naive, innocent, childlike, for they have not yet encountered the abyss that one faces without the possibility of relief. The threat is the dissolution of the evaluative dimension of one's life. There goes with it an incoherence of beliefs, emotions, and the will. For if nothing is believed to matter, if all facts are believed to lack significance, then emotional reactions to them are inappropriate and there is no reason to make an effort to try to change anything in the world or in oneself.

Falling into this state of boredom is one of the worst things that can happen to people, for it destroys the enjoyment of life. Physical existence continues, physiological needs are not silenced, but one's self is assailed and one is a helpless witness to the process of its disintegration. The terrible thing is that the loss of self, of one's individuality, is not the result of malignant external causes, such as torture, which could possibly be resisted or from which one could recover. The loss is caused by oneself, and thus the perpetrator and the victim are one. Resistance or recovery seem hopeless because they depend on the very self that is disintegrating. The cure is rendered ineffective by the sickness it is supposed to alleviate. It is reasonable, therefore, to do what one reasonably can to avoid this threat.

Boredom combines apathy and restlessness.[16] Apathy is the lack of interest. Nothing engages one's attention; nothing is interesting because one is interested in nothing. The lack is not in objects but in oneself. One is disengaged from the world, alienated from other people, finds all activities worthless and pointless, and is dominated by a feeling of emptiness. This is a highly frustrating state of mind because everyone craves stimulation, worthwhile activities, and objects that engage one's interest. Restlessness follows if this craving is left unsatisfied. One craves something, without knowing what it might be, and without finding anything that would assuage the craving. But nothing could because one craves something worth prizing, while refusing to attribute worth to anything. The unsatisfied craving, however, compels the search to go on, but because one has made its satisfaction impossible, the search is doomed to fail. The restlessness thus continues unabated. One's incongruous states of apathy and restlessness collude in sabotaging whatever one tries to do to relieve them.

At any particular time, either apathy or restlessness has the upper hand in the motivation of the bored person. When apathy is dominant, the result is depression. When restlessness rules, the endless quest is on for distractions. The distractions, however, can only hide the truth that the satisfactions they bring are counterfeit. For the real thing would have to be worthwhile, but boredom is the result of the inability to assign worth to anything. When restlessness is combined with the unavailability or with the recognition of the worthlessness of distractions, then boredom creates the condition for evil. It is largely for this reason that in Christian theology acedia is a capital sin. The connection between boredom and evil is, of course, at the center of this chapter, but before I can get to it some further things need to be said about boredom.

What is the source of the apathy that characterizes boredom? Why do some people, enjoying comfort and freedom, become apathetic while others find meaning and purpose in their lives? People have attitudes to their lives and circumstances.[17] These attitudes are composed of the beliefs they hold, the emotions they feel, and the motives that drive their actions. There are considerable variations in the extent to which people are conscious of their attitudes and articulate them to themselves or others, and even more in the extent to which they deliberately shape them. They also have, of course, beliefs, emotions, and motives apart from those that focus on their lives and circumstances. But the ones that are so focused determine how they view their lives, how satisfied or dissatisfied they are with the way things are going for them, and how successful or unsuccessful they are in living as they think they should.

These attitudes may or may not be reasonable, depending in part on whether their constituent beliefs are true, emotions appropriate, and motives realistic. The beliefs may be false because they involve factual error (I have great self-control), or because they are mistaken in the importance they ascribe to some facts (My honor depends on what people think of me). The emotions may be inappropriate because they are directed toward the wrong object (I am ashamed of my impoverished childhood), or because they are stronger or weaker than their objects warrant (My car is my pride in life). And the motives may be unrealistic because their goals are unattainable or self-destructive (I want to communicate with my dead father), or because they are incompatible with one's psychological makeup (I will not compromise my principles, but I will succeed as a politician).

It is not enough, however, to make attitudes reasonable if their constitutive beliefs, emotions, and motives avoid these pitfalls; they must also be integrated rather than fragmented. Integration depends on there being a large area of overlap among the constituents of the attitude. This requires that many of one's beliefs, emotions, and motives should have shared objects. The beliefs, then, inform the emotions, the emotions are directed toward the objects of one's beliefs, and the motives are guided by the joints forces of one's beliefs and emotions. One's attitude is fragmented if this reciprocal reinforcement is lacking. Beliefs about one's life then elicit no emotions, emotions about it are disconnected from the beliefs, and what one is motivated to do is uninformed by what one believes or feels.

The result of such a fragmented attitude is a life that lacks overall direction. One is pulled hither and yon by incongruous beliefs, emotions, and motives; does nothing wholeheartedly; and always has strong reasons against acting on any one of the constituents of the attitude by the contrary promptings of the other constituents. It will seem to one's divided self that the reasons against doing something are always stronger than the reason for doing anything. The predictable outcome of this state of fragmentation is apathy, a state in which nothing seems worth doing, and restlessness, which prompts one to do something, even if it is arbitrary. Boredom follows, whichever alternative dominates, for a life of apathetic inactivity is without interest, and a life of restless arbitrary activity is without purpose.

It must be stressed that serious, chronic boredom that results from such lives is a threat rather than a reality for many people. It is a state into which people fall if they are thoughtful and eschew self-deception. They then stalwartly face what they see as the truth, and the loss of meaning and purpose follows because they reject evasions. Most people sense the threat without being clear about what it is. In the current idiom, "they don't want to go there." They are bored, but they do not allow themselves to be dominated by apathy. What happens instead is that they are restless and seek distractions that would relieve their boredom and stand between them and the threat that clear-sightedness about boredom would make real.

Contemporary popular culture supplies the distractions they seek. Television, recreational drugs, pornography, surfing the Internet, health fads, garage sales, oriental cults, shopping in malls, and spectator sports are some of the familiar forms of distraction. They require little application and energy, give a modicum of pleasure, establish a lukewarm fellow feeling with others who share the same pastime, and can all be viewed as justifiable forms of relaxation to which one is entitled after a day or week of hard work. People can become quite skillful in mixing and varying them so as to avoid jadedness by overindulgence in any one distraction.

This skill helps them to get through their lives in a moderately pleasant way by earning a living and filling in the rest of their time. In our age, these distractions are the opium of the people.

There are some people whose lives are not filled with distractions, even though they are in great need of them. The reasons for this are various: reluctance to deceive themselves; seeing the distractions for what they are; emotions or motives too strong to be lulled into quiescence; having more time on their hands than even skilled manipulation can fill; being too poor to have the necessary resources for self-indulgence; lacking even the small amount of required education; alienation from their society; rebellious temperament; and so forth.

Their position is thus the following: they have adequate comfort and freedom; their attitude to their lives and circumstances is fragmented; they are more or less acutely aware of the threat of unassuaged boredom; they cannot or do not avail themselves of the distractions; they have moved beyond apathy; and they restlessly seek some activity that would relieve their boredom, overcome the fragmentation, and seem worthwhile. And now add to this two further conditions. One is that they regard with indifference or contempt the large majority of their fellows who have succumbed to the distractions. The other is that they have, as indeed most people do, a propensity to one or more of the familiar vices of cruelty, aggression, greed, envy, selfishness, and the like. People in this position are ripe for developing their propensity into a pattern of evil actions.

7.4 The Thrill of Evil

Consider the attractions evil has for people in this position. Evil is far more thrilling than the soporific distractions the evildoers scorn. Unlike most of the distractions, evildoing is active and energetic. It calls on the evildoers' resources because they have to plan, maintain secrecy, leave no clues, and outwit law enforcement agencies. Success gives them a feeling of accomplishment, of having prevailed in difficult circumstances. It proves their independence and self-sufficiency, and thus provides a sense of pride. It expresses their contempt for the sheeplike herd who have fallen for a life of distraction. And their evil actions are authentic, as opposed to the self-deceiving distractions, because they express part of their nature, what they truly are. Their actions stem from their character, not from indoctrination, social conditioning, or external influences of some other kind. In doing evil, they are genuinely exercising their freedom, they assert themselves, and they control the situation they have created. Furthermore, evildoing gives them pleasure apart from the one that any exercise of authentic agency gives. It is the specific pleasure derived from the particular form their evil actions take: of profit, if it is robbery; of feeling strong, if it is battery; of being smart, if it is fraud; of power, if it is murder or rape. And to these must be added the pleasure of release from the restlessness that has led them to search for some worthwhile activity.

But beyond thrill and pleasure there is something else, perhaps more important than either, that makes evil attractive: it is a way of integrating the evildoers' attitude to their lives and circumstances and thus overcoming the fragmentation that is the root cause of boredom.

The cognitive component of their attitude is a set of beliefs about morality and the law. They are seen as arbitrary restrictions enforced by the powerful to protect their own interests and keep the general population in check. Those who are smart enough see through the hypocritical rhetoric used to bamboozle people into conformity. All but fools seek their own advantage, and the only good reason for conformity is to avoid punishment. Reasonable people will conform when the refusal to do so is too costly, but they will act as they please when they can get away with it. Such actions not only bring pleasure and profit; they also demonstrate to the powerful that not everyone is deceived and that outwitting the enforcers is a game that can be won. The emotive component of the attitude is composed of feelings that naturally accompany these beliefs. They include pride at being one of the few who are not deceived and see things as they are; contempt for the herd that stupidly and slavishly conforms; satisfaction at being able to get away with violations; excitement during the planning and the execution of what the powerful call crimes; and self-respect derived from a sense of independence, exercise of freedom, and opposition to arbitrary authority. The motivational component of the attitude is the strong disposition to express these beliefs and feelings in action. It involves taking risks when they seem worthwhile; presenting a facade of conformity when it is advantageous; and, above all, through pretense, cunning, and calculation, maintaining independence and control in the face of the menace of conformity.

Those who possess such an attitude are certainly not bored. They have an integrated attitude to their lives and circumstances. Their beliefs, emotions, and motives form a coherent whole. They are fully and wholeheartedly alive. Their lives have meaning and purpose. But they derive these undoubted benefits from the evil they habitually and predictably do. Indeed, they are evildoers precisely because doing evil enables them to avoid boredom and the sickness of the soul that it threatens.

7.5 Boredom and Evil

We have now reached the end of the argument. Boredom may lead to evil because evil can be thrilling and boredom is a symptom of an empty life lacking in meaning and purpose, a life that everyone wants to avoid. The distractions of popular culture are unlikely to satisfy those who are moderately intelligent and honest with themselves. For such people, the excitement of pitting themselves against the rules of a boring conventional life, outwitting the authorities who try to enforce the rules, and the prospect of profiting from crime may prove attractive enough to override such moral education as they may have received. But the thrill by itself is not a sufficiently strong motive. It must be conjoined with a propensity for cruelty, aggressiveness, greed, and the like. It is, then, the joint forces of a boring life, unappealing distractions from it, the thrill of evil, the propensity for vice, and an inadequate moral education that explain why some people opt for an evil life.

The argument is committed to the claim that the motivation of many psychopaths can be explained in this way, but it allows that there may be differently motivated psychopaths and, certainly, other evildoers who are not psychopaths. The argument does not imply that boredom unavoidably leads to evil, or that the predisposition to vices cannot be resisted, or that the distractions of popular culture are the only ways, short of a life of crime, to alleviate boredom. But if the argument is successful, it explains why habitual evildoing may appear attractive to people who enjoy modern comforts and considerable freedom.

This explanation is important for several reasons. One is that it carries with it the suggestion of what can be done to make it less likely that people will opt for a life dedicated to this kind of evil. What can be done, first, is to make lives more interesting by providing better uses for leisure—through a rigorous and compulsory education—than those offered by popular culture. Second, crimes and the development of the propensity for vice can be made less attractive by making punishment swift, certain, and severe. And third, moral education can be improved by concentrating on the development of character rather than on the inculcation of rules, and by providing a reasoned explanation of why conformity to morality is in the interest of everyone living in a society.

Another reason for the importance of the explanation is that it follows from it that a very widely held belief about human motivation is false. The first expression of this false belief is a paradox Plato puts into Socrates' mouth: no one does evil knowingly. It is a paradox because it seems obviously false. People often know what they are doing, and what they are doing is often evil. But Plato has Socrates deny this on the grounds that when people do evil, they do not realize that what they are doing is evil. They mistakenly believe that their evil actions are in fact good. And they make this mistake because their feelings or desires obscure their reason. If they could reason without interference, they would come to know the good and act on that knowledge. If they do evil, it must result from insufficient or interfered-with knowledge of the good.

The deep assumption underlying this Socratic paradox is that morally good actions always conform to reason and evil actions are always contrary to reason. This is so because the scheme of things is permeated by a moral order. Morality is to live and act in conformity to it. If we do, life goes well for us, and if we do not, we act contrary to our own well-being. The requirements of reason, morality, and human well-being thus coincide. To think otherwise is a symptom of a failure of reason, a mistaking of evil for good, and contrary to one's own well-being.

This has been an immensely influential belief in the history of Western ideas. It is a dominant tendency in Christianity and the Enlightenment; the shared belief of such disparate thinkers as Plato, Aquinas, Leibniz, Spinoza, Kant, and Hegel; the assumption on which optimistic views about human progress and perfectibility rest; and the ground of hope for many religious believers and secular humanists alike. It is nevertheless false.

Its falsehood emerges from understanding the thrill of evil. People who opt for a life of evil in preference to a life of boredom need not be unreasonable, although of course they are immoral. They have good reasons for seeking meaning and purpose in their lives, alleviating their boredom, integrating their fragmented attitude, acting in ways that express their nature rather than succumbing to the mind-numbing distractions of popular culture, and putting to use their intelligence and ingenuity. Evil, therefore, motivates them, and they do not mistake it for good. They do evil knowingly, precisely because it is evil. It thrills them, which it would not do if it were not evil. Their evil actions thus conform to reason. Therefore, the requirements of reason and morality need not coincide.

But what about human well-being? Is it not a requirement of reason to opt for actions that contribute to, rather than detract from, human well-being? The answer depends on whether human well-being is interpreted in collective or individual terms. If it is interpreted collectively, then the psychopaths' actions clearly detract from human well-being, and so they may be regarded as unreasonable. If it is interpreted individually, then the psychopaths' actions clearly contribute to their own well-being, since it improves their boring lives, and so they may be regarded as reasonable. This leaves us with the judgment that psychopaths may have reason for acting as they do and the rest of us have reason to prevent them from so acting.

But are there reasons why psychopaths should interpret their own actions in terms of the collective rather than the individual sense of human well-being? Yes, there are such reasons. They derive from two considerations. One is that it is in the psychopaths' interest to live in a society that contributes to, rather than detracts from, their own well-being. This is a reason for them, therefore, to act in a way that would strengthen, rather than weaken, the society that serves their interest. The other is that if psychopaths weigh the cost of having to bear their society's condemnation of their evil actions against the cost of alleviating their boredom in some socially acceptable way, then the advantage to them of the latter over the former will become obvious. This is a reason for them, therefore, to act in socially acceptable, rather than evil, ways. Psychopaths, of course, may not heed these reasons, but if they seek their own advantage, they should. The force of these two reasons does not depend on the desperate expedient of denying that evildoers may have reasons for doing evil. It is quite enough to show that evildoers also have reasons against doing evil, and that reasons against evil actions outweigh reasons for them.

CHAPTER 8

Taking Stock

> The belief that a thoroughly . . . evil man must be a devil—and
> look his part; that he must be devoid of any positive quality; that
> he must bear the sign of Cain . . . [is a fallacy]. Such devils exist,
> but they are rare. . . . As long as one believes that the evil man
> wears horns, one will not discover an evil man.
>
> —ERICH FROMM, *The Anatomy of Human Destructiveness*

In the preceding six chapters I discussed the Albigensian
Crusaders, Robespierre, Stangl, Manson, the dirty warriors in Argentina,
and the psychopath. These evildoers are similar in some ways, different in
others. They caused serious, excessive, malevolent, and inexcusable harm
to others. But they differed in their motives, times and places, positions in
their societies, education, character, political and moral views, and attitudes to their evil actions. The aim of this chapter is to begin to discuss
the general significance of these cases by way of transition to the more
theoretical second part of the book.

8.1 Sources of Evil

Most people most of the time live everyday lives. If a society is civilized, everyday life in it is routine, mundane, but for all that necessary
because it provides needed resources, order, and predictability. Everyday
life in contemporary Western societies tends to be boring, as we have seen
in chapter 7. This is a contingent fact. Pervasive change, religious enthusi-
asm, political unrest, robust cultural life, hostile external challenge, or
internal moral conflict could make everyday life very interesting. In any
case, there is an understandable tendency not to be content with the

118

comfort and security everyday life in fortunate societies provides. Those who seek no more are scorned by seekers as plodding, cowardly, hypocritical, bourgeois philistines. These are the people Flaubert excoriated, Thomas Mann described in *Buddenbrooks*, Sinclair Lewis and Dreiser exposed, and Galsworthy made memorable as the Forsythes. But, for better or worse, there are many who want more, who feel that their lives are seriously lacking if all they have is social security. Man, as Emerson observed, does not live by bread alone, and adding low-cholesterol margarine is still not enough.

Taking the point of view of an outside observer, I described faith, ideology, ambition, envy, honor, and boredom as motives that may become evil and lead to evil actions, given propensity for vice, favorable circumstances, and weak limits. But they may be described quite differently from the point of view of the evildoers as providing what they seek beyond everyday life, or as pointing toward something that lies beyond creature comforts and they miss. People often say contentedly, if they have it, or wistfully, if they do not, that there has to be more to life. Faith, ideology, ambition, and honor are valued because they may provide an ideal whose pursuit gives meaning to one's life. Each may inspire and motivate, set standards by which people can evaluate actions, other people, institutions, and societies. Each may form an essential component of their identity and psychological security. Envy is an understandable reaction if one sees others succeeding and oneself failing at the pursuit of some ideal. And chronic boredom is an obvious sign that one's life lacks this evaluative dimension.

It should also be recognized that although these motives may become evil, they need not. Faith and ideology may have built-in prohibitions of evil; ambition and honor could spur people in good or morally indifferent directions; and envy and boredom sometimes lead to self-improvement. These possibilities must be acknowledged. But in the cases under discussion they have not been realized, for three reasons. The existing prohibitions of evil were weak, the circumstances favored evil actions, and the motives in question were particularly prone to prompt evil actions because they were infused with passion. The source of this passion is the connection of the motives with having or lacking ideals that make one's life meaningful. It is very hard to view dispassionately the source of one's identity and psychological security. This, in itself, presents no moral danger. Passions can be benign. The danger enters because the importance of these motives in people's lives and the passions associated with them are liable to lead those ruled by them to falsify the relevant facts. The motives and passions provide a point of view that tends to make evildoers systematically miss the significance of their actions. It prevents them from seeing their actions as evil or acknowledging their moral significance.

The crusaders, Robespierre, and the dirty warriors recognized that in normal circumstances their actions would have been evil. They believed, however, that their circumstances were not normal and their actions were morally justified. Their beliefs were grotesquely false, of course, but they did not see that. They sincerely believed otherwise, and so they inflicted horrendous suffering on innocent people, while feeling righteous about it. What made this possible was the falsification of the relevant facts by the crusaders' faith, Robespierre's ideology, and the dirty warriors' honor.

Stangl, Manson, and the psychopath also falsified the facts, but they did it differently. They acknowledged that their actions were evil. Yet Manson and the psychopath believed that their evil actions were justified on non-moral grounds, and Stangl believed that his actions were excusable. Manson thought that the refusal to grant him the recognition he deserved justified his gruesome murders of people he envied, and the psychopath thought that having what he regarded as fun was more important than the mayhem from which he extracted it. Stangl, on the other hand, believed that his actions were coerced because only by doing them could he realize his goals, so he was not responsible for them. The beliefs of these evildoers reflected their perverted hierarchy of importance. They believed that recognition, fun, and rising in the world were more important than the ghastly harm they did. But they could believe this only because envy, boredom, and ambition led them to falsify the relevant facts.

The reason, then, for not taking the evildoers' point of view is that it systematically falsifies the relevant facts. It inflates the importance of the evildoers' concerns and deflates the great harm their concerns lead them to cause. This explains how they could have before their very eyes the immediacy of the mangled people they have tortured, humiliated, and were often about to murder and regard some remote concern of their own as more important than the immediate suffering they were causing. They could reconcile the two only by falsifying the facts of the bleeding bodies in front of them, and they were led to this falsification by the passions that permeated their point of view. That point of view contains the sources of evil.

Taking that point of view, however, is not an aberration, but a consequence of the human tendency to want to have an ideal that makes one's life meaningful. The yearning for it is understandable, and so are the passionate attachment to the ideal once one has it and the deep resentment, which may be turned outward or inward, if one fails to have it. These passions become strong in the various circumstances that may threaten the ideal or prevent one from possessing it. The ideal may be attacked, as the crusaders supposed; its realization may be sabotaged by enemies, as

Robespierre and the dirty warriors believed; one may be coerced to do terrible things in order to achieve it, as Stangl claimed; morality itself may be an obstacle to it, as it was for the psychopath; or one may be deprived of it by misfortune or injustice, as Manson supposed. The strong passions these and similar circumstances provoke make evildoers then see the relevant facts not as they are, but as they are falsified by the passion. The Cathars are seen not as unworldly ascetics, but as enemies of Christendom; disagreements are seen not as routine features of political life, but as symptoms of immorality; victims are seen not as suffering human beings, but as cattle bound for slaughter; robbery and mayhem are seen not as injuries inflicted on innocent victims, but as fun things that alleviate boredom; and the murder of successful people is seen not as the ghastly crime it was, but as just retribution for one's failure. Evildoers thus come to believe sincerely that the facts they have falsified are as they see them, and they hold their sincere beliefs passionately because of their connection with the ideals that make their lives meaningful and sustain their identity and psychological security. The evil they do is the result of this falsification.

8.2 Responsibility

If evildoers are motivated by sincere and yet false beliefs, then the question arises whether it is justified to hold them responsible. A full discussion of this question is the subject of chapter 13, but some preliminary remarks are called for here in order to bring out further implications of the six cases. Numerous softhearted and tender-minded apologists are led by their understanding of the sources of evil actions to exempt the evildoers from responsibility. Underlying this attitude may be the religious view that we are all sinners as a result of the Fall, so we should not be judgmental of each other. "Judge not, that ye be not judged," as Matthew (7.1) says. Or behind it may be the Enlightenment view that we are all basically good and do evil only because bad political arrangements corrupt us. Both views lead to excusing evildoers from responsibility because, having understood the causes of their actions, apologists suppose that anyone might become an evildoer if affected by the same causes. Since people have no control over the causes that affect them, the apologists conclude either that "there but for the grace of God go I" or that it is a matter of luck whether one becomes an evildoer. They then humbly confess that they too might have done what the evildoers did if they had been in the evildoers' place. The apologists thus cultivate a sympathetic fellow feeling for what they tend to describe as the predicament of the evildoer.

The better the apologists succeed at this ill-advised sentimentalism, the closer they come to excusing the evildoers and the more remote becomes the suffering their evil actions have caused. The sympathy they gain for evildoers is at the expense of their sympathy for their victims. The appropriate response to this misdirected attitude is: "I do not know, and it does not much interest me to know, whether in my depths there lurks a murderer, but I do know that . . . I am not a murderer. I know that murderers existed . . . and still exist . . . and that to confuse them with their victims is a moral disease or an aesthetic affectation or a similar sign of complicity; above all, it is a precious service rendered (intentionally or not) to the negators of truth."[1] Normal evildoers in normal circumstances ought to be held responsible for their evil actions because they caused serious, excessive, malevolent, and inexcusable harm.

Apologists, nevertheless, may remain reluctant to proceed from the condemnation of evil actions to holding evildoers responsible. It matters, they may say, why the evildoers did what they did. It is one thing if they intended their actions, and quite another if they did not. Now whether the evildoers we are considering intended their evil actions is unclear. They certainly intended their actions, but they did not see them as they really were. The crusaders, Robespierre, and the dirty warriors intended the actions that grievously harmed their victims, yet they did not intend evil actions because they falsely believed that their actions were morally justified. Manson and the psychopath intended actions they knew were morally unjustified, but they falsely believed that they were justified on other grounds. Stangl also intended his morally unjustified actions, but he falsely believed that they were excusable because he was coerced. All these evildoers, therefore, intended their actions under one description and did not intend them under another.[2] The question is whether the apologists are right in claiming that this unclarity caused by false beliefs makes evil actions unintentional and thus excuses the evildoers from responsibility.

It is obvious, I think, that it does not. To show this, let us accept for the sake of argument as true the false beliefs that the Cathars were trying to subvert Christendom, the moderates in the French Revolution were enemies of humanity, the dirty war was waged against fanatical terrorists, and the crusaders, Robespierre, and the dirty warriors were protecting morally good ideals against these attackers. If these false beliefs were true, a case might be made that these people were morally justified to do what was necessary to protect their ideals. But what they in fact did was far in excess of what might be covered by this moral justification.

The crusaders murdered children, threw people in wells, blinded and cut off the ears and noses of countless people, and burned alive thousands as their favored method of execution. Robespierre had people lynched, buried alive, hacked to pieces, slowly drowned, publicly humiliated, and parts of their still warm bodies devoured by the mob. And the dirty warriors subjected their victims to weeks of bastinado, flaying, and electric shocks to their genitals, and kept them nude and blindfolded until they were thrown out of airplanes. The moral justification these evildoers falsely believed themselves to have cannot even begin to account for the savage, inhuman cruelty and ferocious malevolence of their actions. Even if it was necessary to kill their victims, it was not necessary to torture and humiliate them beforehand. And, of course, killing them was not necessary either. They could have been exiled or imprisoned.

Stangl, Manson, and the psychopath were as passionately committed to their ideals as the crusaders, Robespierre, and dirty warriors, and they falsified the facts as much as the others, but not by seeing evil as morally justified. Manson and the psychopath were indifferent to moral justification, while believing themselves to have nonmoral justifications for their evil actions. Manson's supposed justification was his resentment for being unappreciated. This may explain his motivation, but how could it justify the horrendous murder of strangers who offended him because they seemed to be successful? The psychopath's justification was the desire to fill his empty life. This is understandable, but it comes nowhere near to justifying him in maiming and robbing countless people, ignoring their suffering, and regarding the pleasure he took in his actions as fun. Stangl did not claim to have either moral or nonmoral justification. He claimed instead that his mass murder should be excused because he was coerced. But what coerced him was his inclination to do whatever was necessary for rising in the world. Who could seriously suppose that evil actions are excusable because the evildoer was unscrupulous?

Thus excusing evildoers from responsibility because their false beliefs made their evil actions unintentional would be a mistake. For the evildoers would be responsible even if their false beliefs were true: their supposed moral justifications do not account for their excesses and malevolence; nonmoral justifications do nothing to show the inappropriateness of holding them *morally* responsible; and excusing them because character defects forced them to do evil merely adds evil character to evil actions as reasons for holding them responsible.

These attempts to condemn evil actions but exempt evildoers from responsibility are, therefore, unconvincing. Seeing what is wrong with them, however, helps to explain that evil actions cause excessive and malevolent harm because of the evildoers' passions. These passions are aroused because evildoers see their victims as threatening the ideal that makes, or would make, their lives meaningful and is, or would be, the source of their identity and psychological security. Their excesses and malevolence are due to the passions with which they are defending what is most important in their lives. Evildoers, of course, are rarely aware that this is what motivates them, and their victims are rarely attacking them. Layers and layers of falsification lie between how the evildoers see the facts and the facts themselves.

Suppose, however, that these falsifications are somehow removed. The evildoers become clear-sighted enough to know what they are doing and why. They see themselves as committed to an ideal that makes their lives meaningful and sustains their identity and psychological security. They are aware of their passionate commitment to an ideal and see what they failed to see before, that the ideal may motivate them to evil actions. It is crucial to understanding evil that the achievement of this clarity is likely to lead to continued evil actions. For their newfound clarity will not diminish the importance they attach to their ideal or make them less passionately committed. The difference clarity is likely to make is that they now do evil with full understanding, whereas previously they did it without it. Clarity may merely transform self-deceiving into clear-sighted evildoers. For what makes people evildoers is not just their knowledge or ignorance of the moral status of their actions, but also their motives. The replacement of ignorance with knowledge may leave their motives as they were.

The achievement of such clarity, however, is rare. Most evildoers find it easier to pay lip service to morality and to convince themselves that the harm they are causing is not serious, excessive, or malevolent, or that it is excusable. There are few people who have not internalized at least to some extent the morality of their society. They prefer not to be judged adversely by other people and by their own—however weak—conscience. So they falsify the facts. But to exempt them from responsibility, as the apologists aim to do, because their falsifications obscure from them the true nature of their actions is indefensible.

At the center of the issue about responsibility are the ideals that motivate evil actions. Religious, political, patriotic, or personal ideals are rarely evil pure and simple. Nazism was that, but this is just what makes it an unsuitable example for the discussion of more complex cases. When evil is regularly done in the name of an ideal, the ideal is more likely to leave room for evil actions than actually prompt them. Faith, ideology, honor, and ambition did not prompt the Albigensian Crusade, the Terror, the dirty war, and Treblinka. But they allowed these horrors to occur. They lent themselves to evil uses by people who adopted these ideals and used them to express their evil propensities in situations in which the opportunity presented itself and the limits prohibiting evil actions were weak. Some ideals are much more easily abused than others: faith because it tends to spurn reason; ideology because it tends to demonize its opponents; honor because it tends to treat political disagreements as personal insults; and ambition because it tends to be unchoosy about means.

The result is that the explanation of evil actions done in the name of an ideal must take account of both the nature of the ideal and the motivation of the evildoer. But this does mean that the evildoers are not responsible for their evil actions. An ideal cannot be held responsible for anything because it is incapable of causing harm. Harm may be caused by people who adopt the ideal and act in its name. If the ideal is evil pure and simple, or if it readily lends itself to evil uses, that is a good reason to hold those responsible who adopted the ideal and caused evil in its name.

There may be a temptation here not to hold people responsible if, as a result of indoctrination, they did not have a choice in adopting an ideal or did not know that it lends itself to evil actions. This temptation, however, should be resisted. People, of course, can be indoctrinated, but they cannot be prevented from seeing that their own actions—prompted or allowed by their ideal—regularly cause serious harm. They cannot be oblivious to the smell of burning flesh, agonized screams, and bleeding wounds of tortured bodies caused by their actions. This ought to make them question their ideal regardless of whether they hold it by choice or indoctrination. They may be told that they are morally justified in inflicting these harms. Then they ought to question the putative moral justification. A justification is moral if ultimately it has to do with protecting human well-being. The question these evildoers should ask is how their actions could possibly protect human well-being by maiming, torturing, and murdering their victims. There could be reasonable answers: extreme situations may call for extreme actions. But the failure to ask these questions about evil actions does not diminish the responsibility for doing them.

8.3 Intention

Responsibility and intention are, of course, intimately connected. People are normally responsible for their intentional actions, that is, for actions they choose and whose moral significance they understand. There are complications, but I shall gloss over them until chapter 13. Here I want to raise two questions: Why should responsibility be thought to depend *only* on psychological processes that go on inside evildoers? And why should people be held responsible *only* for their intentional actions? These questions are connected, but let us begin with the first.

One main reason for holding people responsible is that they caused serious, excessive, malevolent, and inexcusable harm. The ascription of responsibility is thus a response to evil having been done. Holding people responsible is aptly characterized as a reactive attitude to them.[3] This attitude is appropriate if they have done evil; otherwise it is inappropriate. But might it not be inappropriate even if evil has been done? Yes, it might be, if they were insane or seriously incapacitated in some other way. For then, suffering from the incapacity, they could not form intentions because they could not choose or understand the significance of their choices. This, however, does not show that responsibility depends on intention. It shows, at most, that excusing people from responsibility depends on the impairment of their capacity to form intentions. But it does not show even that much because if the impairment is their fault, they may well be held responsible for both the impairment and the evil action that resulted from it. The evil action of an insane person is one thing; that of someone who got drunk is another. So it might—or might not—be appropriate to hold people responsible for evil actions even if they were not intentional. Much depends on why their evil actions were not intentional.

Although much depends on this, responsibility need not. Consider two people with identical intentions to perform an evil action, say to torture an innocent person. One does, but the other does not because the intended victim has contrived to escape. If responsibility depends on intention, then the successful and would-be torturers have the same responsibility. But of course they do not. The would-be torturer has done no harm, whereas the successful torturer has. We may deplore the intention of the would-be torturer, but only because we know that such intentions normally lead to evil actions. The upshot is that we can now see that responsibility depends on evil actions, not on intention. Intentions normally matter to the assignment of responsibility, but only because of their connection with actions. If this connection did not exist, intentions would be as irrelevant to responsibility as nightmares.

If this line of thought is correct, there should be cases in which it is appropriate to hold people responsible for their unintentionally evil actions. This brings us to the second question raised above: Are people responsible *only* for their intentional actions? But we have already seen that the answer is no. For people may be responsible for the impairment of their capacity to perform intentional actions. The same answer may also be reached in another way.

Take a slave owner in a society where slavery is and has been an accepted practice ever since anyone can remember. The status of slaves is halfway between those of domestic animals and servants. If anyone questions the practice of slavery, the answer is that slaves are not fully human, so they ought not be treated as if they were. This particular slave owner treats them no better or worse than is the prevailing norm: he buys and sells them, works them as hard as it is prudent, awards them for sexual uses to faithful servants, thinks nothing of separating slave parents and children, and has them flogged when he thinks they are lazy or unruly. In acting this way, he is doing what other people around him are doing and what his family has always done. He is as little concerned to justify the practice as he is to justify employing servants, keeping dogs, or having trees around his house. Of course, he has a choice about being slave owner, but he does not understand the significance of the choice he has made about slaves because he falsely believes that the slaves are subhuman. He is not, therefore, an intentional slave owner. But who can reasonably doubt that his unintentional actions were evil and that he is responsible for them?

The answers to the two questions I have asked follow from what has been said: first, responsibility depends also on actions, not just on what psychological processes may or may not precede actions; and second, people may be held responsible for both intentional and unintentional actions. The first answer does not mean, of course, that psychological processes are irrelevant to responsibility. Most of the time, responsibility and intention go together. What I deny is that they must go together, that there can be no responsibility without intention. Nor does the second answer mean that people are responsible for all their unintentionally evil actions. Lack of intention may excuse people from responsibility. What I deny is that it is always inappropriate to hold evildoers responsible for their unintentionally evil actions.

These questions matter because how we answer them has a central bearing on how we understand and respond to evil. I have argued that the evildoers in the six cases acted as they did partly because they held false beliefs about their motives, victims, and the justifiability and significance of their actions. If it were inappropriate to hold people responsible for unintentional actions, and if intention requires understanding the significance of one's action, then it would be inappropriate to hold the evildoers responsible for their evil actions since their false beliefs made them misunderstand the significance of their actions. This would lead to the absurd conclusion that the moral condemnation of these evildoers is unjustified. The apologists would, then, be right: it is reasonable to condemn their evil actions, but it is unreasonable to condemn those who did the actions. The result is that if the apologists were right, we would be left without moral resources to respond to the crusaders, Robespierre, Stangl, Manson, the dirty warriors, and the psychopath. Since morality is concerned with protecting human well-being, and since these evildoers could not be morally condemned for their egregious violations of human well-being, morality cannot do what it is meant to do. The collapse of morality is thus the—unintended—consequence of the apologists' position. The way to avoid this consequence is to abandon the assumptions from which it follows, namely, that responsibility depends *only* on the psychological processes of the evildoers, and that people should be held responsible *only* for their intentional actions.

The fundamental defect of the apologists' position is a misplaced emphasis. They stress the importance of the evildoers' intentions at the expense of the harm caused by evil actions. They are correct in recognizing that normally intention has an important bearing on responsibility, but they are wrong in failing to recognize that the reason why intention is important is that it may lead to evil actions that cause harm. The right view recognizes that responsibility is primarily for evil actions. They are the pivot on which responsibility turns. Intentions matter only secondarily because they are normally correlated with actions.

But why do the apologists get wrong the respective importance of evil actions and intentions to the assignment of responsibility? Because they suppose that if they succeed in explaining what led evildoers to evil actions, then they will also have succeeded in determining whether the evildoers should be held responsible for their evil actions. This supposition, however, is mistaken. The explanation of actions and the assignment of responsibility are different questions. The right answer to one is different from the right answer to the other. The explanation of actions depends on identifying the psychological processes that led a person to an action. The assignment of responsibility depends on ascertaining whether an action has caused serious, excessive, malevolent, and inexcusable harm. The explanation of actions looks to what goes on inside those who act. The assignment of responsibility looks also to what goes on outside those who act, to how their actions affect others. The apologists fail to see this difference, and that is the root of their error.

8.4 Realism about Evil

Realism about evil calls for recognizing that evil is widespread and seriously endangers human well-being; that evildoers must be held responsible for causing it; that coping with it depends on preventing evil actions; and that prevention, in turn, depends on understanding why evildoers do evil. One would think that realism about evil is taken for granted by all who think about it, but this is not so. There is long-standing opposition to realism. In fact, much of past and present thinking about evil goes to great lengths, involving the most ingenious intellectual contortions, to evade realism because it is incompatible with religious beliefs about the scheme of things and with Enlightenment beliefs about human beings.

A manifestation of this incompatibility is that the oddest collection of thinkers simply deny that evil is comprehensible. The following is an early, but representative, expression of this view: "After all is said and done, we must agree we understand neither the causes nor the reasons [for evil]: it is better to admit it at the beginning and stop here. We should look upon the objections of philosophers as only so much caviling and wrangling and oppose them only with silence and the shield of faith."[4] There are many later expressions of the same view.[5]

What some, but by no means all, religious and Enlightenment thinkers find incomprehensible, however, is not evil in itself, but evil if the scheme of things or human beings were as they assume. If God were the perfectly good and powerful creator, as defenders of the Judeo-Christian tradition assume, then the existence of evil might be incomprehensible. If human beings were basically good and reasonable, as they are assumed to be by many Enlightenment thinkers, then it might be incomprehensible why they cause evil contrary to goodness and reason. Those religious and Enlightenment thinkers who find evil incomprehensible cannot deny the fact of evil; cannot bring themselves to give up their assumptions; throw up their hands and fall into a metaphysical panic or despair about the future of humanity; and declare that what they prevent themselves from understanding is incomprehensible. They prefer to denigrate reason over recognizing that they are themselves unreasonable. Their rejection of realism, however, is not merely a mistake about reason, but also a practical obstacle to coping with evil. For by regarding evil as incomprehensible, they commit themselves to denying that there could be a reasonable way of coping with it.

Nietzsche also seems to reject realism about evil even though he is a violent critic of the religious tradition and does not share the Enlightenment illusions about human reason and goodness. His view about evil is inseparably connected with his criticism of the Judeo-Christian approach to morality. He thinks that the evil of this approach is a sham, the invention of what he calls slave-morality. It is a value constructed by the weak to resist the power of the strong. The strong affirm life by trying to make the most of its possibilities. They are creative, either of great works of art or of themselves, their lives, which they try to make into works of art. They are noble, fearless, impose their will on their surroundings, and thus set an example for the rest of humanity of what life could be. The weak deny life. They fear for themselves. Their shortcomings leave them no choice but to resign themselves to the miserable conditions of their existence. But they see the lives, virtues, and achievements of the strong, and they envy and resent them. This leads them to want to curtail the creative exploration of human possibilities by the strong. What they, the weak, call morality is a stratagem they have invented to achieve control over the strong. The key moral terms, good and evil, are expressions of this ignoble denial of all that makes life worth living. They call evil what the strong have to do to pursue their aims. And what they call good is what serves the interest of the weak. True morality, Nietzsche thinks, rejects these notions of good and evil as pernicious shams, and recognizes that good is what contributes to the creative activities of the strong, and bad is what stands in their way. Nietzsche thus thinks that seeing evil is to see through it. As a result, he denies the reality of evil; it exists only as a product of resentful weak minds.[6]

Nietzsche does not make it easy to sympathize with his work. But if we try, we can see a point in both what he rejects and what he values. There has been much stupidity and arbitrary moralizing in the tradition he rails against. Sex outside of marriage, homosexuality, masturbation, work on Sunday, collecting interest on loans, playing cards, resisting tyrants, and many more activities have all been called evil at one time or another. One can also admire people who live their lives with verve and relish, who are creative and take risks in exploring possibilities that frighten timid souls. But none of this warrants the denial of the reality of evil in the basic sense I have been understanding it.

In this sense, evil is the violation of limits that protect minimum conditions of human well-being. These conditions are required by whatever forms human lives may take. Creative lives depend on them as much as insipid ones. They have to do with such matters as murder, torture, and mutilation. Evil actions violate these basic limits, and evil people do it regularly, excessively, malevolently, and inexcusably. The existence of these conditions and their protection are minimum requirements of human well-being, not the self-serving inventions of anyone. They are as undeniable facts about human beings as the analogous conditions are for any other organic or inorganic entity. Human beings, of course, have a special interest in protecting the conditions that affect them, but that interest is common to all human beings.

On this basic level, it is uncontroversial that evil exists and what it is. If Nietzsche denies its reality, he is committed to the absurd and morally offensive view that the crusaders, Robespierre, Stangl, Manson, the dirty warriors, and the psychopath were not evildoers but admirable pioneers exploring the possibilities of human life. If, on the other hand, he is protesting against the moralizing imposition of arbitrary limits on acceptable forms of sex, work, creativity, risk taking, and so forth, then he should have said so more clearly. In either case, Nietzsche has given no reason to doubt the importance of realism about evil.

The Stoic-Spinozistic view is another rejection of realism about evil. Its defenders acknowledge that evil appears to exist, but they regard this appearance as an illusion to which human beings succumb because of misdirected desires.[7] Such desires are bound to be frustrated because they are contrary to the natural order implicit in the scheme of things. Evil, according to this view, is nothing but the unavoidable frustration of these unsatisfiable desires. If the misdirection of such desires is recognized, then the frustration they cause will be seen as emotional detritus that has been misidentified as evil. The key to coping with what is taken to be evil is to train oneself not to have misdirected desires, for then the frustration will be replaced by peace of mind.

It is undoubtedly true that what appears to be evil may not be and that greater self-knowledge and self-control would make it possible to avoid much unnecessary frustration caused by misdirected desires. But this view is advanced not merely as a way of alleviating experiences misidentified as evil but as an explanation of all evil. As such, however, it is a failure, for two reasons. First, it cannot be reasonably supposed that all desires are misdirected, for human life requires having and satisfying some desires. Rightly directed desires, however, are often frustrated, and their frustration often causes real evil that cannot be alleviated by growth in self-knowledge and self-control. Second, this view is committed to holding that all occurrences of evil are apparent, not real. This would mean that the crusaders, Robespierre, Stangl, Manson, the dirty warriors, and the psychopath were not evildoers because their actions were not evil but merely the consequences of their victims' misdirected desires. This is as absurd and morally offensive as Nietzsche's denial of the reality of evil.

The importance of realism about evil is one of the main threads that runs through the preceding arguments, as well as those that follow. An essential part of it is that any realistic treatment of evil must be concrete. There must be actual cases of undeniable evil at hand, and theories, explanations, generalizations, and abstractions about evil must be tested by and do justice to the concrete cases. Another thread in the argument is the need to humanize evil. Evil people and actions are parts of human life. They are, unfortunately, not rare. They must be understandable in human terms. There are moral monsters, but they are as exceptional as moral saints. Most evildoers are not monsters. They are people with common propensities, such as selfishness, greed, aggression, cruelty, and the like. They hold a mixture of beliefs about themselves and their actions, beliefs that are influenced by self-deception; simple or ingenious falsifications; pressing circumstances; passionate hopes, fears, and resentments;

the norms and expectations of their society; and their personal history. The explanation of evil depends on understanding how these complex influences motivate them to cause evil and make them habitual evildoers. As the next three chapters will show, the obstacles in the way of such an explanation are considerable. Realism about evil shatters illusions and provides no comforting answers. It sees human beings as flawed and the human prospect as uncertain. It has the virtue, however, of facing facts without which coping with evil is impossible.

8.5 The Approach

The explanations I shall consider in the next three chapters have a history. Much has been written about them throughout the ages, and there are many books tracing the history of each. But this book is about evil, not about the history of unsuccessful explanations of it. These explanations matter, for present purposes, only insofar as they help us arrive at the right explanation. I shall, therefore, consider only their logic and pay scant regard to their details or historical context. The notes to these chapters are intended to help explore further what I ignore.

In the course of the preceding discussion some minimum conditions have emerged that a successful explanation of evil must meet. It must recognize the existence of evil: the fact that human actions cause serious, excessive, malevolent, and inexcusable harm to other human beings. There can be reasonable disagreements about whether an action is evil. But there are also many unarguably evil actions, such as those considered in chapters 2–7. A successful explanation must recognize all uncontroversially evil actions as such and recognize that they are widespread. Its central task, of course, is to explain why evil actions are often done. The explanation must identify their cause (or causes), and this cannot merely be to postulate a hypothetical entity. To explain what is not understood by appealing to something that is no better understood is no explanation. Both the supposed cause of evil and evil itself must first be identified independently of each other, and only then can the connection between them be established. The explanation must also provide an account of how the cause produces the effect. A successful explanation, thus, must (a) acknowledge that evil exists; (b) recognize that it is widespread; (c) identify its cause; and (d) explain how its cause produces the effect.

It may be thought that these conditions are so obvious as not to be worth mentioning. This would be a mistake, however, because the conditions disqualify some widely held explanations of evil: (a) those that deny the reality of evil (like those of Nietzsche and the Stoic-Spinozistic view); (b) those (such as given by Sade and the more extreme Romantics) that attribute widespread evil to monsters who aim to subvert the whole of morality, on the grounds that moral monsters are rare and must depend on the cooperation of numerous mundane evildoers who take advantage of morality rather than rebel against it; (c) views that regard evil as incomprehensible (see note 5 of this chapter); and (d) explanations that attribute evil to occult entities such as the Devil (as do both simple-minded fundamentalists who read the Bible literally and some very thoughtful Christian apologists)[8], because they fail to provide a reason for supposing that such entities exist or an explanation of how they cause evil. I shall consider whether the yet-to-be-discussed explanations are inadequate because they do not meet one or more of these minimum conditions, or for some other reason.

Part Two

EXPLANATIONS OF EVIL

CHAPTER 9

External Explanations

The unchanged horrors of human life, the savage and obvious
evils . . . scarcely vary from culture to culture or from age to age:
massacre, starvation, imprisonment, torture, death and mutilation in war, tyranny and humiliation—in fact, the evening and
the morning news. Whatever the divergences in conceptions of
the good, these primary evils stay constant and undeniable as
evils to be at all costs averted, or almost all costs.

—STUART HAMPSHIRE, *Justice Is Conflict*

9.1 Four Types of Explanation

There is no shortage of explanations of evil. Plato, the Stoics,
Augustine, Aquinas, Hobbes, Leibniz, Spinoza, Butler, Kant, Bradley, and
Freud, among others, have offered historically influential answers to the
questions of what causes evil and why there is so much of it. There are
numerous contemporary explanations as well. It is possible, I believe, to
classify these explanations as being one of four types. I must qualify this at
once by emphasizing that the types I have in mind are ideal. Actual explanations conform to one type or another imperfectly because they incor-
porate elements of the other types. But if we recognize that some
elements are central and some peripheral, then it becomes plausible to
classify explanations on the basis of their central elements.

The classification depends on two distinctions regarding the supposed
causes of evil. One is between external and internal causes, the other
between passive and active ones. Both distinctions require explanation. It is
common ground among the many explanations that the immediate causes
of evil are human actions. The differences among them emerge when they

attempt to explain the causes of evil actions themselves. The two distinctions are drawn on the basis of the differences among the supposed causes.

The causes may be external or internal to the evildoers. External causes are metaphysical or natural influences, such as God's design or human injustice, that lead people to evil actions. Internal causes are psychological, such as ignorance or cruelty. One difference, then, between explanations of evil actions is whether they locate their causes within evildoers or in conditions outside them.

The causes of evil actions may also be active or passive. Active causes spur evildoers to evil actions. These causes may be internal, such as intending, calculating, desiring, or resenting, or they may be religious, ideological, or economic external influences. The causes are passive if evil actions are the result of either something evildoers lack, such as reason, knowledge, or self-control, or the absence of external limits, like moral prohibitions or strict laws. Thus an active cause prompts evildoers to do something, whereas a passive cause allows them to do it, and both their actions and inactions cause serious, excessive, malevolent, and inexcusable harm to others.

These two distinctions, then, yield four types of explanation: external-passive, external-active, internal-passive, and internal-active. I discuss the first two in this chapter and the last two in chapter 11; chapter 10 is about a biological explanation that combines external and internal elements. The accompanying table provides a graphic representation of the explanations.

	Passive	Active
External	The causes of evil actions are outside influences that make evil intrinsic to the scheme of things.	The causes of evil actions are outside influences that corrupt evildoers and prompt them to perform evil actions.
Internal	The causes of evil actions are psychological processes that malfunction and prevent evildoers from seeing their actions as evil.	The causes of evil actions are psychological processes that prompt evildoers to perform evil actions.

Singling out some outside influences or psychological processes as causes does not mean that they are sufficient to explain why evil actions are done. Actions, evil or not, depend on countless conditions. In order to act, people must be alive, conscious, have enough oxygen, be able to move, and so on and on. Their actions unavoidably reflect their upbringing, education, work, interests, the conventions of their society, and so forth. These conditions can normally be taken for granted. They are necessary but not sufficient for explaining actions, and certainly not evil actions. Explanations of evil actions claim that certain specific outside influences on or psychological processes of evildoers are also necessary, and that, in conjunction with these other conditions whose presence can normally be assumed, the specific influences or processes are sufficient for causing evil actions. The specific influences or processes are singled out because they are supposed to have crucial importance in explaining evil actions. Their supposed importance may be brought out by the claim that although actions could be done, evil actions would not be done if it were not for these specific influences or processes. Their importance is that they will lead to evil actions if the other conditions are present. For this reason they are the central elements of the explanation, although the explanation can and should recognize that there are also other necessary but peripheral elements.

What type an explanation of evil action is depends, then, on whether it regards as central outside influences or psychological processes, and whether the central elements are thought to be active or passive. But each of the four types of explanation has different versions, which identify different specific active or passive influences or processes as central and thus the supposed causes of evil actions. It is important to bear in mind that these are *supposed* causes. For as we shall see, all four types fail as explanations of evil actions. They rest on questionable assumptions; regard elements as peripheral when they are central; and leave numerous uncontroversially evil actions unaccounted for. They are nevertheless worth discussing because they contain elements that a successful explanation cannot ignore.

9.2 Evil as Unavoidable

External-passive explanations acknowledge the existence of evil and recognize that there is much of it. According to them, there is a morally good order permeating the scheme of things, and its very existence requires the existence of evil. Part of the goodness of that order is that evil is kept to the unavoidable minimum. Such explanations are external because they attribute evil to a morally good order that exists independently of human beings. They are also passive because they suppose that evil actions reflect incapacities intrinsic to human beings and prevent us from understanding the workings of the morally good order and the unavoidable part evil plays in it. Evil appears bad because we fail to understand that the world in which we live is the best one possible.

Consider as an illustration fighting a just war. If a nation ruled by a vicious tyrant attacks another nation without a morally acceptable reason, the nation attacked is surely in the right in resisting the aggressor. But in the course of fighting the war, people will be killed or maimed, many lives will be irreparably damaged, and the families of the dead and the incapacitated will also suffer. This is unavoidable, however, because there is no other way of avoiding even greater evil. What a morally good order requires is that in the course of fighting the war the least possible amount of evil be caused. And this explanation claims that this is just the nature of the moral order that informs the scheme of things. One must regret, of course, the evil there is. A larger view, however, based on a fuller understanding than what the participants have, will recognize that what is happening is, all things considered, for the best because any alternative would be worse.

The assumption on which this type of explanation rests, then, is not only that a morally good order governs the scheme of things, but also that this order is arranged so as to sustain the most favorable ratio between good and evil, given that some evil is unavoidable. Just as the free market in classical economic theory is supposed to guarantee that the unrestricted economic activities of individuals jointly maximize everyone's economic welfare, so the free activities of human beings jointly maximize human welfare. As the favorable outcome of the economic order is supposed to be governed by an invisible hand (in Adam Smith's apt phrase), so is the favorable outcome of the moral order. The difference is that in economics the invisible hand supposedly governs a spontaneous unintended order, whereas in morality the invisible hand is attributed to God, who has designed the order intentionally to produce the most possible good and least possible evil for the imperfect creatures we are.

There is, thus, a cosmic optimism informing invisible-hand explanations, an optimism that fully recognizes the facts and frequency of evil and is undeterred by the misery and suffering of humanity. A well-known and influential expression of it is Pope's:

> All Nature is but Art, unknown to thee;
> All Chance, Direction, which thou canst not see;
> All Discord, Harmony, not understood;
> All partial Evil, universal Good:
> And in spite of Pride, in erring Reason's spite,
> One truth is clear, WHATEVER IS, IS RIGHT.[1]

Perhaps the most sustained attempt to defend this type of explanation and the optimism that goes with it is Leibniz's.[2] His attempt was criticized almost as soon as he made it public. Its best-known critic was Voltaire, who ridiculed Leibniz's claim that this is the best possible world on the grounds that it absurdly denies the existence of evil. Leibniz, however, recognized its existence. He claimed that any other world would be worse than ours because it would have even more evil. Their disagreement is thus that Leibniz denies and Voltaire asserts that the facts of evil are incompatible with a morally good order in the scheme of things. Although Voltaire failed to appreciate the depth and logical ingenuity of Leibniz's explanation, Voltaire still has the better of their disagreement.

9.3 Reasons against Explaining Evil as Unavoidable

There are, it seems to me, three reasons to doubt such explanations of evil. The first is that the explanations confuse morally bad and evil actions. Even if they explain the former, they simply ignore the latter. It may be true that a morally good order requires occasional morally impermissible actions. There may be good reasons to tell a lie or break a promise (e.g., to avoid aiding an evildoer) and even to murder (e.g., to remove a tyrant), but evil actions are much worse than morally bad. They cause excessive and malevolent harm. Only those who ignore the concrete details of evil actions can suppose that they are unavoidable parts of a morally good order. Perhaps the crusade against the Cathars was necessary for the defense of the church, and the Cathars had to be killed. But they did not have to be slowly burned, or be blinded, or have their noses and ears cut off. Perhaps the French Revolution was necessary for the moral improvement of humanity. But it was not necessary to disembowel, bury alive, humiliate, and lynch people who did not even oppose it. And it is obscene to speculate about the greater good that Nazi death camps might be supposed to have served.

Explanations that regard evil as the unavoidable minimum in a morally good order systematically ignore that evil actions cause excessive and malevolent harm, that is, more harm than is necessary for the achievement of whatever aim evil actions may have. The excesses involved in them are malevolent because they reflect the impassioned cruelty, rage, fanaticism, and so on of the evildoers. Their excesses are not means to or parts of any conceivable morally good order. They are the self-expressions of evil people who vent their corrupt urges at the cost of causing enormous harm to their wretched victims. Any explanation of evil that glosses over the gory details that evil actions concretely involve is inadequate. Although the indignation and ridicule such explanations often elicit are readily understandable, they are not good reasons. A good reason is that an explanation that fails to account for the facts it is meant to explain is indefensible.

It may be said in response that the failure to explain the excesses and the malevolent motives evil actions involve is not the fault of the explanation, but yet another indication of the limitations of human understanding. Even the excesses and the malevolence would be explainable if only we understood fully the morally good order. Just because something seems evil to us does not mean that it really is evil. And even if it were, it may be an instance of those unavoidable evils that the morally good order keeps to the absolute minimum. This, or something close to it, is in essence what God said to Job as he complained about what happened to him.

The second reason against the external-passive explanation is that to ascribe the inability to explain evil actions to the limitations of human understanding rather than to the failure of the explanation has unacceptable consequences that its defenders certainly do not intend. To begin with, any criticism could be deflected in this way. There is no fact, argument, or inconsistency adduced against the explanation that could not be treated as evidence for limited understanding rather than as evidence against the explanation. But then, since the explanation excludes nothing and is compatible with everything, it cannot explain anything. An explanation must say: the reason why evil actions are done is . . . , and then replace the dots with its account. But this explanation replaces the dots with saying that the limitations of human understanding prevent us from seeing the reason. And that is simply an admission that the promised explanation has not been delivered. It is a complicated way of saying what an explanation of evil actions cannot say, namely, that it is not understandable by limited human beings why evil actions are done. If this turned out to be truth, we would have to accept it, but under no circumstances would we have to accept it as an explanation of evil actions.

Suppose for the sake of argument that there is a morally good order and the truth is that we cannot explain how evil actions fit into it. All we know is that they must fit in some way or another. This would have the consequence that the condemnation of evil actions would be morally wrong since it would be the condemnation of the morally good order into which evil actions fit. And if it were wrong to condemn them, it would be wrong to try to prevent them or to hold people responsible for doing them. If we lacked the understanding, then the whole of morality—which rests on our supposed understanding of good and evil—would have to be abandoned. People could then do whatever they pleased, thinking of themselves as representing the morally good order, and if they happened to do evil, they and we could be confident that it was for the good, even if we do not understand how. The immediate consequence of this explanation is that if it were correct, we would have to approve of the actions of the evildoers discussed in chapters 2–7 because our limited understanding prevents us from seeing their actions as unavoidable parts of the best order we could possibly have. Its ultimate consequence would be moral anarchy. No morally committed person could accept an explanation that led to such a conclusion.

An argument sometimes given in favor of a morally good order having to have evil in it is that there could be something good only in contrast with evil. The contrast may be thought of in naturalistic or evaluative terms. If it is taken to be naturalistic, the relation between good and evil is seen on the model of mountain peaks and slopes or obverse sides of a coin. Having one requires having the other. But whatever may be true of natural relations in general, it is not true of the relation between good and evil. It is absurd to suppose that there can be kindness only if there is cruelty, or freedom only if there is tyranny. Defenders of this argument, therefore, tend to think of the contrast as necessary for evaluating actions in terms of good and evil. The problem with this is that even if their contrast were necessary for evaluation, it would not require the existence of evil. The good could be properly appreciated even in contrast with imaginative depictions of evil. It is, for instance, unnecessary to have people actually drawn and quartered in order to maintain a lively appreciation of one's good health. Nor is it required for the appreciation of the good that it be contrasted with evil. Contrasts with neutral or indifferent things would serve just as well. The knowledge of people dying in their sleep, without being tortured to death, is sufficient for one's appreciation of the good of being alive.

The third reason against the external-passive explanation is that it rests on the groundless assumption that a morally good order exists independently of human beings. If there were such an order, it would have to be supernatural, since in the natural world with which we are familiar no morally good order is discernible. The most casual reading of history makes us see, as Hegel says, "the evil, the ruin that has befallen the most flourishing kingdoms which the mind of man created," and "we can hardly avoid being filled with . . . a moral sadness, a revolt of the good will—if indeed it has any place within us. Without rhetorical exaggeration, a simple truthful account of the miseries that have overwhelmed the noblest nations and finest exemplars of virtue forms a most fearful picture and excites emotions of the profoundest and most hopeless sadness."[3]

The problem with assuming that the moral order is supernatural is that we are confined to the natural world and have no direct access to the supposed supernatural world. The only kind of evidence we have and can have comes from the natural world. We can, of course, speculate about whether anything lies beyond the natural world and what it might be. We can ask whether the evidence we have implies anything beyond itself. And we can test various speculations by asking whether they are logically consistent and account for the relevant facts. But we must be very clear that there have been and will be numerous speculations that pass these tests and yet are incompatible with one another. There can be no reason for favoring any one of them over the others.

Perhaps there is a moral order beyond the natural world, but it is bad, not good, or just indifferent to human beings. Perhaps there are many gods at odds with one another, or perhaps there are none. Perhaps we are an experimental project of superbly intelligent extraterrestrial beings. Perhaps there is a God and we are to Him as ants are to us. There is no reason to accept any of these speculations. Nor is there any reason to suppose that changes in the natural world move in any particular direction, toward any particular goal. But if there were such a movement there would still be no reason to assume that its goal was in any sense moral.

We have good reason to believe that morality is a human effort to secure the conditions of human well-being. Evil is a practical problem because it violates those conditions. Unless we solve it, life will go badly for us. And solving it means finding the causes of evil and minimizing their efficacy. To treat evil as if it were the theoretical problem of reconciling the speculation that there is a morally good order with the undeniable facts of life is to miss its significance. Seeing the problem in this way encourages logical ingenuity and imaginative conjectures, but it will do nothing to help us cope with evil. It is right to condemn this sort of approach as much cleverness in aid of nothing. For even if—per impossibile—this speculation turned out to be true, it would not explain how the morally good order leads to evil actions, how evil actions that are part of the moral order are to be distinguished from evil actions that are not, how we could make evil less widespread if it is an unavoidable part of a supernatural order, and how a supernatural order that ordains the egregious excesses and malevolence of the evildoers we have earlier discussed could be thought of as good.

It may be asked, if the external-passive explanation of evil is guilty as charged, why waste time discussing it? Why not just throw it on the dust heap of history to keep company with phrenology, witchcraft, and similar abuses of reason? The answer is that the explanation has rightly stressed the importance of two considerations that a successful explanation of evil must take into account. One is that evil may be an unavoidable part of human life. In that case, however, coping with it cannot take the form of envisaging a possible state of affairs from which evil is absent and then trying to make it actual. Coping with evil may well be a matter of minimizing

particular occurrences of it, while knowing that it will recur in one particular form or another. The other is that we must recognize that the more
remote consequences of evil, just like the supposed activities of the invisible hand, are hidden from us. Our responses to evil, therefore, ought to
be based on ameliorating the particular harm it has caused rather than
constructing policies based on unreliable conjectures about the future.
Both considerations imply that learning from the past is a better
approach to coping with evil than trying to realize a future ideal. This has
important practical consequences, and the merit of the external-passive
explanation is that it points toward them.

9.4 Evil as Corruption

The cosmic optimism that permeates the external-passive explanation is virtually invulnerable to criticism. Showing that the reasons supporting it are untenable not only fails to weaken it, but actually
strengthens the optimists' belief that better reasons must be available. As
John Stuart Mill rightly pointed out: "So long as an opinion is strongly
rooted in the feelings, it gains rather than loses in stability by having a
preponderating weight of argument against it. For if it were accepted as a
result of argument, the refutation of the argument might shake the valid-
ity of the conviction; but when it rests solely on feeling, the worse it fares
in argumentative context, the more persuaded its adherents are that their
feelings must have some deeper ground, which the arguments do not
reach."[4] Some of the feelings that support this optimism are the wish for a
better world, concern for human well-being, pity for suffering, fear of cosmic indifference, hope that in the long run everything will turn out well,
and the comfort of regarding the world as hospitable to humanity.

These feelings are strong enough in many religious believers to override
the lack of reasons for believing in a supernaturally guaranteed order. But
the feelings are also strong in countless nonbelievers who repudiate religion and rest their optimism on the supposed basic goodness or perfectibility of human beings. The existence and prevalence of evil, however,
is a serious challenge for both religious and secular optimists because it
calls into question the appropriateness of their feelings. They struggle,
therefore, to meet the challenge. The external-active explanation of evil I
shall now consider is one of the main ways in which nonbelievers attempt
to account for evil while maintaining a secular optimism.

This type of explanation is active because it recognizes that evildoers
are guided by vices, such as greed, aggression, cruelty, and selfishness, to
take positive actions rather than to passively refrain from acting. It denies,

however, that these vices originate in human beings. People are motivated by vices, but only because they have been corrupted by external influences. These influences are usually political and take the form of evil institutions, laws, and practices. Being victimized by evil conditions of life poisons people's minds and prevents them from understanding the moral significance of their actions. They do evil, but they do not see what they do as evil because they are terrorized, enraged, deprived, brutalized, or humiliated. They are benighted by the evil political conditions of their lives, not by intrinsic moral failings. Just as the external-passive explanation accounts for evil as the working of a benign invisible hand, so the external-active explanation accounts for it as the effect of poisoned minds. Both aim to sustain optimism in the face of evil. I have given reasons against the first, and we now have to see whether the second does better.

Rousseau's *Emile* begins thus: "God made all things good; man meddles with them and they become evil."[5] The implied view may be seen as a bridge leading from Christianity to the Enlightenment. The external-active explanation of evil as the effect of poisoned minds is perhaps the dominant view in the Enlightenment as represented by the Encyclopedists.[6] Some of them believed in God, some were atheists. They all agreed, however, in seeking a natural explanation of evil and appealing to God, if at all, only as a being who set the world in motion. They saw evil as a result of our failure to act in accordance with reason. But they attributed this failure to interference with natural human development rather than to deficiencies intrinsic to us. They saw human beings as malleable and, given the right conditions, perfectible. The key was to remove impediments from the way, to overcome corrupting influences, and to encourage by education the development of the natural and inborn human propensities for the good. As Kant put it: "Enlightenment is man's emergence from his self-imposed immaturity. Immaturity is the inability to use one's understanding without guidance from another. This immaturity is self-imposed when its cause lies not in lack of understanding, but in lack of resolve and courage to use it without guidance from another. *Sapere Aude!* 'Have the courage to use your own understanding!'—that is the motto of enlightenment."[7]

The optimism that characterizes the Enlightenment and is reflected by these lines of Kant rests on the assumptions that human well-being depends on human effort; we are capable of making the right effort; the rightness of the effort depends on our will and reason; and the right employment of will and reason depends on individuals who must free themselves from corrupting external influences, use reason to decide how they ought to live and act, and use will to act according to reason. Evil actions are the result of the misuse of will and/or reason, and their misuse is caused by outside forces. The corollary is that if we resist outside forces, use our will and reason rightly, then there will be no obstacles to human well-being, for the world can be changed by our efforts and we have the capacities required for making the right changes.

There were differences among those who accepted these assumptions: they disagreed about God, the respective importance of will and reason, the seriousness of the threat of evil, the likelihood of our success, and the extent to which it depended on science. But I shall ignore these differences because they do not affect the underlying view that we cause evil only because we have been corrupted by external influences. If our minds were not poisoned, our actions would be good, not evil.

From Rousseau, the Enlightenment, and Kant it is but a small step to contemporary liberalism, which spells out the moral and political implications of this optimistic view. If human beings are as claimed, we all possess equal moral capacities. Since human well-being depends on the development and exercise of these capacities, the conditions enabling this to happen ought to be guaranteed for everyone equally. Human rights protect these conditions; individual freedom provides the opportunity we all need to make the most of our capacities; and justice is nothing but fairness in guaranteeing for everyone the availability of these conditions. If we are free, equal, and enjoy rights and justice, we are able to live autonomous lives. We understand then the importance of protecting these conditions for everyone, and we refrain from actions that violate them. The existence and prevalence of evil now is merely a symptom of the extent to which we fall short of this ideal state of affairs. The right course of action for us is to implement policies that bring us ever closer to this most desirable goal.

The feelings that motivate secular optimists show that their hearts are in the right place: on the side of humanity. The problem is that these feelings are allowed to grow into passions, color their beliefs, make them accept an untenable explanation of evil, and lead to a sentimental falsification of human propensities. There is no good reason to believe that human beings are basically good and/or perfectible, that *the* causes of evil are corrupting external influences, or that if freedom, equality, rights, and justice were guaranteed, evil would not be prevalent. Denying the truth of these assumptions on which the poisoned-mind explanation rests is not, of course, to deny that *some* human beings can change for the better, or that the improvement of bad political conditions might eliminate *some* evil, or that *some* people can be corrupted by external influences. The assumptions commit those who accept them to the much stronger general claims that changing for the better is the natural and normal propensity of *all* or *most* human beings, and it is changing for the worse that is exceptional; that *all* or *most* evil would be eliminated by the improvement of bad political conditions; and that *all* or *most* evil is the result of corrupting external influences. The following reasons against this view are intended to show that these claims are not generally true without denying that they may be sometimes true.

9.5 Reasons against Explaining Evil as Corruption

Since the external-active explanation is naturalistic, it must begin with the observable facts of past and present human actions. The relevant fact is that there is a multitude of good and evil human actions. There are many general explanations compatible with this fact. One is that human beings are naturally good and they do evil only when externally corrupted. Another is that human beings are naturally evil and they do good only when improved by external influences. Yet another is that human beings are naturally ambivalent and they do good or evil depending on external influences. A further one is that human beings are naturally good, or evil, or ambivalent and they do good or evil depending primarily on the respective internal strengths of their propensities, external influences having only a secondary effect on their actions. The external-active explanation assumes that the first of these general explanations is true and the others are false. But for this assumption no reason is given. It is the assumption with which defenders of this Enlightenment view start. The minimum required to make this assumption reasonable is to give reasons for preferring it and reasons against rejecting its rivals. This, however, has not been done. The assumption is taken for granted, and its rivals are ignored.

It makes matters much worse that not only is there no good reason for accepting the external-active explanation, but there are good reasons for rejecting it. The first of these reason is that if evil actions were caused by political conditions that corrupted those subject to them, then evil actions should vary with political conditions. But there is no such variation. The political conditions of Stalin's Soviet Union, Hitler's Germany, Mao's China, Ataturk's Turkey, Pol Pot's Cambodia, Khomeni's Iran, Saddam's Iraq, Milosevic's Yugoslavia, and so on were evil but very different. But the evil actions were the same: the arrest, torture, and execution of masses of people who were often innocent of any wrongdoing and when guilty their offense was reluctance to lend full support to a vicious regime. The dictators did evil because they wanted power, and their henchmen did it out of a mixture of fanaticism, ambition, and fear. Evil thus remains the same even though external influences differ, and this is contrary to what the poisoned-mind explanation leads one to expect. It seems that much of human motivation does not alter as conditions alter. If this were not so, we would find the actions of historical figures and literary characters in contexts very different from our own incomprehensible.

The second reason for rejecting the external-active explanation is that according to it human beings are corrupted by external influences that poison their minds and cause them to do evil. It has to be granted, of course, that all human beings are subject to external influences and their actions reflect these influences. But the external-active explanation is committed to the much stronger claim that external influences are the primary causes of evil actions. It must claim that if the external influences were not present, evil actions normally would not be taken; and if the external influences were present, evil actions would normally follow. If it did not accept this stronger claim, it would not constitute even an attempted explanation of evil. If external influences were merely one of the antecedents of evil actions, they would no more account for evil actions than such other antecedents as the presence of oxygen or the availability of food. But the stronger claim to which the external-active explanation must be committed is obviously false because different people subject to the same external influences routinely perform different actions, some of which are evil, some good, and some morally neutral. Injustice may embitter some and lead to evil actions, or it may turn others into impassioned defenders of justice, or it may prompt the morally neutral action of leaving the unjust society and seeking a better life elsewhere.

Consider as an illustration of this criticism some of the previously discussed concrete cases. It cannot be that Manson's brutalized childhood by itself was sufficient to turn him into a mass murderer because many people with equally brutalized childhoods did not become mass murderers. It cannot be that the semi-fascist ethos of the military was enough by itself to turn the Argentinean dirty warriors into torturers and murderers because there were numerous officers imbued with the same ethos who resigned rather than torture and murder. Nor can Catholicism alone explain the Albigensian Crusade because there were priests who sympathized with the Cathars and tried to save them from the horror that befell them. Of course, external influences had something to do with these evil actions, but the first can explain the second only in conjunction with the internal psychological conditions of those who, influenced by the same conditions, did evil and those who did not. The external-active explanation attributes evil to corrupting external influences, but it fails to explain why some minds are and some are not poisoned by the same external influences.

The third reason for rejecting the external-active explanation is its failure to ask the obvious question of what causes the external influences that corrupt people by poisoning their minds. Let us suppose, as defenders of this secular optimism typically do, that the corrupting external influences are evil political conditions: murder, torture, persecution, and so forth. But what are the causes of these evil political conditions? Political conditions are created and maintained by people. If there is murder, torture, or persecution, it is because there are murderers, torturers, and persecutors. It may be said that people cause these evils because they have also been corrupted by evil political conditions. But what are the causes of *those* evil political conditions? Sooner or later it must be acknowledged that political conditions are created and maintained by people through their actions. If the conditions are evil, it is because the people who create and maintain them are evil. People come first, and the conditions they create and maintain come only after them. Ultimately, therefore, it is political conditions that must be explained with reference to the people who create and maintain them, rather than the other way around. Nevertheless, it is the other way around that the external-active explanation proceeds. For the sentimentality of its defenders about human goodness and perfectibility can be sustained only by shifting responsibility for evil actions from the internal propensities of evildoers to external influences that are falsely supposed to explain the internal propensities and the evil actions they cause. This consideration, especially when combined with the preceding two, provides, I think, decisive reasons against the external-active explanation.

Seeing that, however, is compatible with recognizing that this explanation contributes to an adequate explanation of evil in two ways. It rightly assumes that evil is not supernatural, but something human beings cause, and, presumably, human beings can, if not eliminate, at least ameliorate. And it is right also in recognizing that what goes on within evildoers is crucial to explaining the evil they do. The external-active explanation goes wrong in supposing that in order to explain what goes on within evildoers, we have to look to causes outside them. Internal explanations do not go wrong in this way.

CHAPTER 10

A Biological Explanation

We play fast and loose with the words *human* and *inhuman,* flattering ourselves by making *human* mean only the good things in our makeup or simply what we approve. The historian cannot subscribe to this policy, knowing as he does that cruelty, murder, and massacre are among the most characteristic human acts.

—JACQUES BARZUN, *From Dawn to Decadence*

10.1 Natural Goodness and Defect

This chapter is a critical examination of Philippa Foot's attempt to explain evil in natural terms.[1] It is partly an external and partly an internal explanation. According to it, evil is a natural defect that leads evildoers to act contrary to the human good. What is good is determined by the facts of human nature, and from the good follow the requirements of reason. Evil actions are contrary to nature and reason. The natural facts this explanation regards as crucial are biological. It thus attempts to explain good and evil in biological terms.

Foot's book supplies perhaps the most important argument that can be used to defend the Enlightenment view of human beings as basically good. Foot recognizes, even if not explicitly, that evil presents a problem for this view. She has written a humane and tough-minded work affirming that good and evil do not just depend on what attitudes people happen to have and yet refusing to seek a supernatural explanation of them. It deserves a chapter on its own merits, even though her argument will be found wanting. A further reason for discussing it at length is that its failings point toward considerations that a satisfactory natural explanation of evil must take into account.

Foot's book is about "natural goodness and defect in living things" (3). She says, "I want to show moral evil as 'a kind of natural defect'" (5), and claims that "acting morally is part of practical rationality" (9). Evil actions violate practical reason: "no one can act with full practical rationality in the pursuit of a bad end" (14), and "one who acts badly *ipso facto* acts in a way that is contrary to practical reason" (62). (Reasoning is practical if it aims at successful action, as opposed to theoretical reason, which aims at true propositions.) I shall discuss first Foot's claim that the good is natural and evil is a defect in its pursuit. Then I shall turn to her claim that the good is required and evil is prohibited by practical reason.

According to Foot, "the grounding of a moral argument is ultimately in facts about human life." "It is obvious," she says, "that there are objective, factual evaluations of such things as human sight, hearing, memory, and concentration, based on the life form of our species." Similarly, "the evaluation of the human will [i.e., what prompts human choices and actions] should be determined by facts about the nature of human beings and the life of our species" (24). What, then, are the facts that determine the evaluation of our will, choices, and actions?

Foot's answer is to "start from the fact that it is the particular life form of a species . . . that determines how an individual [of that species] . . . should be. . . . The way an individual *should be* is determined by what is needed for development, self-maintenance, and reproduction; in most species involving defence, and in some the raising of the young." The way an individual should be sets "norms rather than statistical normalities" (32–33). And "by an application of these norms to an individual member of the relevant species it [is] . . . judged to be as it should be or, by contrast, to a lesser or greater degree defective in a certain respect" (34). Again, "if we have a true natural-history proposition to the effect that S's [members of a species] are F [possess a certain species-preserving characteristic], then if a certain individual S . . . is not F it is therefore not as it should be, but rather weak, diseased, or in some other way defective" (30). Foot says that "my belief is that for all the differences . . . between the evaluation of plants and animals . . . and the moral evaluation of humans . . . these evaluations share a basic logical structure and status. . . . Moral defect is a form of natural defect" (27).

The differences between the human and other species Foot has in mind have to do with the different requirements of the good of different species. These differences are considerable because of "human communication and reasoning. . . . The goods that hang on human cooperation, and hang too on such things as respect for truth, art, and scholarship, are much more diverse and much harder to delineate than are animal goods" (16). "Nevertheless, for all the diversities of human life, it is possible to give some quite general account of human necessities, that is, of what is generally needed for human good. . . . Human beings need the mental capacities for learning language; they also need powers of imagination that allow them to understand stories, to join in songs and dances—and laugh at jokes. Without such things human beings may survive and reproduce themselves, but they are deprived. And what could be more natural than to say on this account that we have introduced the subject of possible human defects; calling them 'natural defects'" (43). Foot, therefore, understands the good of the species much more broadly than just survival. It also requires that individual members of the species should live a characteristically human form of life. The good of the species in general and of its individual members in particular is to live according to this requirement.

10.2 The Human Good

It is plain common sense to suppose with Foot that many characteristics good for human beings collectively as a species are good for members of the species individually. Intelligence, benevolence, and courage are such characteristics. But Foot's claim is stronger than this. An obvious interpretation of it is that the characteristics that are good for the species collectively *determine* what is good for individual members of it. This, however, cannot be right. It would be good for the species to be merciless in killing defective infants and the feeble old, for it would prevent the deterioration of the gene pool and ease pressure on scarce resources. It would also be good for the species to despise underachievers, for it would spur them to do better. But merciless treatment or being despised is not good for the individuals who suffer from the actions prompted by these characteristics. And that means that what may be good or bad for the species collectively may not be good or bad for individual members of it.

History is full of moral outrages that have been perpetrated in the belief that the good of individuals is determined by the good of such collectives as state, party, race, and religion. Foot would be ill-advised to propose species as yet another collective that sets the standard of good and evil. But, then, how should she be understood in saying that "the particular life form of a species . . . determines how an individual . . . should be" (32) or that the life form sets "norms . . . and by the application of these norms to an individual member of the relevant species it . . . [is] judged to be as it should be or, by contrast, to a lesser or greater degree defective in a certain respect" (34)?

Perhaps a clue to what she means can be found in the following: "the idea of a good life for a human being . . . is . . . deeply problematic. . . . Nevertheless, for all the diversities of human life, it is possible to give some quite general account of human necessities, that is, of what is quite generally needed for human good" (43). This seems right. Human beings belong to the same species because they share certain biological characteristics, and the human good requires the satisfaction of the needs created by these characteristics. But the ambiguity of "the human good" still creates problems.

Genocide, slavery, and the torture of innocent people deprive individuals of the necessities of life, freedom, and physical security. They are evil if anything is, yet their practice in history had no discernible effect on the good of the species. They had a terrible effect on their victims, but since they constituted only a fraction of the species, the good of the species was not endangered by the undeservedly miserable lives and deaths of a small minority of its individual members. Foot, then, may be interpreted as having in mind general patterns of actions, not individual ones. She may be saying that good and evil actions are those that, if generally performed, would contribute or be detrimental to the good of the species. Even if we ignore doubts about the assumed connection between collective and individual goods, this still does not show what needs to be shown, namely, that genocide, slavery, and the torture of the innocent are evil *because* they endanger the good of the species. Of course they are evil, but not merely because their general practice would endanger the good of the species. They would be evil even if the species as a whole would not be affected by them. They are evil because they cause serious, excessive, malevolent, and inexcusable harm to individuals. It is what these practices do to individuals, not to the species, that makes them evil.

Foot may reply by saying that the biological characteristics of the species are still basic to this evaluation because the practices harm individuals only because they have the nature that makes them members of the human species. Foot is surely correct in that human nature sets universal and objective requirements of the good of individuals. Human beings have basic biological needs, and their good requires that these needs be satisfied. This is an objective, factual truth about all members of the species, and the truth holds regardless of what beliefs or attitudes anyone has. From this truth it follows that there are goods necessary for all human beings regardless of how diverse they are in other respects. But it is also a universal and objective truth that these goods, while necessary, are not sufficient because good human lives require more than the satisfaction of basic needs. Lives in which only the basic needs are satisfied are fit for beasts, not humans. Foot recognizes that the human good must include such diverse goods as "respect for truth, art, and scholarship" (16) and "mental capacities for learning language . . . imagination . . . laugh[ing] at jokes," and that "without such things human beings may survive and reproduce themselves, but they are deprived" (43). The human good, then, depends on both universal and diverse goods. The former are the same for all members of the species. The latter vary with history, culture, and individuality, but there is no variation in the requirement that good lives must have some combination of these or other diverse goods.

Both universal and diverse goods are natural. They are not supernatural; their goodness depends on natural facts, not on human beliefs or attitudes about them; objectively true or false statements can be made about them; and they are biologically based. But Foot does not notice that universal and diverse goods are biologically based in significantly different ways. Universal goods are biologically determined. They are required because they satisfy a basic need in a specific way—hunger by the intake of calories, fatigue by rest, and so forth. The failure to have biologically determined universal goods endangers survival. Diverse goods, by contrast, are biologically undetermined because the needs they satisfy are not satisfied in specific ways. Human beings need love, but they can live without it, and the form in which they have it may be familial, erotic, or patriotic; real or imagined; reciprocal or one-sided; calm or passionate. Human beings also need meaningful activities in their lives, but their survival is not endangered by their lack, and their need may be satisfied by various activities, such as aesthetic, scholarly, competitive, horticultural, or creative; cooperative or solitary; goal-directed or recreational; active or passive. The lack of such biologically undetermined diverse goods does not affect survival, but it endangers good lives.

Diverse goods are no less biologically based than universal ones. It is in the nature of members of our species to need both. Yet there is an essential difference between them. Human nature dictates what universal goods we need, when, and how much. Human nature also dictates that we need diverse goods, but it leaves open what would satisfy that need. Specific universal goods are necessary; specific diverse goods are optional. This is why historical, cultural, and individual variation in universal goods is minimal, whereas variation in diverse goods is considerable.

One consequence of this difference between universal and diverse goods is that Foot's explanation of evil is inadequate. She says: "I want to show moral evil as 'a kind of natural defect.' *Life* will be at the centre of my discussion, and the fact that a human action or disposition is good of its kind will be taken to be simply a fact about a given feature of a certain kind of living thing" (5). Again, "the meaning of the words 'good' and 'bad' is not different when used of features of plants on the one hand and humans on the other, but is rather the same as applied, in judgements of natural goodness and defect, in the case of all living things" (47).

These claims may be true of universal goods, but not of diverse ones. A general practice that deprives people of specific universal goods may be evil because it endangers the survival of the species. In this respect, plants, animals, and humans are alike. But a general practice that deprives people of specific diverse goods does not endanger the survival of the species. It may be an evil because it endangers the possibility of good lives for individuals. In this respect, humans are unlike plants and animals. Humans need and can enjoy biologically undetermined diverse goods; plants and animals cannot because their goods are universal and biologically determined. It may be an evil to deprive individuals of a diverse good they need for good lives. Plants and animals, however, cannot be harmed in this way, so it is a mistake to claim, as Foot does, that "the meaning of the words 'good' and 'bad' is . . . the same as applied, in judgements of natural goodness and defect, in the case of all living things" (47). There is a uniquely human kind of good and evil that other living things lack.

Foot's explanation of that kind of evil thus cannot be right. A satisfactory explanation of evil must recognize that evil may endanger good lives, not just survival, and there is more to endangering good lives than an exclusively biological explanation could account for. It is, for instance, clearly evil to betray a person one loves for a paltry sum, to destroy a child's self-confidence simply for fun, or to corrupt an innocent person in order to win a bet. A satisfactory explanation of evil must do more than provide a biological account of the relevant actions. What has gone wrong with Foot's explanation of evil is that she glosses over the crucial difference between universal and diverse goods. She supposes herself to have explained all evil as a biologically determined natural defect that endangers the good of individuals, whereas she has explained only evil actions that endanger universal goods but not diverse ones.

It may be supposed that this criticism of Foot's explanation can be muted by claiming that the universal goods and evils that have to do with survival are bound to be vastly more important than the diverse goods and evils that affect good lives. If so, Foot would be right to concentrate on universal goods and evils and to regard diverse ones as dependent on them. But three considerations count against this defense.

First, the diverse goods and evils of religion, art, politics, science, law, medicine, and so forth routinely interfere with the satisfaction of basic biological needs. These diverse goods and evils set limits to permissible ways of obtaining and distributing universal goods and avoiding universal evils; they guide the evaluation of the respective importance of incompatible universal goods and evils; they help judge what quantity or quality of them is acceptable or unacceptable; and they determine who can legitimately adjudicate the unavoidable disputes about these matters. Such disputes raise questions about the requirements of the human good, about the forms human lives should take in a particular context. Answering them requires deciding which of many ways of living are better for individuals. But the decisions cannot be made if one thinks of the better exclusively in biological terms, since all reasonable answers recognize the importance of satisfying biological needs and dispute about questions beyond the biological level.

Second, one of the biologically undetermined diverse goods is the attitude individuals have toward their lives. It is essential for good lives that their attitude be favorable. A favorable attitude may take a large variety of forms, some of which are that they should be happy, satisfied, or content with how they live; they should not regard their activities as boring, pointless drudgery; they should be hopeful, enthusiastic, or wholehearted about what they do; they should not be lastingly frustrated, guilty, ashamed, or fearful; they should have much pleasure and little pain; in short, they should enjoy or approve of their lives and activities. Survival requires none of this. It makes no difference to it what attitudes individual members of the species have so long as their biologically determined universal needs are satisfied. Good lives require more, and that shows that there are diverse goods and evils as important for good lives to have or to avoid as are universal goods and evils.

Third, it often happens that individuals reasonably regard some diverse goods in their lives as more important than universal ones. They willingly and knowingly forgo universal goods for the sake of some diverse good they value more highly. This is what happens when individuals sacrifice their lives for their children, cause, or country. Or when they judge that without some particular diverse good their life is not worth living, as they do in choosing death over dishonor, sacrilege, or the disintegration of the culture that sustains them. We thus find once again that Foot's disregard of diverse goods and concentration on universal goods makes it impossible to provide an adequate explanation of all human goods and evils.

Foot's explanation of evil as a natural defect that endangers good lives is inadequate because biologically determined universal goods provide only part of what good lives need. She is right: evil is natural because its source is an objective, factual matter, open to observation. She is also right: evil is a defect. But the defect need not be that evil is inimical to survival. The defect may rather be that evil endangers good lives understood as particular combinations of universal and diverse goods. Foot's explanation of good and evil thus faces a dilemma it can neither avoid nor satisfactorily resolve.[2] If it relies exclusively on biological facts, it cannot account for biologically undetermined diverse goods, so it fails in its own terms as an explanation of the good. If it goes beyond biological facts, it cannot explain all evil as a biological defect detrimental to survival, so it fails in its own terms as an explanation of evil. In either case, it fails to explain what it was meant to explain.

10.3 Practical Reason

Foot's second claim is that practical reason requires good actions and prohibits evil ones. This claim is unaffected by doubts about the first one because it can be held regardless of how far the facts of biology can be used to explain good and evil. Foot says that "acting morally is part of practical rationality" (9) and that "the rationality of, say, telling the truth, keeping promises, or helping a neighbour is *on a par* with the rationality of self-preserving action" (11). In explaining what she means by practical rationality, Foot distinguishes between "what N should do relative to a certain consideration" and "what N should do 'all things considered' (a.t.c.)" (57). She says that "the special characteristic of an a.t.c. or final 'should' is its conceptual connection with practical rationality" (59). Thus practical reason calls for doing what one all things considered should do. The consideration of all things yields as a conclusion what is "the only rational thing to do." The actions of anyone who does not do what "is the only rational thing to do are ipso facto defective . . . contrary to practical rationality" (59). And what practical rationality requires is that human actions should be guided by the goods necessary for human beings. Morality consists in being so guided. "Anyone who thinks about it can see that for human beings the teaching and following of morality is something necessary" (16–17). The requirements of morality, therefore, are also requirements of practical reason. The connecting link between them is the conclusion formed on the basis of having considered all things. That conclusion will also be to perform the action that, in a particular context, best secures the goods necessary for human beings. Such actions are good and reasonable, whereas evil actions are contrary to the human good and thus unreasonable.

The history of moral thought is a graveyard of attempts to show that good actions are rational and evil actions are irrational. Foot attempts the same, but instead of basing it on the usual metaphysical or epistemological grounds, she appeals to biological considerations. Her attempt, however, is as unsuccessful as the earlier ones proved to be. This becomes evident if we recognize that the consideration of all things may be done from at least three different points of view and none yields the conclusion she draws from it.

Let us think about the position of individuals who have to decide in a particular context what they should do. Suppose they want to do what is rational and moral. They try to reach a decision, as Foot says they must, by considering all things. The first obstacle they cannot but run into is that they cannot possibly consider *all* things because they are too numerous. They must focus their efforts, therefore, on considering all *relevant* things. At this point, they have to face the second obstacle of deciding what makes a thing relevant. If they follow Foot, they decide that what is relevant depends on what contributes to the human good. And so they come to the third obstacle. They see that very few people indeed are ever in a position to do anything that might directly affect all of humanity. Whatever they end up doing will directly affect only very few individuals. It is only through them—indirectly—that they can contribute to the human good. In order to surmount this obstacle, they have to decide who the individuals are whose good they should aim at. They have roughly three options: everyone likely to be affected by their action; intimates to whom they feel loyal; or only themselves. As they deliberate about which option to choose, it must become obvious to them that they have reasons both for and against acting on any one of the three options.

The reason for aiming at everyone's good is that the human good depends on cooperation and individuals would be unlikely to cooperate unless by doing so the likelihood of their own good would be substantially increased. The reason against proceeding in this way is that aiming at the good of intimates or oneself is often incompatible with aiming at everyone's good. Loyalty and self-interest provide reasons against resolving such conflicts in favor of everyone's good. Typical conflicts of this sort occur in the distribution of scarce resources at one's disposal, or in weighing the respective importance of the impersonal obligations of patriotism or one's job over against either personal obligations to intimates or commitment to a personal project that gives meaning to one's life.

The reason for aiming at the good of intimates is that human life is made immeasurably better by ties of loyalty and that maintaining them requires honoring reciprocal obligations and having special concern and preference for intimates over strangers. The reason against it is that it may violate personal obligations or weaken the system of cooperation, and its demands often interfere with personal projects, which are as important to a life worth living as intimate relationships.

The reason for aiming at one's own good is that unless it is secured, there is diminished possibility of aiming at anything else. Given normal human psychology and the rarity of saints, one's continued enjoyment of goods is a condition of caring about the good of others. The reason against it is that securing goods for oneself depends on the cooperation of others, and ties of loyalty, requiring one to care about the good of intimates, are among the goods one wants for oneself.

The upshot is that when individuals proceed in the manner recommended by Foot, they routinely find that their consideration of all things yields reasons both for and against particular courses of action. What these reasons are depends on the point of view from which they are considering all things. This conclusion cannot be avoided by claiming that if they really consider *all* things, then they will have reason to adopt one of these points of view and not the others. For as we have seen, while they will have reason to adopt one of these points of view, they will also have reason to adopt the others, as well as reasons against adopting any one of them. Urging them to weigh the respective importance of these reasons will not help because they will have to do the weighing from one point of view or another. Different points of view will result in the assignment of different weights to these reasons, and there will be reasons for and against each weighting. As a result, it is a mistake to suppose, as Foot does, that the consideration of all things will yield the action that will be "the only rational thing to do" (59). Perhaps each point of view will yield one and only one rational action, but that action may well vary with points of view and the individuals who adopt them.

10.4 What Reason Requires and Allows

The source of Foot's mistake is a failure to draw the crucial distinction between what practical reason requires and what it allows. The distinction makes clear what practical reason can and cannot do and what has gone wrong with Foot's use of it.[3] Practical reason requires that deliberations about what one should do meet the following conditions: be logically consistent, take account of relevant facts, consider reasons both for and against possible actions, and evaluate their alternatives on the basis of these requirements. The reason for these requirements is that conformity to them increases the likelihood of succeeding at whatever one aims at and violating them virtually guarantees that the deliberation will go astray. Practical reason, therefore, requires conformity to these conditions and prohibits violation of them. Rational actions meet these conditions; irrational ones do not. One relevant fact practical reason requires taking into account is how one's actions are likely to affect the human good. For if individuals fail to do so, they fail to take into account anyone's good, including their intimates' and their own, and that would make their actions self-defeating.

Practical reason, however, allows various ways of doing what it requires, and it also allows doing many things that it neither requires nor prohibits. Practical reason thus allows the consideration of the effects of actions from any one of the three points of view discussed above. What it does not allow, what it forbids, is ignoring how actions affect the human good from one point of view or another. Thus, an action contrary to a requirement of practical reason is irrational. If, however, an action is contrary to another that is allowed by practical reason, it may still be rational. There is no rational alternative to conforming to a requirement of practical reason, but there are rational alternatives to acting in one of the several ways practical reason allows.

Foot is right to claim that practical reason requires human beings to consider how their actions are likely to affect the human good. But she is wrong to claim that practical reason requires considering it from one of the three points of view; it allows considering it from any one of the three. Foot's view of evil, therefore, is mistaken. Evil is supposed to be the natural defect of acting contrary to the human good. But there are three points of view from which the human good could be considered.

There is a clear tendency in Foot—although there is no explicit statement of it since she does not acknowledge the significance of these different points of view—to consider the good of the species from the point of view of everyone likely to be affected by an action. Let us suppose, if only for the sake of argument, that those who identify morality with impartial benevolence are right. Then the point of view that considers everyone's good, not just intimates' and one's own, is the moral point of view. An evil action, then, becomes one that is contrary to everyone's good. And evil actions, according to Foot, are contrary to practical reason. But if the human good is considered from the point of view of intimates or oneself, then individuals are allowed by practical reason to act contrary to everyone's good if it would mean acting for the good of people they are loyal to or of themselves. Actions that Foot regards as evil, then, may not be contrary to practical reason. Practical reason thus allows some evil actions. Foot's attempt to show that all evil actions are irrational, therefore, fails because it fails to distinguish between what practical reason requires and what it allows.

It is undeniable that people often have reasons for their evil actions. It is a plain fact, for instance, that the evildoers discussed in chapters 2–7 had reasons for the ghastly things they did. The crusaders' and Robespierre's reason was that they were acting for the good of everyone; Stangl's and the dirty warriors' reason was that they were acting for their own good and the good of their family (Stangl) or the good of their country (dirty warriors); and Manson's and the psychopath's reason was that they were acting for their own good.

It does not change the fact that these evildoers had reasons that their reasons were based on false beliefs. For they did not know that their beliefs were false, and they took them to be true at least at the time of their actions. Of course, they ought not to have taken their beliefs to be true, but this is a judgment about their morality, not about their reasons. Their beliefs followed from the point of view from which they were considering the relevant facts, and what the judgment expresses is that they ought not to have taken that point of view since it led them to cause great evil. The correctness of this moral judgment, however, does not mean that the evildoers acted irrationally; it means that morality requires people not to act on such reasons as these evildoers had.

Nor does it change the fact that the evildoers had reasons for their actions that they also had reasons against them. For they weighed their reasons and found that the evil-producing ones outweighed the others. All of them deliberated; they were all at least normally intelligent; they violated no rule of logic; they were not ignorant of the relevant facts; they considered alternatives and criticisms; and they all reached their decisions reflectively over a period of time. Of course, they ought not have made the decisions they made, but as before, this is a moral claim about the use they made of their reasons, not a claim about their lack of reasons. Reason, therefore, allows what they did; it is morality that prohibits it. Reason would have prohibited their actions only if they had ignored considerations of how their actions are likely to affect the good. But they had considered it, and they had reason to do what they did. That the good of their victims ought to have prevented their evil actions is, I repeat, a moral judgment about how people ought to weigh their reasons—a judgment that presupposes that people have reasons for at least some of their evil actions. And that means that Foot is mistaken in claiming that "acting morally is part of practical rationality" (9) or that "no one can act with full practical rationality in the pursuit of a bad end" (14).

10.5 Nature and Evil

The larger significance of Foot's view is that it can be used to provide badly needed rational support for the secular optimism of the Enlightenment. What reason is there for believing that human nature is basically good if it is denied that reality is permeated by a divinely created good order? If nature is all there is to reality, and if it is a morally indifferent jumble of things and processes, then how did the minute segment of it that constitutes human nature come to possess the characteristic of goodness that nothing else is known to have? What is the justification of the secular optimism that sees history as the march—with some unfortunate detours, perhaps—toward the betterment of the human condition? Foot's answers draw on evolutionary theory and explain human nature and its basic goodness as products of the evolution of our species.

Essential to evolution is a long, slow, and gradual process of adaptation in the course of which propensities that aided survival replaced propensities detrimental to it. Had it been otherwise, our species would have become extinct. The propensities favored by evolution are, according to Foot, good, whereas disfavored ones are natural defects, which she regards as evil. Good propensities must significantly outnumber evil ones, for the species could not have survived if it had been otherwise. This is why human propensities are basically good and why evil propensities are bound to be infrequent defects. Foot thus sees the species as living in harmony with nature. This is not because nature is hospitable to our species, but because the species had managed to adapt itself to natural conditions. The contents of the good are simply the propensities that made the evolutionary success of the species possible. The explanation of our possession of these propensities is that other propensities have been systematically bred out of us as a result of being maladaptive. Individual members of the species deficient in good propensities perished, whereas those who were well endowed in these respects produced offspring that were better and better endowed until good propensities became basic and dominant and evil ones became gradually diminishing recessive defects. The undoubted evils of history are the symptoms of the persistence of these defects. It is, however, not misplaced optimism to believe that they will gradually diminish further as a result of being maladaptive.

If the human good were identical with the biologically determined universal goods necessary for the survival of the species, this view would be unobjectionable. But as Foot recognizes, the human good also requires diverse goods, which are biologically undetermined and satisfy requirements other than those of survival. These diverse goods are constituents of the characteristically human forms of life our evolutionary success made possible. That success has freed us from necessity and provided the opportunity to make choices about how we live and act. To be sure, nature, including our nature, sets limits within which our choices must fall, but within these limits we can shape our lives. Morality is one of the strategies we have developed to guide our choices. If the propensities we have developed to make our survival more likely were also propensities that would make our enjoyment of diverse goods more likely, we would have no need of morality because our natural propensities would guide our choices in the right direction. But this is plainly not so. Many of our propensities are vices, such as aggression, greed, selfishness, cruelty, envy, and hatred. And many of our actions, prompted by these vices, are evil without endangering the survival of the species—actions such as holding slaves, torturing, prostituting children, persecuting political or religious opponents, and blinding or mutilating people in order to extract obedience from others. We need morality to control these vices and actions. As history shows, they are widespread and they occur in a large variety of societies, cultures, and circumstances. They are as much a part of human nature and conduct as kindness, generosity, altruism, love, and the actions that express them. Perhaps we came by our vices in the same way as we came by our virtues: in the course of evolution they were adaptive. But there is no reason to suppose that the propensities that were conducive to biological adaptation are also conducive to living characteristically human forms of life, and history provides ample evidence to suppose otherwise. There can be no reasonable doubt about our possession of many propensities that endanger the human good.[4]

My fundamental disagreement with Foot's explanation of evil hinges on our different ways of understanding human nature. She thinks of our natural propensities as basically good; if we act according to their promptings, our actions will be good. I think that some of our natural propensities are good, others are evil, and neither is more basic than the other; if we act according to their promptings, some of our actions will be good and some will be evil. The reason for rejecting Foot's view is that it fails as an explanation of evil. If our nature were as Foot says, evil should not be as widespread as it is; evil should not be caused by the same vices that recur again and again in contexts separated by time, space, and circumstance. But since evil is widespread and it is caused by vices that have not changed much in recorded history, it is reasonable to attribute evil to propensities that may have aided us in the distant past but are now detrimental to human life. The conclusion that follows from this examination of Foot's view is that a satisfactory explanation of evil must treat evil as a natural, but not merely a biological, fact; recognize that evildoers may have reasons for the evil they do; and accept that the secular optimism of the Enlightenment is unfounded because good and evil propensities are both basic in human nature.

It must be said finally that even if the doubts I have expressed about Foot's view were misplaced and all she claims were true, her view would still fall very far short of an adequate explanation of evil because it leaves crucial questions unanswered. Some of them are: What is the difference between merely bad and truly evil actions? Why is it that some people do and others do not act on their evil-prompting motives? What is the role in explaining evil of such external factors as circumstances favoring evil and weak limits? If evil is a biologically determined natural defect, should evildoers be held responsible? Is the presence or absence of intention relevant to explaining evil? Is evil merely what prompts an action or does it also depend on the harm inflicted on victims? A satisfactory explanation of evil must consider and provide defensible answers to such questions.

Internal Explanations

There is no such thing as "eradicating evil" [because] the deepest essence of human nature consists of instinctual impulses
which are of an elementary nature . . . and which aim at the satisfaction of certain primal needs.

—SIGMUND FREUD, *Thoughts for the Times*

11.1 Evil as Malfunction

Internal explanations identify some psychological process within
evildoers as the primary cause of evil. Such explanations, being psychological, contrast with both external and biological explanations. Internal
psychological explanations may be passive or active. The passive one
claims that the malfunction of the intellect or the will is the primary cause
of evil. This is the explanation I will now consider. The internal-active
explanation attributes evil to some psychological process that actively
motivates people to perform evil actions. I will discuss it next.

The internal-passive explanation, then, regards defective beliefs or
motives as the primary cause of evil. Probably the first and certainly the
most influential explanation of this kind is the one Plato has Socrates
express: those "who don't recognize evils for what they are, don't desire
evil but what they think is good, though in fact it is evil; those who . . . mistake bad things for good obviously desire the good."[1] From this follows
what has been called one of the Socratic paradoxes: No one does evil
intentionally.[2] Intentional actions, of course, are sometimes evil, but the
evildoers mistakenly fail to see them as such. They intend the actions, but
only because they see them as good, not evil. If they saw them as evil, they
would not intend them. But why do evildoers fail to see their evil actions

164

as evil? To this question traditional and contemporary versions of the Platonic explanation give divergent answers.

The thought behind the apparent falsehood of the Socratic paradox is that people are normally motivated in their actions to achieve some purpose that seems good to them. The internal-passive explanation of evil actions, therefore, must be either that evildoers are ignorant of the good and perform evil actions in the mistaken belief that they are good, or that, although they know what the good is, they do evil because some motivational defect prevents their actions from reflecting their knowledge. According to the Platonic explanation, then, evil actions result from either a cognitive or a volitional malfunction. The remedy in either case is moral education that imparts genuine knowledge and strengthens the will to act on it.

The Platonic explanation, however, is driven to rely on a supernatural assumption about the nature of reality and its influence on human motivation in order to explain the source and motivational importance of knowledge of the good. For since history and experience amply testify that what appear to be knowledge of the good and good intentions are compatible with evil actions, it must be supposed that history and experience are misleading because they fail to reflect the reality behind appearances. The supernatural assumption the Platonic explanation must depend on, then, is that beyond the appearances of the morally ambivalent world there is a supernatural realm in which a morally good order prevails. Knowledge of the good is knowledge of this morally good order. Lives will be good to the extent to which they are guided by knowledge of the morally good order rather than by the misleading beliefs to which appearances give rise. Thus, the Platonic explanation is that evil is caused by ignorance of the good or by misdirected intentions to act according to it. Evil exists and it is widespread because of human malfunction.

This supernatural assumption and the explanation of evil implied by it have passed from Greek thought to Christian theology through the works of Augustine and Aquinas.[3] Guided by their influence, a dominant tendency in Christian thought is to attribute to an all-knowing, all-powerful, all-good God the creation of the morally good order that permeates reality. Evil is the effect of original sin, the propensity of human beings to malfunction, choose evil over the good, and thereby pit themselves against God's morally good order. Although this type of Christian thinking about evil dominated Western thought until the Enlightenment, it must nevertheless be seen, ignoring some twists and turns of theological sophistication, as an adaptation and articulation of the supernatural assumption and explanation of evil first advanced by Plato's Socrates.

11.2 Reasons against Explaining Evil as Malfunction

There are four reasons to doubt internal-passive explanations. The first has to do with the groundlessness of the supernatural assumption on which the explanation rests. There is no need to belabor this since the reasons against the assumption have already been given in chapter 9, where I discussed Leibniz's similar assumption. Any evidence that may be cited in favor of the supposed existence of a morally good order beyond the natural world must be derived from the world as it appears to normal human observers, for there is no other kind of evidence open to human beings. That evidence, however, cannot be reasonably taken to point to anything supernatural beyond the observable natural world because the most such evidence can indicate is that human knowledge is limited and fallible. We cannot have evidence of what, if anything, lies beyond all evidence to which we could possibly have access.

If, undeterred by this obstacle, defenders of the supernatural assumption advance speculative inferences from the evidence to which we do have access, then they must recognize that evidentially unsupported inferences can be derived both in favor and against their assumption. If the existence of a morally good supernatural order is inferred from observed instances of goodness in the world known to us, then the existence of a morally evil supernatural order must be analogously inferable from observed instances of evil. And the same goes for possible inferences about a morally mixed or indifferent supernatural order. Any logically consistent speculation about a supernatural order that accounts for the relevant facts is as reasonable or unreasonable as any other. Nor is there any more reason to accept the implied view that human beings do evil when they lose sight of the good than the implicitly denied alternative that human beings do good when they lose sight of evil.

The fact is that speculations about what may lie beyond all possible evidence cannot be reasonably advanced as explanations of anything. Arbitrarily picking one possible speculative assumption from among many other equally speculative ones is to advance a wild guess, not a causal explanation. An acceptable explanation must identify the supposed cause, and the effect to be explained, independently of each other, and then give reasons for correlating them. The Platonic version of the internal-passive explanation fails to identify the supposed cause or establish its correlation with the supposed effect. The first objection to the internal-passive explanation is that it is vitiated by the groundlessness of the supernatural assumption to which it is committed.

The second reason why the Platonic explanation fails is its psychological implausibility. This becomes apparent if we reflect on the claim that no one does evil intentionally. Suppose for the sake of argument that evil is done unintentionally because evildoers do not see that what they are doing is evil. They have strong feelings or desires that lead them to act in evil ways, but they fail to understand or evaluate their actions correctly. They mistakenly think that they are just, principled, or objective, but in fact they are cruel, fanatical, or prejudiced. They are led to their mistaken views by strong feelings and desires and by a weak commitment to morality. Suppose they are made to understand that what they are doing is really evil, and that their previous understanding and evaluation of their actions were mistaken. The Platonic explanation assumes that their newfound understanding will lead them to change their actions. This is what makes the view implausible. For there is no good reason to suppose that if evildoers recognize themselves as such, then they will alter their conduct, and there are good reasons to suppose that they may simply continue as before.

It must be remembered that their unintentionally evil actions were motivated by their strong feelings and desires and by their weak commitment to morality. Why would these motives change if evildoers come to understand that their actions are evil? If they had a strong commitment to morality, they might change their actions. But if they had that, they would not have performed evil actions in the first place, and of course, their initial moral commitment is weak. Nor is the understanding they have gained likely to diminish the strength of their feelings and desires. Their predictable reaction to understanding the true nature of their action would be to say with a shrug, that is the way I am, and carry on as before.

The motivation of such evildoers is not mysterious. They may understand the requirements of morality and hold that the requirements of their personal projects, political allegiances, religious convictions, aesthetic preferences, or familial or ethnic ties are more important than moral requirements. The Platonic explanation assumes that if people understand what morality requires, they will do it. The fact is that they may not because they may regard other requirements as more important. And if those requirements conflict with the moral ones, they may do evil intentionally. Countless religious fanatics, terrorists, criminals, and ideologues stand as lamentable testimony to the psychological implausibility of the Platonic explanation.

Several of the evildoers I discussed earlier are cases in point. Manson knew precisely what he was doing, he knew the moral status of the ghastly murders he had arranged and committed, and he had reasons for his evil actions, namely, to punish those who were successful while he was a failure. The psychopath also knew the difference between good and evil actions, but he chose the evil ones because he found them exciting, in contrast with good actions, which he regarded as boring. It is simply psychologically naive to suppose that those who know the difference between good and evil, have the capacity and the opportunity to act in one or the other way, will invariably do good, not evil.

The third reason counts not so much against the Platonic explanation as against a contemporary Christian version of it.[4] R. G. Collingwood's succinct statement of this version is that "evil . . . must have a cause; and the cause of evil in me can only be some other evil outside myself. And therefore we postulate a Devil as the First Cause of Evil" (175). Gordon Graham elaborates: the explanation of "great evils . . . must lie in some conception of malfunctioning, the 'natural' going wrong" (120). He finds that "our modern, humanistic, scientific sensibility lacks an adequate explanation of evil" (154); he concludes that evildoers causing these great evils "have been seduced by evil . . . that there is not merely seduction, but a seducer" (145), and offers the "hypothesis that evil is the outcome of supernatural spiritual agencies" (157). Evildoers "were *chosen,* just as a seducer chooses his victim"; because "they displayed a susceptibility that made them suitable candidates for Satanic purposes, [they were] individuals who could be successfully seduced by evil" (157–58). Graham, then, places all this into "a cosmic narrative," according to which "there has been war in heaven, which is where the fundamental struggle between good and evil takes place, and Satan has been forced to retreat to the earth" (178). This cosmic narrative "provides us with a new understanding of the present evils of this world, one which alters . . . their moral meaning. They become explicable as horrible acts in the final struggle of an evil intelligence that knows itself to be defeated" (179).

The first thing to say about this is what Arendt said in her review of de Rougemont's virtually identical view: "instead of facing the music of man's genuine capacity for evil and analyzing the nature of man, he . . . ventures into a flight from reality and writes on the nature of the Devil, thereby . . . evading the responsibility of man for his deeds," and she rightly deplores "this metaphysical opportunism, this escape from reality into a cosmic fight in which man has only to join the forces of light to be saved from the forces of darkness."[5]

Defenders of this view would reply that they are forced to postulate the Devil as a supernatural explanation of great evil by the failure of natural explanations. In this they are doubly mistaken. To begin with, the great evils committed by the evildoers discussed in chapters 2–7 have been explained in natural terms, if by that is meant explaining in psychological terms why they did what they did. There is no reason to seek a supernatural explanation beyond the motives of faith, ideology, ambition, envy, honor, and boredom as motives that moved these evildoers. It may be said, however, that there is a reason: an explanation of evil must find a single cause for all evil. There must be some cause, it may be supposed, that underlies these various forms of evil. But this supposition is groundless. Nothing compels the highly implausible supposition that complex and multiform events, such as prosperity, love, surgery, war, storytelling, or playacting, have a single cause. Why, then, must evil have one? And if one seeks the implausibly postulated single cause of evil, why must it be the Devil? Why not a Manichean evil divinity; why not a minor heavenly functionary who misunderstood his instructions; why not the Greek gods, who, in order to settle a dispute among themselves, explore the limits of human evil, much as the Book of Job tells us God and Satan did? Or, indeed, why not a God who is not as perfect as Christians believe he is? To these questions there are no plausible answers.

Suppose, however, what is false: all natural explanations of evil have failed. We just do not know what leads people to become evildoers. It would do nothing toward dissipating our ignorance to say that the Devil is responsible for making people into evildoers. For this to qualify as an explanation, it would have to explain *how* the Devil accomplishes this. Graham says that it is through the susceptibility of potential evildoers. That, however, explains nothing unless it tells us just how the Devil makes people susceptible; why some people are susceptible and others not; why the susceptibility results in many different forms of evil; why some people can and others cannot suppress the evil impulses to which they are susceptible; and so forth. An explanation has to be concrete. It must identify the psychological process that the Devil instills or sets into motion that transforms a priest into a crusading murderer, a provincial lawyer into a bloodthirsty tyrant, a naval officer into a torturer, a petty criminal into a serial killer, or a police officer into the *Kommandant* of a death camp. The explanations that answer these questions are, as we have seen, psychological, and thus natural. If these explanations were unsuccessful, then postulating the Devil would still not supply the psychological explanation that is needed.

The fourth reason against the explanation of evil as malfunction emerges from the context of a contemporary view with ancient roots, according to which there is a crucial asymmetry between good and evil: the good motivates actions, but evil does not. Many accept the famous opening sentence of Aristotle's *Nicomachean Ethics:* "Every art and every inquiry, and similarly every action and choice, is thought to aim at some good; and for this reason the good has rightly been declared to be that at which all things aim."[6] Anscombe's recent restatement of this view is that "the man who says 'Evil be thou my good' . . . is committing errors of thought" because "'wanting' introduces good as its object. . . . Goodness is ascribed to wanting in virtue of the goodness . . . of what is wanted." But "the notion 'good' that has to be introduced in an account of wanting is not that of what is really good but what the agent conceives to be good; what the agent wants would have to be characterisable as good by him."[7] From this follows the widely held view that evildoers must want what they believe is good, but they malfunction and mistake evil for good.[8]

Let us begin with the unclarity of the good that supposedly motivates people who are not malfunctioning. Does this motive aim at a moral or a nonmoral good? If it is moral, it may be interpreted as impartial benevolence, or whatever else is supposed to be the mark of a moral motive. But then the claim that people are either morally motivated or malfunction is false. For they may be motivated by some nonmoral good—ideological, aesthetic, commercial, religious, prudential, and so forth. If moral and nonmoral goods come into conflict, people may opt for the nonmoral good, and do evil while being motivated by the (nonmoral) good. This is precisely what several of the evildoers in chapters 2–7 have done. If, however, the good is interpreted as nonmoral, then people motivated by it may act contrary to the moral good without malfunctioning, and once again end up doing evil. Neither interpretation succeeds in showing that evil actions are the result of some malfunction in evildoers.

Consider next another problem arising from the interpretation of good and evil. Good and evil are general, abstract terms, and it is exceptional to be motivated by them. People are motivated by concrete considerations, such as wanting to be healthy, help a friend, make a profit, avenge an insult, or keep out of trouble. Their actions may turn out to be good or evil, but that is rarely their reason for doing them. If not to be motivated by the good is to malfunction, then the vast majority of humanity malfunctions all the time. And they are malfunctioning even when what they do is morally good because they do not do it for what the asymmetry view regards as the only right reason. If, then, most morally good, morally evil, and nonmoral actions alike are attributed to malfunction, it is legitimate to wonder why normal functioning should be held to be faulty. The answer appears to be that defenders of the asymmetry view refuse to admit that rightly functioning human beings may be motivated by other than what is morally good. That, however, is wishful thinking, not a reason.

This brings us to the psychological implausibility, which is the most direct reason against the asymmetry view. It is a fact of life and common human experience that evil actions are often motivated by faith, ideology, ambition, honor, envy, or boredom. These motives may reflect the deepest values of evildoers, motives they have examined and endorsed because it seemed to them preferable to alternatives. Evildoers thus may have reasons for the evil they do. An adequate explanation of evil must acknowledge and take into account this fact rather than attempt to falsify it as the malfunction of basically good human propensities.

These four reasons taken together are strong enough to render doubtful both traditional and contemporary versions of the Platonic explanation. An adequate explanation of evil must account, at the very least, for most cases of evil actions. The Platonic explanation does not do so. It is undoubtedly true that evildoers sometimes do not realize that their actions are evil because some cognitive or volitional malfunction prevents it. But it is equally true that many evil actions are done by people who know very well what they are doing, have reasons for doing it, and are not prevented by circumstances or defects from acting differently.

11.3 Evil as Natural

According to the internal-active explanation, human beings have a propensity to perform evil actions. This propensity is an active motivating force, part of human psychology and normal functioning. It is not the result of a psychological malfunction, corruption by external influences, or a biological defect. It is a propensity as natural to humans as ferocity is to sharks, hunting to tigers, acquisitiveness to squirrels, and playing with their prey to cats, but in humans it takes psychological forms. These are the familiar vices: cruelty, aggression, greed, selfishness, and the like. The propensity motivates corresponding action in appropriate circumstances, unless it is controlled or interfered with in some other way. Evildoers tend to give free rein to such propensities, and the episodic evil actions of morally committed people result from the momentarily unimpeded promptings of the propensities.

Human beings, of course, also have propensities to perform good actions. They have virtues as well as vices. They can be kind, peaceful, generous, and altruistic. These propensities are also natural constituents of the human psychological makeup. Good and evil propensities often conflict and motivate incompatible actions. How their conflicts are resolved is rarely a foregone conclusion. Whether good prevails over evil or vice versa depends on the particularities of the circumstances, the character and education of the subjects, the foreseeable consequences of the incompatible actions, the prevailing state of morality, and so forth.

This type of explanation has been defended, among others, by Hobbes, Butler, Kant, Bradley, and Freud.[9] They differ because they describe the nature of evil, as well as good, propensities in different ways, and also because they disagree about the relative strengths of the conflicting propensities. By and large, Butler, Kant, and Bradley optimistically believe that if good propensities are reinforced by reason, they will prevail over evil ones. Hobbes and Freud pessimistically hold that reason is insufficient to control evil propensities; authoritative external measures are also needed, and even they may not suffice. The optimists think that the propensity for evil is not the strongest because good propensities and the ideal of the human good will lead reasonable people to understand that their good is inseparably connected with the good of others. This will motivate them to act on their good propensities and control evil ones. The pessimists think that the propensity for evil is so strong as to permeate all other propensities, as well as the efforts of reason to control them. This propensity may be "a perpetuall and restlesse desire of Power after power that ceaseth onely in Death,"[10] as Hobbes thought, or, as Freud claimed, "there is no such thing as 'eradicating evil' [because] the deepest essence of human nature consists of instinctual impulses which are of an elementary nature . . . and which aim at the satisfaction of certain primal needs."[11]

The optimists are optimistic for different reasons. Butler thinks that actions dictated by self-love and altruism usually coincide, and when they do not, the authority of conscience weighs in to strengthen altruism. Kant thinks that reason is universal and it leads autonomous people to an impartial, objective evaluation in which their own concerns count no more than the concerns of anyone else. And Bradley thinks that the ideal set by one's good self, if all goes well, has sufficient attractions to resist the promptings of one's bad self. The pessimistic view is deeper. Hobbes and Freud doubt that any psychological process can be guaranteed to be immune to invasion by evil propensities. Their response to reliance on altruism, reason, or the ideal of one's good self would be that they cannot be relied on to ensure morally desirable actions because they are as liable to be put to evil uses as any other psychological process. That people may believe that they are motivated by altruism, reason, or their good self counts for very little because their beliefs may be rationalizations of their evil propensities. Much evil has been caused by the false beliefs that it is for the victims' own good, or that it is dictated by reason, or that it is called for by a high ideal. And the evil is not lessened if the evildoers hold their false beliefs sincerely.

The merits of the pessimistic version of the internal-active explanation of evil are considerable, especially in contrast with the other attempted explanations. It does not rely on speculation about a supposed supernatural order. It does not attribute evil to nonhuman causes. It does not deny the complexities of evildoing by holding them to be biological defects. It does not falsify human motivation by regarding all evil as the product of ignorance or weakness. It does not accept the myth that human beings are basically good. It does not refuse to face the evidence provided by history and personal experience. It does not confuse cause and effect by regarding political injustice as the cause and evil as its effect. And it does not suppose that if evildoers realized that their actions were evil, they would be bound to stop acting that way. It recognizes, in short, that the cause of evil is a natural human psychological propensity.

11.4 Reasons against Explaining Evil as Natural

These merits notwithstanding, there are two reasons for doubting this explanation of evil as well. The first is a mirror image of one of the reasons that counts against the external-active explanation. That explanation regards external influences as the primary causes of evil. The unacceptable consequence is the explanation's incapacity to account for the facts that some people do and others do not become evildoers even though they are subject to the same external influences and that evildoers are motivated by the same familiar vices under radically different circumstances. Part of the reason, then, why the external-active explanation is inadequate is that it does not recognize the importance of the psychological propensities of evildoers. One reason against the internal-active explanation is that it does not take sufficient notice of the external circumstances of the evildoers. Consequently, it lacks an account of why some people do and others do not become evildoers even though they have the same psychological propensities. External influences clearly have an important bearing on what psychological propensities turn into vices, and the internal-active explanation needs to recognize this.

The concrete cases discussed in chapters 2–7 illustrate this. It is not enough to explain the evil that was done to say that the crusaders were motivated by faith, Robespierre by ideology, Stangl by ambition, Manson by envy, the dirty warriors by honor, and the psychopath by boredom. These psychological propensities may cause no harm if people's circumstances include rigorously enforced limits on acting on their propensities, or if they are subject to external influences that counter the motivational force of their potentially evil psychological propensities. Robespierre might have lived out his life as a harmless provincial lawyer with quaint radical ideas if the French Revolution had not occurred. Stangl might have remained a law-abiding official in the Austrian police if there had been no Nazism. And the dirty warriors might have nurtured their honor in melodramatic posturing without serious immorality. These people became evildoers not only because of their psychological propensities, but also because external influences encouraged their expression and the limits prohibiting evil actions were weak. Part of the trouble with the internal-active explanation is that it regards psychological propensities as the primary causes of evil and fails to recognize that external influences favorable to evil and the absence of strong prohibitions are just as important.

The second reason why the internal-active explanation of evil fails is the assumption of its defenders that the explanation of evil depends on identifying *the* propensity that is its cause. What is at fault is the assumption that evil has a single cause. Hobbes thought that it was the quest for power and Freud that it was destructiveness, or as he called it, the death instinct. The problem is not so much with the propensity they singled out, but with the very idea that the explanation of evil requires finding a single cause. It is not merely that it stretches explanatory ingenuity too far to see, say, faith and boredom as forms of seeking power, or ambition and honor as manifestations of the death instinct. It is also that the very idea that the explanation of evil should reduce the multiplicity of evil-producing propensities to one is flawed. As there are many virtues, so there are many vices.

Much evil is motivated by selfishness, but terrorists and ideologues may be selflessly dedicated to their causes. Evildoers often deceive themselves about their motives and actions, but moral monsters and psychopaths may be quite clear about what they are doing and why. Many evil actions are motivated by cruelty, but evildoers may be impersonal, impartial, and disinterested executors of someone else's orders. Evil is frequently done out of greed, but vengeful, thrill-seeking, sadistic, and fanatical evildoers may be indifferent to possessions. Generally speaking, no good reason has been given for the assumption that evil has a single cause, and the great variety of evil actions motivated by a great variety of propensities are good reasons for rejecting it.

It adds force to this second reason against internal-active explanations if we consider the problems with Colin McGinn's contemporary versions of it. McGinn says that his "aim is to develop the outlines of a moral psychology of evil in which its structure is laid bare."[12] And "the basic idea is that an evil character is one that derives pleasure from pain and pain from pleasure" (62). He explains that he is "discussing what we might call *pure* evil as opposed to *instrumental* evil—malice for its own sake, not as a means to achieving some other goal. . . . I am concerned with cases in which the other's pain is prized for its own sake, in which the motive is precisely to cause suffering. This is not egoistic in the traditional sense, since no benefit to the agent accrues from the other's pain, aside from the pleasure afforded by it" (63).

McGinn adds that "the paradigm is the torturer" (68) and that "pleasure in the infliction of pain by means of physical violence is the prime example of evil in the defined sense" (69). Then he goes on to provide a very interesting and, as far as I can see, correct analysis of the motivation of the sadist (77–81), and discusses the connection between envy and evil (81–83). He also recognizes that it may be rational to be evil (85–87). His account is natural, internal, active, and psychological, and although it deplores evil on moral grounds, it does not make the mistake of supposing that what is immoral is ipso facto irrational. In all this, I agree with him. What, then, is wrong with McGinn's explanation of evil?

Consider the crucial component of his account of an evil character as one who takes "pleasure in the infliction of pain by means of physical violence" (69). If this is what makes a character evil, then a torturer who takes no pleasure in torturing is not evil. There is no reason to suppose that the crusaders or the dirty warriors took pleasure in the torture they inflicted, and there is good reason to suppose that Stangl was actually pained (until he numbed himself) by the suffering of his victims. On McGinn's account these obviously evil people were not evil, and that shows that it is a mistake to make pleasure central to the explanation of *all* evil. McGinn may well be right about pleasure being central to the evil of sadism, but evil takes many forms, of which sadism is only one. McGinn's explanation does not cover other forms.

We can reach the same point in a different way. Take the victim of a crime who feels pleasure at the pain of the apprehended and jailed criminal because he thinks that the criminal is suffering just punishment. If McGinn were right, the victim would be evil. But of course, he is not because he has done nothing wrong. Or take a boxer who takes pleasure in causing pain to his opponents. Does that make him evil? Are people evil if they take pleasure in causing pain by witticisms, obscenity, or exposing hypocrites? We may not think of all these people as having sterling characters, but surely they fall far short of having an evil one. What has gone wrong with McGinn's account, in addition to not fitting many cases of evil, is that it makes people evil who obviously are not. McGinn does not recognize that evil is connected with actually causing harm, not merely meaning to; that the harm must be serious enough to prevent the normal functioning of its victim; and that although taking pleasure in the deserved pain of others is not good, it is hardly evil. McGinn does not distinguish between what is merely morally bad and evil, which is much worse. There are good reasons, then, against accepting his version of the internal-active explanation as an account of all forms of evil.

11.5 Transition to Mixed Explanation

Arendt's explanation of evil is about halfway between an internal-active explanation and the mixed explanation I shall defend in chapter 12. There are reasons against accepting her explanation, but of all the ones I have so far discussed, hers comes closest, in my opinion, to being right. She discusses evil in two works: one general, the other particular.[13] I begin with the particular, which concerns Adolf Eichmann, an evildoer not very different from Stangl (the subject of chapter 4). Eichmann was born into a lower-middle-class German family in 1906. After an unremarkable early life, in 1932 he joined the Nazi Party and the SS, and in 1934 he applied to and was accepted into the SD, the section of the SS in charge of the Final Solution, that is, the extermination of the Jews. He eventually rose to a rank equivalent to lieutenant colonel and was given the job of arranging the transportation of Jews from all over Europe to the forced labor and death camps. He was responsible for the murder of millions of innocent people. After the collapse of Nazi Germany, he escaped to Argentina. He was traced and caught by Israeli security forces in 1960, brought to Israel, tried, sentenced to death, and in 1962 hanged. Arendt's book is a record of his trial and her reflection on it.

Arendt concludes her account of the trial by saying that Eichmann's "long course in human wickedness had taught us . . . the lesson of . . . the banality of evil" (EJ 252). This comment was widely misunderstood by people who took Arendt to be minimizing and thus extenuating the evil Eichmann committed. What she meant to communicate, however, was the banality of the evildoer. For this mass murderer turned out to be a very ordinary bureaucrat who, although showing "extraordinary diligence in looking out for his personal advancement" (EJ 287), was not the bloodthirsty, sadistic monster many people expected. That his job involved the killing of millions was a matter of indifference to him. He just wanted to be good at whatever task he was given. "Despite all the efforts of the prosecution, anybody could see that this man was not a 'monster'" (EJ 54). He showed "utter ignorance of everything that was not directly, technically and bureaucratically, connected with his job" (EJ 54). "He was not stupid. It was sheer thoughtlessness—something by no means identical with stupidity—that predisposed him to become one of the greatest criminals. . . . If this is 'banal' . . . if with the best will in the world one cannot extract any diabolical or demonic profundity from Eichmann, that is still far from calling it commonplace. . . . That such remoteness from reality and such thoughtlessness can wreak more havoc than all the evil instincts taken together which, perhaps, are inherent in man—that was, in fact, the lesson one could learn in Jerusalem" (EJ 288). Eichmann "acted not as a man but as a mere functionary whose functions could just as easily been carried out by anyone else . . . it was mere accident that he did it and not someone else" (EJ 289). And so Arendt is at a loss to connect "the unspeakable horror of the deeds" (EJ 54) and the "sheer thoughtlessness" (EJ 288) of the man who perpetrated them. She cannot understand how this murderer of millions "except for his . . . personal advancement . . . had no motives at all" (EJ 287).

Arendt's puzzlement about why Eichmann did what he did is very odd indeed because in the book about the trial she supplies the answer specifically about Eichmann and in her earlier theoretical work she describes what makes people instruments of the totalitarian state. As for Eichmann, "as the months and the years went by, he lost the need to feel anything at all. This was the way things were, this was the new law of the land, based on the Führer's order; whatever he did he did, as far as he could see, as a law-abiding citizen. He did his *duty*, as he told the police and court over and over again; he not only obeyed *orders*, he also obeyed the *law*" (EJ 135). During the pre-trial examinations, he "declared with great emphasis that he had lived his whole life according to Kant's moral precepts, and especially according to a Kantian definition of duty. . . . To the surprise of everybody, Eichmann came up with an approximately correct definition of the categorical imperative: . . . 'the principle of my will must always be such that it can become the principle of general laws'" (EJ 135–36). But Eichmann also explained that "from the moment he was charged with carrying out the Final Solution he had ceased to live according to Kantian principles, that he had known it, and that he had consoled himself with the thought that he no longer 'was master of his own deeds,' that he was unable 'to change anything.'" Arendt adds that Eichmann distorted the Kantian formula "to read: . . . 'Act in such a way that the Führer, if he knew your action, would approve it'" (EJ 136). What motivated Eichmann was "the demand that a man do more than obey the law, that he go beyond the mere call of obedience and identify his own will with the principle behind the law . . . [which] was the will of the Führer." And Arendt says that "there is not the slightest doubt that in one respect Eichmann did indeed follow Kant's precepts: a law is a law, there could be no exceptions" (EJ 136–37). So Eichmann did what he did because of what he saw as his duty and because of his "extraordinary diligence in looking out for his personal advancement" (EJ 287). His supposed duty happily coincided with his supposed self-interest. Their combined motivational force, relentless Nazi propaganda, the authority of his superiors, and his physical distance from the murder of his victims were strong enough to silence any qualms he may have had about doing his share in murdering millions. This seems to me a good explanation of the evil Eichmann did.

Arendt, however, gives even more because she explains how it happens that people in totalitarian states identify their own will with that of the regime. This is one great theme of her theoretical work on totalitarianism. She distinguishes between limited and radical evil. "Murder is only limited evil. The murderer who kills a man . . . still moves within the realm of life and death familiar to us" (OT 442). In contrast, "the real horror of the concentration and extermination camps lies in the fact that . . . here murder is as impersonal as squashing a gnat . . . there are neither political nor historical nor simply moral standards. . . . [This] is the appearance of radical evil" (OT 443). Limited evil serves the purpose of an individual. Radical evil, however, is different. "The concentration camp was not established for the sake of any possible labor yield. . . . The incredibility of the horrors is closely bound up with their economic uselessness. The Nazis carried this uselessness to the point of open anti-utility. . . . In the eyes of a strictly utilitarian world the obvious contradiction between these acts and . . . expediency gave the whole enterprise an air of mad unreality. This atmosphere of madness and unreality, created by the apparent lack of purpose, is the real iron curtain which hides all forms of concentration camps. . . . Seen from the outside, they and the things that happen in them can be described only in images drawn from a life . . . removed from earthly purposes" (OT 444–45).

Evil is radical when it shows that "everything is possible" (OT 441). It makes "evident that things which for thousands of years human imagination had banished to a realm beyond human competence . . . can be established by the most modern methods of destruction" (OT 446). Evil is radical because it destroys the possibility of civilized life. If everything is possible, then there are no limits, no rules, no laws. Anything, then, can be done to anyone. "It is inherent in our entire philosophical tradition that we cannot conceive of a 'radical evil.' . . . We actually have nothing to fall back on in order to understand a phenomenon that nevertheless confronts us with its overpowering reality and breaks down all standards we know" (OT 459). "There is a great temptation to explain away the intrinsically incredible by means of liberal rationalizations. In each one of us, there lurks such a liberal, wheedling us with the voice of common sense" (OT 439–40). "What common sense and 'normal people' refuse to believe is that everything is possible" (OT 440–41). That is the radical evil concentration camps show.

"Concentration camps are the most consequential institutions of totalitarian rule . . . indispensable for the understanding of totalitarianism" (OT 441). "The uselessness of the camps . . . is only apparent. In reality they are more essential to the preservation of the regime's power than any of its other institutions. Without concentration camps, without the undefined fear they inspire . . . a totalitarian state can neither inspire its nuclear troops with fanaticism nor maintain a whole people in complete apathy" (OT 456). Individuals living in a totalitarian state have three choices: they can resist, sink into apathy, or identify with the state. Eichmann, with his "extraordinary diligence in looking out for his personal advancement" (EJ 287), chose to identify with the state. He stopped thinking for himself, adopted as his will the Führer's command, and made his duty what his superiors in the SS said it was. Since his duty was to transport millions to their death, that is what he did, and was rewarded for it. This is the explanation of his thoughtlessness, of his fervent declarations that what he did was his duty, and of how this ordinary man came to do extraordinary evil.

I find this a convincing explanation of the evil Eichmann did, although with two reservations. One is that Arendt explicitly denies that she has offered an explanation. She says that what she concluded about Eichmann "was a lesson, neither an explanation of the phenomenon nor a theory about it" (EJ 288). I do not know why Arendt denies that she has given an explanation, or why she remained puzzled about Eichmann's motivation after having made plain that it was the combination of his ambition, misguided sense of duty, identification with Nazism, and the opportunity and direction provided by his position in the SD. My other reservation is that I do not think that either Communism or Nazism has ever achieved the sort of absolute control she attributes to totalitarian regimes, and if they have not, then what regime has? Even during the worst days of Stalinist terror and the fear instilled by the Gestapo and the SS, people knew that there were alternatives to the life that was imposed on them. They knew it either from having lived under a different regime, or from travel, foreign radio, and books. Others knew it secondhand through acquaintance with people who had firsthand knowledge. The memory of another way of life certainly persisted in Germany, where the Nazis were in full power for less than ten years, and it persisted even in Russia, where the regime lasted for about seventy years. Individuality, therefore, did not become extinguished, although, of course, it was deeply threatened. These reservations aside, however, Arendt's explanation of Eichmann's motivation seems to me to be a skillful description of how private vice, public encouragement of its expression, and the removal of moral limits caused him to become a mass murderer.

Explaining Eichmann's motivation, however, is one thing; explaining evil is quite another. Arendt sees that, and she denies having written "a theoretical treatise on the nature of evil" (EJ 285). It is well to remember that. What she says about evil fits Eichmann and the very similar case of Stangl. But it does not fit the crusaders, Robespierre, the dirty warriors,

Manson, or the psychopath. Arendt's account illustrates how both internal and external explanations are necessary for understanding evil. It is an example of an explanation that succeeds. It succeeds, however, in explaining only one form of evil, and there are many others.

In conclusion, I have argued in chapters 9–11 that there are good reasons against accepting external, biological, and internal explanations of evil. But the arguments have identified important elements that a better explanation must embody. In the next chapter, I attempt to provide that better explanation.

The Mixed Explanation

I feel at times identified with the good, as though all my self were in it; there are certain good habits and pursuits . . . which are natural to me, and in which I feel at home. And then again there are certain bad habits and pursuits . . . in which perhaps I feel no less at home, in which also I feel myself to be myself . . . whichever way I go, I satisfy myself and yet fail to do so. . . . I am driven to believe that two opposing principles are at war in me, and make me at war with myself; each of which loves what the other hates, and hates what the other loves.

—F. H. BRADLEY, *Ethical Studies*

12.1 Preamble

There is a charming fable in one of John Godfrey Saxe's poems:[1]

It was six men of Indostan
To learning much inclined,
Who went to see the Elephant
(Though all of them were blind),
That each by observation
Might satisfy his mind.

The first, having bumped into the elephant's flank, declared that it was like a wall; the second concluded after groping around its tusk that it was a kind of spear; the third compared it to a snake because he felt the length of its trunk; others claimed that it was really a tree, a fan, and a rope because they fingered its leg, ear, and tail.

181

And so these men of Indostan
Disputed loud and long,
Each in his own opinion
Exceeding stiff and strong,
Though each was partly in the right,
They all were in the wrong!

The elephant before us is evil. The explanations discussed in chapters 9–11 are each partly in the right, although they are all in the wrong. Each concentrates on an undeniable condition of evil, but denies other equally undeniable conditions. The aim of this chapter is to provide an explanation that incorporates all the conditions.

The explanation is *mixed* because it has internal, external, active, and passive conditions, and because it recognizes the central importance of each condition. It thus differs from previous explanations because they stress the importance of one or two of these conditions and neglect the importance of the others. At the same time, it overlaps with the other explanations because it incorporates the conditions they regard as pivotal. The proposed explanation is also *multicausal* because it holds that different forms of evil have different causes. This is another way it differs from previous explanations, which vainly seek to identify *the* single cause of evil. Nevertheless, the failures of previous explanations are not total because they all identify some conditions a successful explanation must recognize. The contribution of previous explanations, of course, is the reason for the detailed discussion of them in chapters 9–11. And the reason for the similarly detailed discussion of the cases in chapters 2–7 is to make concrete the particular and grievous harms evil causes. These cases are, as it were, the raw data a successful explanation of evil must account for.

12.2 The Conditions

Let us now assemble the conditions that have emerged up to this point. They are at once constituents of the mixed explanation I aim to provide and conditions of its adequacy. To begin with, the explanation must account for the concrete cases of serious, excessive, malevolent, and inexcusable harm (in chapters 2–7), and it must recognize that cases like them abound. The explanation, therefore, excludes the views (in 8.5) that attribute evil to moral monsters who are bound to be rare and could not account for the prevalence of evil and those that regard evil as incomprehensible and reject the very possibility of explanation. Since the explanation is multicausal, it must identify the different causes of various forms of evil. It thus excludes both single-cause explanations (in chapters 9–11) and explanations that identify a cause but do not explain how it and its supposed effect are linked (in 11.2). So it excludes the Devil and bad political arrangements as explanations because they do not specify how these putative causes produce evil effects and why they affect some people but not others. Then, since the explanation is naturalistic, objective, factual, and psychological, it must identify the psychological facts or processes that constitute the causes, the effects, and the links between them that jointly make up evil. Consequently, the explanation excludes the appeal to anything supernatural (in 9.2 and 11.1), the attempt to treat evil merely as a matter of the adverse attitude a society or an individual has toward otherwise morally neutral facts (in 8.4), and the explanation of evil in purely biological terms (in chapter 10).

The explanation must also recognize that human beings are ambivalent toward good and evil. There are basic human propensities leading to both good and evil actions, such as altruism and selfishness, love and hate, justice and injustice, kindness and cruelty. The development of these propensities is encouraged or discouraged by the characters and circumstances of individuals, but all of them are present in normal human lives as possibilities that may or may not be acted on. This excludes the optimism—inspired by the Enlightenment or by our evolutionary success—that regards good propensities as basic and evil ones as derivative defects caused by the malfunctioning of good propensities (in 9.4, chapter 10, and 11.1). It also excludes the religious optimism according to which good propensities are in harmony with the scheme of things and evil ones are contrary to it. The exclusion of secular and religious optimism does not mean, however, that the explanation is committed to pessimism as a result of supposed human wickedness. Human beings are basically neither good nor bad, but ambivalent. Reason favors uncertainty about the future, not optimism or pessimism.

The mixed explanation, therefore, has both internal and external conditions. The first specifies the particular propensities that motivate evil actions. The second specifies the particular circumstances that influence the development of these propensities and form the context of evil actions. Both conditions have an active and a passive aspect. Internal propensities motivate not only action but also inaction, not only the development of propensities but also their suppression. And external circumstances provide both possibilities and limits, encouragements and discouragements of actions. The mixed explanation thus excludes all attempts to attribute evil to one of these conditions or aspects and downplay the importance of the others (in chapters 9–11).

The explanation must also take into account the complex connection between reason and evil. Evil actions need not be irrational: some are prohibited by reason, but others are allowed by it. This requires spelling out the requirements of reason and explaining why evil actions may or may not meet them. One way of doing this is to distinguish between universal goods required for everyone's well-being and diverse goods that are socially and individually variable (in 10.2). Evil actions are normally contrary to universal goods, but they need not be contrary to diverse goods. If diverse goods conflict with universal ones, there may be reasons to prefer diverse goods even if doing so requires actions contrary to universal goods. Such actions may be both evil and allowed by reason. The recognition that evil actions may be allowed by reason excludes all explanations committed to the claim that evil actions are by their very nature contrary to reason (in chapters 9–11).

Lastly, the explanation must note that evil actions may be either intentional or unintentional. Actions are intentional if their agents want to perform them because they understand and favorably evaluate their significance, whereas mistakes in understanding and evaluation make an action unintentional. Intentional evil actions thus reflect a considered preference for evil over good. Unintentional actions may reflect a culpable or nonculpable deficiency in people's understanding or evaluation of their actions. This excludes explanations that deny the possibility of intentional evil actions (in 11.2).

An explanation that takes account of all these considerations must be mixed because of the indispensability of external, internal, active, and passive conditions. It must also be multicausal because the causal role of these conditions varies with the characters and circumstances of evildoers and with their particular motives and actions. There is good reason to suppose that the causes of the evil actions of the crusaders, Robespierre, Stangl, the dirty warriors, Manson, and the psychopath—separated by great differences in time, place, character, and context—were different. What needs to be explained, then, are the causes of such evil actions.

The general form of the explanation is that evil actions are caused by the combination of internal psychological propensities and external circumstances. The internal condition of the explanation identifies the specific psychological propensity that led to a particular evil action, and it gives an account of why that propensity was acted on rather than any one of the numerous others possessed by the evildoer. This part of the explanation, therefore, has an active aspect that explains the motivational force of a specific propensity and a passive aspect that explains why other propensities lacked sufficient motivational force. The external condition identifies the social conditions conducive to the performance of the evil action. It also has an active aspect that points at the specific conditions that elicit the evil action, and a passive aspect that explains why the prohibitions proved insufficient in that context. I must emphasize that this is the *general form* of the mixed explanation, but it is not, of course, the explanation itself. The explanation must be *particular* because specific propensities and social conditions differ from case to case, and because the relative causal efficacy of the internal, external, active, and passive conditions of the explanation is also likely to differ. The result of these differences is that the explanation of an evil action cannot be generalized to other evil actions. This is what doomed previous explanations that sought *the* cause of evil actions.

12.3 The Internal Condition

If explanations of evil actions must be particular, then doing what I now must do, namely, show what a successful explanation is like, must be done with reference to specific cases. The cases in point are the ones discussed in chapters 2–7. I shall proceed by identifying their different conditions, beginning with internal active propensities. The crusaders were motivated by their faith, Robespierre by his ideology, Stangl by ambition, Manson by envy, the dirty warriors by honor, and the psychopath by boredom. These are psychological propensities, not just biological ones: they are not simple, direct responses to stimuli, like closing one's eyes when sneezing, but complex, indirect responses mediated by the beliefs, feelings, experiences, and evaluations of evildoers.

Each of these propensities is a readily understandable and widely shared human tendency. Faith and ideology are responses to the generally felt human need to make sense of the scheme of things. People also tend to assess their lives, and if their assessment yields an adverse judgment, one response is ambition to improve it; another is to envy those whose lives are better; and yet another is the listless, apathetic boredom that results from the lack of meaning. Nor are many people without honor that embodies their sense of identity and the values by which they want to live. None of these propensities has a necessary connection with evil actions, but each is easily transformed into a powerful urge to cause serious, excessive, malevolent, and inexcusable harm to those who are thought to threaten a person's manner of living.

The reason why these threats elicit extreme reactions is the importance attributed to what is threatened. People's faith, ideology, and honor make their lives meaningful. Ambition, envy, and boredom are different ways of coping with the dissatisfactions of their lives. To threaten them is to threaten either what makes their lives worth living or the stratagem they have constructed to cope with their unsatisfactory lives. The threats are thus directed against people's psychological security and attempts to avoid hopelessness. No wonder they are passionately attached to what they believe is threatened and are fiercely protective of it.

This passion is an important part of the explanation of why the psychological propensities in question so easily come to motivate evil actions. For the passion leads to the systematic falsification of the moral significance of the relevant facts. Faith, ideology, and honor provide, in different ways, the moral outlook of their adherents. Passionate attachment to them is seen as an expression of righteousness, and dissension as immoral. The supposed immorality, however, is seen not simply as a failing, but as a challenge to what makes life worth living. Living and acting contrary to the faith, ideology, or honor are thus condemned for falling short of the true and the good. This may happen as a result of ignorance, in which case the remedy is to inform the uninformed. But the real threat comes from those who are not ignorant, who knowingly reject the faith, ideology, or honor. Such people are thought of as guilty of willful immorality and endangering human well-being. They are blamed not for the familiar and comparatively minor failure to do what morality requires, but for the radical subversion of morality itself. This is what aroused the passions of the crusaders, Robespierre, and the dirty warriors, what they blamed their victims for, and what supposedly justified them in treating their victims in ways they knew were normally immoral, but under the exceptional circumstances warranted.

The passions behind envy and boredom led to a different type of falsification. Manson and the psychopath did not think that their actions were morally justified. But they thought that they were justified by nonmoral considerations, which overrode moral prohibitions. The source of Manson's deep resentment of those who succeeded where he failed and the psychopath's frantic search for excitement was the fact that they were both talentless petty criminals, uneducated and unloved, vegetating with empty lives, and having no hope for a better future. This led them to reject the standards by which they were condemned, and changed them from petty thieves into evildoers. They supposed themselves to see through the phoniness of the standards and the hypocrisy of those who live according to them. They were enraged by what they took to be the injustice of others enjoying their lives and possessions in contrast with their own miserable existence. So they appointed themselves scourges of humanity, Manson to vent his envy and the psychopath to alleviate his boredom. The evil actions by means of which they proceeded were justified in their eyes by their own deprivations.

The passion behind Stangl's ambition was to rise in the world. When this made him a mass murderer, he did not think his actions were justifiable morally or otherwise, but he thought they were excusable because he had not intended to be a mass murderer. His falsification involved desensitizing himself to the ghastly facts of the death camp and ignoring his ambition to rise, so that he could see himself as coerced by circumstances that left him no options. What coerced him, however, was the ambition that was his ruling passion, not his circumstances. He believed that his evil actions were excused by coercion, but his belief was false because his ambition blinded him to the existence of other options.

None of these evildoers set out to do evil. They did what they did, but they saw it under a different description: as doing God's work, benefiting humanity, being conscientious, resenting injustice, saving one's country, or having fun. They knew that their actions would normally be regarded as evil, they knew about the requirements of morality, and part of what led them to try to describe their actions in acceptable terms was to avoid being condemned by others and by themselves. There is no reason to suppose that their misdescriptions of what they were doing were insincere. They seemed to have genuinely believed that their actions were justified or excusable.

It is amazing that they could have sustained this belief as they came face to face with the agony of their victims, with their cries, blood, and mutilated bodies. These evildoers were not desk murderers, like Eichmann, who ordered others to do the evil deeds. They personally were the murderers, torturers, and agents of mayhem. The passions that enabled them to falsify their descriptions, to sustain their false beliefs, to justify or excuse the horror of what they inflicted on their victims had to be extremely strong. Understanding how they could have done what they did depends on understanding the strength of the passions that led to their falsifications and disguised from them the true nature of their evil actions. The explanation I have proposed is that these evildoers believed that their victims threatened the very core of their psychological security and sense of values. Their excesses and malevolence were enraged reactions to what they took to be unprovoked attacks on what made or would have made their lives worth living.

It is essential to bear in mind that this is very far from a complete explanation. First, it does not account for moral monsters who set out to do evil and do not falsify to themselves what they are doing. Second, it should not be supposed that if the falsifications were removed, the evildoers would stop doing evil. For they may just continue to do knowingly what they did before in self-imposed ignorance. Falsification is merely an effect of the passion that motivates them; removing this effect would leave the underlying passion intact. They would still be enraged at being threatened, and they might do intentionally the evil they did before unintentionally. Or they might not. The explanation says nothing yet about what they might do, so more is needed to make it complete. Third, if the falsifications were in place, the passions had motivating force, and the evil actions under some misdescription were intended, evil might still not be done if external conditions prevent it. A complete explanation of evil actions, therefore, cannot be only internal. Fourth, even the internal condition of the explanation must go beyond what has so far been said. For it must explain why the passions were not controlled, why the falsifications were so readily accepted. This last point leads to the internal passive propensities of evildoers.

If human beings are ambivalent toward good and evil, then evildoers will have good propensities, not just evil ones. Their evil propensities are dominant, but a complete explanation owes an account of why they are dominant, why their good propensities are suppressed enough to prevent them from interfering with their own attempts at falsification. In short, it must be explained why their conscience is silent. The explanation is that they are deficient in self-knowledge. Self-knowledge needs to be developed; they have not done so; consequently, they lack the inner resources that could prevent their falsifications. Their conscience is silent because they fail to know that there is something it should condemn. But why have they not developed self-knowledge?

Part of the explanation has to do with the external conditions of their lives, and I shall discuss them in the next section. Another part of the explanation, however, is internal. It is that evildoers are vaguely aware that what self-knowledge might reveal would force them to call into question the stratagem they hit upon to make their lives tolerable. It would raise doubts about their motives for adhering to their faith, ideology, or honor, or for coping with their dissatisfactions through ambition, envy, or resistance to boredom. Self-knowledge would open up the possibility that it is their need to make sense of their lives that motivates their faith, ideology, or honor and not whatever intrinsic merits their systems of value may be supposed to have. It would make them suspect that their ambition, envy, or boredom might be an attempt to disguise their own deficiencies rather than a reaction to the adverse conditions in which they live. It might suggest that it is with themselves that they should be dissatisfied, not with the world. And that would lead to despair because if they themselves were deficient, their hope for a better future would be undermined by their own handicaps. Evildoers thus have a strong impetus not to develop self-knowledge. A noteworthy feature of this impetus is that its source is the same as the source of their evil actions. They are both attempts—one turned inward, the other outward—to protect what makes their lives worth living. One does it passively by resisting the very possibility of questioning it, the other by actively savaging those who are thought to threaten it.

The just-completed account of the internal condition of the mixed explanation has an active aspect, which identifies the specific propensity that motivates a specific evil action, and a passive aspect, which points at the specific deficiency that prevents evildoers from seeing their evil action as evil. Permeating both aspects and explaining their dominant role in the psychology of evildoers is the passion with which they are protecting what makes their lives worth living and sustains their hope for a better future. This account incorporates central portions of both the internal active and the internal passive explanations discussed earlier (in chapter 11). The explanation of evil actions *is* connected with a specific propensity and with a malfunction of the evildoer. But these are only parts of a full explanation, and they must be amended by the recognition that both the specific propensity and the malfunction occur in many different forms. A full explanation of an evil action, therefore, must be particular because it must identify the specific propensity and the specific form of the malfunction.

12.4 The External Condition

A clue to the indispensability of the external condition is the ordinariness of the evildoers I have been discussing. This is the feature Arendt described as the banality of evil (see 11.5). But her description is misleading because it is evildoers who may be banal, not the evil they do; not all of them are banal, for moral monsters are anything but; and even evildoers who are banal are so only if viewed independently of the evil they do. Suitably qualified, however, Arendt's description points to something important. Take, for instance, Robespierre and Stangl. During the Terror and in Treblinka each assumed monstrous proportions as the merciless dispenser of immense suffering to a very large number of innocent victims. But imagine Robespierre if the French Revolution had not occurred or Stangl in an Austria without Nazism and the *Anschluss*. Robespierre might have spent his life as a provincial lawyer, and Stangl might have been an official in the Austrian police. It is essential to understanding their evil actions that it was the Revolution and Nazism that elicited them. If these upheavals had not changed their lives and encouraged the development of their evil propensities, they would have been very unlikely to become the great evildoers they in fact were.

If human beings are basically ambivalent, then they all have evil propensities. But not all of them develop and act on them. One reason why they might do so is that their social conditions favor evildoing. This happened to Robespierre and Stangl, and their evil actions cannot be explained without taking into account the large role social conditions had in causing them. The radical alteration of their earlier conditions encouraged Robespierre and Stangl to act on their evil propensities and suppress good ones. They both saw opportunities in the upheavals surrounding them, and they changed their manner of living accordingly. These changes gradually drew them deeper and deeper into identifying their interests with those of the French Revolution and Nazism, which in turn encouraged them more and more to continue and to intensify their murderous activities.

The social conditions of the crusaders and the dirty warriors also changed as a result of the Cathars and Marxist terrorism in Argentina, but these changes did not influence them to change their manner of living, as they did Robespierre and Stangl. For the crusaders had long before dedicated their lives to serving their faith, and the dirty warriors had from childhood on been trained in the code of honor that formed their self-image. Both continued in their previous manner of living; the change was merely that they had to serve the cause they had made their own in new circumstances. Their superiors told them that their cause was threatened and had to be defended, and both the priests and the soldiers rose to the occasion. This, however, did not mean that they obeyed commands against their will. For what they willed was identical with what their superiors willed. The commands they obeyed merely directed their actions in the light of information their superiors had and they lacked. They, like Robespierre and Stangl, acted under the influence of their social conditions. The difference was that the crusaders and the dirty warriors acted under the influence of lifelong social conditions, whereas those of Robespierre and Stangl provided them with opportunities and allegiances they previously lacked. But all of them were prompted by different external influences to develop and act on their evil propensities, and they did so. If their social conditions had been different, they might not have become evildoers. If their good propensities had been stronger than their evil ones, they might have resisted external influences. It was the combination of their dominating evil propensities and social conditions encouraging them to act on their propensities that made them into the evildoers they were.

Social conditions also influenced Manson and the psychopath, but in a way that was yet again different from the four other cases. Once the others committed themselves, the general direction their actions had to take was clear. They had to eliminate the enemies of the Revolution, run the death camp, suppress the Cathars, and get rid of suspected subversives. But the social conditions of Manson and the psychopath gave them no direction. They were dissatisfied with their conditions and spurred by them to action, but not to any particular action. They belonged to no authoritarian organization that told them what to do, like the church, the Nazi Party, or the Argentinean navy; they were not swept up in an upheaval, like the French Revolution, the *Anschluss,* or terrorism. They lived in mid-twentieth-century America, which was relatively stable, orderly, and committed to curtailing the political role of authoritarian organizations. Social conditions, therefore, influenced Manson and the psychopath to do something to escape their dissatisfactions without suggesting what they might do. They had to rely on their own resources much more than the other four, but because they were barely literate and totally undisciplined, their resources were meager. Their limited knowledge led them to reject what surrounded them, and since that involved morality, they rejected that too, thus allowing their evil propensities to dictate whatever they had the inclination and the opportunity to do.

There is, however, one respect in which all six of these evildoers were similarly influenced by their social conditions: the conditions discouraged them from developing the self-knowledge that might have led them to question their evil actions. The authoritarian organizations to which the crusaders, Stangl, and the dirty warriors belonged gave them clear ideas of what they ought to do and wherein good and evil, right and wrong lay. If they had any doubts, their superiors had ready answers for them. They felt no need for self-knowledge because they had no questions to which self-knowledge might have given them the answers. Robespierre was fully engaged in the feverish activities of the Revolution and had no leisure and energy for the reflection self-knowledge requires. Manson and the psychopath were busy fending for their daily needs, usually by thievery, and they lacked the discipline to think systematically even about simple matters, let alone something as complicated as the distinction between their apparent and real motives. So even though the social conditions in the six cases were alike in discouraging self-knowledge, they differed considerably in how they did it.

The combination of evil propensities and social conditions that encourage their expression in action and discourage self-knowledge is still not sufficient to explain evil actions in the cases we are considering. For if the social conditions had also included strong limits, then the opportunities for evil actions would have been severely curtailed. Thus a further condition of the mixed explanation must be the failure to set and enforce strong enough limits to prohibit evil actions. The crusaders' faith, Robespierre's ideology, Stangl's ambition, Manson's envy, the dirty warriors' honor, and the psychopath's boredom led to evil actions partly because the limits in their social conditions failed to rule them out. This makes it necessary to understand these limits.

The limits are meant to prohibit evil actions, which deprive people of universal goods and thus violate basic requirements of human well-being. The limits, therefore, protect goods everyone needs. A viable society must have such limits, for if it did not, its members would have no reason to pay taxes, obey the laws, or participate in its institutions. The limits are the bulwarks of civilized life. If they are breached, barbarism and savagery follow. The limits, however, are prima facie, not absolute. They may be justifiably violated in war, defense against terrorism, or the punishment of evildoers. In such cases, serious harm is caused, but it is justifiable, provided it is not excessive and malevolent. What can justify it is that it is required as protection from even greater harm. Apart from cases of this sort, however, a society must either set and enforce strong limits prohibiting evil actions or risk disintegration.

The social conditions of the six evildoers were different in many ways, but they were alike in not including strong enough limits to prevent them from causing great evil. Yet the particular ways the limits failed varied considerably. In the contexts of the crusaders and the dirty warriors, there were strong limits and they knew what they were. But the limits were not strong enough to prevent their evil actions based on the false belief that their victims violated the limits and that this justified the harm they inflicted on them. In the cases of Robespierre and Stangl, the previously recognized limits had broken down. As a result of the upheavals created by the French Revolution and Nazism, there were virtually no limits on what might be done, provided the Jacobins and the Nazis approved of it. The circumstances of Manson and the psychopath included limits, but they were weak as a result of a misguided reluctance to enforce them. It was—and still is—widely believed that a free society is incompatible with the enforcement of strong limits, but the belief was—and remains—mistaken because the enforcement of strong limits is not incompatible with a free society, but a condition of it.

The external condition of the mixed explanation, therefore, must have also a passive aspect, which attributes evil actions partly to the failure to set or to enforce strong limits. Although this general form of the explanation fits each of the six cases, its generality hides important differences in the ways in which the failure occurred. As a result, there is yet a further reason for insisting that a successful explanation of evil actions must go beyond the general form and be particular.

In sum, the mixed explanation aims to show, constructively, that the most general form of explanations of evil actions must combine internal, external, active, and passive conditions. And it aims to show, critically, why the explanations discussed earlier—each of which stressed one condition and ignored or minimized the importance of the others—were bound to fail. It aims also to show that this form, while still general, can be made less so by specifying that the internal-active conditions are evil propensities inherent in human psychology; the internal-passive conditions are failures to develop self-knowledge; the external-active conditions are social conditions that encourage the expression of evil propensities; and the external-passive conditions are failures to maintain strong limits. A satisfactory explanation, however, must go beyond even this less general form by specifying the particular evil propensities and social conditions and the particular reasons for the failures of self-knowledge and limits involved in the evil actions of a particular evildoer. I hope to have provided this specificity in the six cases I have considered.

If specificity makes mixed explanations particular, it also makes them multicausal because the conditions that jointly constitute the cause of evil actions are bound to vary with contexts and individuals. This variation contributes to the particularity of the explanations in two ways. One is the result of differences in propensities, conditions, and reasons for failures. The other is the result of differences in the comparative causal efficacy of the various specific conditions. The strength of evil propensities, the conduciveness of social conditions to evil actions, the obstacles to developing self-knowledge, and the degree to which limits are weak also vary with contexts and individuals. And this provides additional support for my claim that mixed explanations of evil actions must be particular and multicausal.

In the interest of avoiding misunderstanding, I must add that there may be evil actions whose cause does not include all four of these conditions. An evil action need not be motivated by an evil propensity because even a good or morally indifferent propensity could prompt an action that causes serious, excessive, malevolent, and inexcusable harm. It would not alter the evil they did if the crusaders or the dirty warriors had not been motivated by evil propensities. Similarly, the failure of self-knowledge is not essential to an evil action, as shown by moral monsters who typically know perfectly well what motivates their actions. Nor do evil actions require weak limits, since determined evildoers may transgress limits regardless of how strong they are. Lastly, an action may be evil without causing serious harm, if the evildoer fully intends it but accidentally fails because, say, the bomb exploded sooner than planned. Actions may be evil, therefore, even if one of the four conditions is missing, provided the causal efficacy of one of the other conditions is sufficiently strong to compensate for the absence of the causal efficacy of the missing condition. I must also add that the explanations I have given are of evil *actions*. There remains the centrally important question of the relation between evil actions and the people who do them. I have so far said little about this, which, of course, concerns the responsibility of evildoers. That is the subject of the next chapter.

12.5 Reason

The explanation of evil actions is one thing, their evaluation another. Understanding evil actions does not exclude condemning them. In fact, knowledge of their causes may strengthen the outrage they provoke. But what if evildoers had reasons for their actions? Might that not justify or excuse them? In order to consider this possibility, we need to resume the discussion (in 10.3–4) of the relation between reasons and evil actions. Reasons may be theoretical or practical. The former guide what should be believed, the latter what should be done. These two aspects of reason are connected, but I shall concentrate on the practical one because the question before us is whether there might be reasons for evil actions. This question is ambiguous: it may be asking whether reason might require evil actions, or whether reason might allow them. The difference is important. It is irrational not to do what reason requires, but it is not irrational not to do what reason allows. The requirements of reason are few and strict; the allowances of reason are many and loose.

The specific requirements of reason are that decisions about which of several actions one should perform be logically consistent; take into account relevant facts; consider reasons for and against possible actions; and evaluate possibilities on the basis of these requirements. Rational actions conform to these requirements; irrational ones violate them. In most normal circumstances, several rational actions are possible and doing one is incompatible with doing another. Any one of these actions is allowed by reason. The requirements of rational action are normally low, many actions typically meet them, and there is rarely just one particular action that reason requires. Consequently, decisions about which of several actions allowed by reason one should do are often guided by moral, aesthetic, personal, prudential, religious, political, and other considerations, which conform to and go beyond the requirements of reason.

Say that it is lunchtime and I am hungry. I could buy a sandwich, have a gourmet meal, fast, diet, give my lunch money to a cause I favor, ignore my hunger and continue to work, or wait for a friend so that we could eat together, and so on. All these actions are allowed by reason. What reason requires is that sooner or later, in one way or another, I should decide what to do about my hunger, even if the decision is to starve myself to death. To the question why one should do what reason requires, the answer is that reason is the best guide to successful action, whatever one's aim happens to be. Anyone who wants to act successfully, therefore, should act as reason requires.

The distinction between what reason requires and allows bears on evil actions. Reason requires a society to set and enforce strong limits that prohibit evil actions. Evil actions deprive people of universal goods, which are basic requirements of human well-being. Part of the reason for living in a society is that it protects these basic requirements of its members, and this is what strong limits should do. Societies, of course, may fail in various ways to do what they should: strong limits may be used to protect diverse goods, not universal ones; or they may protect only some members; or they may not be enforced; or their enforcement may be overdone and thereby drastically interfere with possibilities the limits were meant to guarantee. Whether a society goes wrong in these or other ways is often a difficult question. The difficulty, however, consists not in knowing that reason requires strong limits that prohibit evil actions, but in knowing how to do what reason requires given the conditions of a particular society, having the will to do it, and bearing the costs.

What reason requires of a society is not the same as what it requires of individuals who live in it. It is clearly in the interest of each individual that there be strong limits prohibiting evil actions. But it does not follow that reason requires individuals to conform to these limits. The interest of individuals is that they themselves should be protected, not that everyone should be. And their interest is to have not just universal goods protected by the limits, but also diverse ones whose protection is not a requirement of reason. These two kinds of goods often conflict, and individuals may have reasons to resolve such conflicts in favor of diverse goods.

Diverse goods, it will be remembered, vary with time, place, individual, and circumstance. But they may be just as, or more, important for the well-being of individuals as universal goods. Universal goods satisfy simple basic needs for nutrition, rest, companionship, health, and so on. Diverse goods satisfy complex needs created by moral convictions, political allegiances, aesthetic preferences, intimate relationships, religious commitments, financial security, or personal projects that give meaning to life. Individuals often have reasons to regard such diverse goods as essential to their well-being. And then, if they have to deprive others of a universal good in order to obtain an essential diverse good for themselves, they would have reason to violate the limits prohibiting evil actions.

The crusaders, Robespierre, Stangl, Manson, the dirty warriors, and the psychopath had just this reason for their evil actions. They thought, respectively, that the diverse goods of their faith, ideology, ambition, envy, honor, and alleviation of boredom were important enough to override the universal goods of their victims. Their actions were evil, but not because they violated requirements of reason: they did not fail to be logically consistent, to take account of relevant facts, to consider reasons for and against possible actions, or to evaluate their possibilities. Their evil actions were thus allowed by reason, but they were still unjustified. What made them unjustified, however, was morality, not rationality. The fact nonetheless remains that in deliberations about actions, morality is only one consideration among others and individuals may have nonmoral reasons for evil actions.

This, however, is an incomplete account of the deliberations of evildoers because they typically have not only nonmoral reasons for evil actions, but also nonmoral reasons against them. These latter reasons are of different kinds. The simplest one is prudence. There are limits prohibiting at least some evil actions in all societies, and the violation of limits is punished, often severely. Prudence dictates that potential evildoers count the risk of punishment and the cost of disguising their evil actions as reasons against doing evil. How strong these reasons are depends on the context. In a society with weak limits, the risk of punishment is likely to be small and the cost of hiding the true nature of evil actions need not be high. In other societies, evil may actually be countenanced or even encouraged, provided it takes certain forms, such as the torture of suspected dissenters or the extermination of a minority.

Another kind of nonmoral reason against evil actions is the ease of life. All societies pay at least lip service to opposing what is regarded there as evil. There is always a more or less sincere official line praising the good and professing abhorrence of evil. Life is less complicated, less strenuous, involves less anxiety, calculation, and pretense for those who toe the official line and have nothing to hide. Evil actions usually need to be hidden, and the difficulty of hiding them, of living in a way that requires much dissimulation, makes life harder than it needs to be. If potential evildoers are reasonable, they recognize this as a reason against evil actions. But again, how strong a reason this is depends on just how genuine is the public support of the prevailing morality and how likely it is that evildoing will be unmasked.

A third kind of reason against evil actions is the ambivalence of most evildoers. Evildoers tend to be motivated by evil propensities, but they also have good ones. Their good propensities are likely to be developed to some extent because it is virtually impossible to come to age in a society without having received at least rudimentary moral education. They must know the simple dos and don'ts of morality; they must be familiar with ideas like reciprocity, indebtedness, and honesty; and they are likely to have been taught to ask themselves "how would you like that done to you?" The combination of good propensities and their training makes it rare to find people without some fellow feeling tied to the humanity of their intended victims. And this gives further reasons against evil actions. But of course, such reasons may be weak; if strong, they may still be outweighed by even stronger ones originating in evil propensities and in passions aroused when people regard themselves as threatened; and moral education in some contexts may be indoctrination with an evil moral code. How strong these reasons are again varies with individuals and social contexts.

The deliberations of evildoers, therefore, typically involve weighing reasons for and against evil actions. Evildoers are what they are because their reasons for evil actions habitually outweigh their reasons against them. But this could happen only because they have reasons and are aware of at least some of them. In this respect, the deliberations of evildoers do not differ from the deliberations of morally good people. Apart from the exceptional saints and monsters, good and evil people both have reasons for and against their actions, weigh their reasons, and decide to act one way or another. Therefore, the Platonic view—shared by many religious believers, champions of the Enlightenment, and biologically influenced optimists—that good actions are rational and evil ones are irrational is mistaken. It is certainly true that people ought to do good actions and ought not to do evil ones, but the "ought" expresses the requirements of morality, not of rationality.

Why ought people do what morality requires? The honest answer, I think, is that they ought to do it only if they care about the well-being of others; wish to live in harmony with them; want to avoid a life likely to be solitary, nasty, brutish, and short; are moved by examples of good lives; and are repelled by examples of evil ones. Such people are the friends of humanity. Humanity also has enemies, and that is what evildoers indifferent to the moral "ought" are. It is important to bear in mind that evildoers are not mere backsliders who lie, steal, or cheat, but people whose actions cause monstrous harm. They do not just violate moral limits, but reveal a depraved attitude toward them. They are the sort of people who snatch an old woman from her deathbed in order to burn her alive, like the crusaders; who enjoy a cozy lunch between two bouts of mass murder, like Stangl; and who incite a mob to dismember and cannibalize live victims on mere suspicion of political dissent, like Robespierre. To think of such evildoers as enemies of humanity is not too strong a condemnation and to treat them as such is well deserved. If potential evildoers are reasonable, they will consider whether they are willing to accept such consequences of their actions. The next chapter is about these consequences.

CHAPTER 13

Responsibility

This is the excellent foppery of the world, that, when we are sick
in fortune . . . we make guilty of our disasters the sun, the moon,
the stars; as if we were villains by necessity, fools by compulsion,
knaves, thieves, and treachers by spherical predominance,
drunkards, liars, and adulterers by an enforced obedience to
planetary influence; and all that we are evil in, by a divine thrust-
ing on: an admirable evasion of whoremaster man.

—WILLIAM SHAKESPEARE, *King Lear*

13.1 The Approach

It is clear that evildoers should be held responsible for their
actions, but it is not clear what that involves, what the conditions of the
justified ascription of responsibility are, what may exempt evildoers from
responsibility or mitigate the responsibility they have. The aim of this
chapter is to give an account of responsibility that answers these questions. The account will not be a general theory because it is concerned
only with moral responsibility, not with legal, political, professional, or
official ones; it concentrates on responsibility for evil actions, not for
merely bad actions, omissions, the performance of duties, or the dis-
charge of obligations; it deals with the responsibility of individuals, not of
societies, governments, corporations, institutions, and other collectives;
it considers only the responsibility of individuals toward others in their
society, not toward human beings in general; and it is about backward-
looking responsibility for evil actions done in the past, not about future
responsibilities individuals or collectives may have.

Responsibility, as I shall treat it, is *for* evil actions, but it is the responsibility *of* the evildoers that is to be considered. And their responsibility is

199

for patterns of evil action, not for isolated episodes. The evil actions of the crusaders, Robespierre, Stangl, Manson, the dirty warriors, and the psychopath flow from and reflect their characters. They are not episodic but habitual evildoers. Their actions reveal the kind of persons they are. The appropriateness of holding them responsible, therefore, cannot be questioned on the ground that their actions may reflect only external influences that led them to do what they would not have done without those influences. There are cases of this sort, but the six I am concerned with are not among them. The psychological propensities of these evildoers play a central role in motivating their actions. Patterns of action are thus normally reliable indicators of character, and that is why the account of responsibility will concentrate on patterns rather than on isolated episodes.

The nature of evil sets further conditions that an account of responsibility must meet. First, responsibility is for causing serious harm, such as murder, torture, and mutilation, and the harm prevents its victims from functioning as normal human beings. It is a straightforward factual question whether serious harm has been caused by a particular person. If the answer is affirmative, the evildoer is causally responsible for the action. Moral responsibility, however, requires more because people may cause even patterns of serious harm through no fault of their own. This points to the importance of a second condition. Responsibility is for having caused harm that is not only serious but also excessive, that is, disproportionately greater than what is needed to achieve the evildoer's goal. The goal of the crusaders, Robespierre, and the dirty warriors, for instance, was to stamp out heresy, political dissent, and subversion. They could have achieved these goals by exiling or jailing their victims. There was no need to burn them alive, hand them to the mob to be mutilated and cannibalized, or force them to crouch motionless, blindfolded, and naked for months on end before throwing them out of an airplane. Such excesses are partly what made their patterns of action evil, which is much worse than morally bad. Responsibility is also for malevolent actions, like burying children alive, throwing live babies into crematoria, or slowly suffocating a heavily pregnant woman by hanging her from a rafter and plunging a knife into her dozens of times, as Robespierre, Stangl, and Manson incited their underlings to do. The excess and malevolence of such actions reveal the evil motives of evildoers. They are not callously indifferent to the suffering of their victims, but passionately bent on causing maximal suffering to them. Holding them morally responsible, therefore, is not just for the serious harm they cause, but also for the manner in which they cause it. Nor should it be forgotten that their actions are not uncharacteristic episodes but habitual patterns in which serious, excessive, malevolent harm is caused again and again to victims who have done nothing to deserve it.

The second condition depends on psychological propensities that motivate the evildoers' excesses and malevolence. What these propensities are is also a factual question, but it is often less straightforward than the question of whether serious harm has been done. For what goes on inside evildoers must be inferred from the nature, manner, and context of their actions, and from what they themselves say about them. Such inferences are fallible, and the testimonies of evildoers are unreliable. Although there is a factual answer to the question of whether their actions were excessive or malevolent, it may be unclear what the answer is. In the six cases, however, there is no such unclarity because the evidence is sufficient, the excess and malevolence unquestionable, and the seriousness of the harm obvious.

The third condition is that there be no excuse that might justify evil actions, exempt evildoers from responsibility, or mitigate the responsibility they have. An excuse does not diminish the seriousness of the harm the evildoers have caused, but makes it inappropriate to hold them morally responsible. Although they caused evil, the excuse shows that the connection between their evil actions and their character is lacking. I will discuss later (in 13.3) how it might be decided what a justifying, exempting, or mitigating condition is, but it may be helpful to have an example here of each. A justifying condition is if evil actions are the only ways of preventing much worse evil. The simplest exempting conditions are insanity and imbecility. A mitigating condition is illustrated by the case of SS lieutenant Kurt Gerstein, who did the evil actions his superiors expected of him, but he joined the SS in order to combat it from the inside and really helped victims when he could.[1] Whether exemption, justification, or mitigation is appropriate in a particular case is a matter of judgment. The available facts about the evildoer's character, actions, and context must be interpreted, their comparative salience evaluated, and how the evildoer saw, or could or should have seen, the context must be reconstructed. What the judgment should be is not always clear. In the six cases, however, there can be no doubt that the evildoers should be held morally responsible. If they were not, it would be hard to see how anyone could be.

These conditions jointly imply that holding evildoers morally responsible depends on both their motives and the consequences of their actions. The consequences are the serious harm they have done. The motives are the psychological propensities that led to the excess and malevolence of their actions. If either consequences or motives were missing, there would be no moral responsibility because there would be no evil action for which responsibility could be ascribed. Actions could be morally bad without causing serious, excessive, and malevolent harm, but they could not be evil. The presence of the appropriate kind of motive and consequence is necessary for holding people morally responsible. But their presence is not sufficient because even patterns of evil action may be excused. If, however, there is no excuse, the motive and consequence are present, and the evil actions form a pattern, the conditions are sufficient for holding the evildoer morally responsible.

13.2 The Account

The account consists in the explanation of the following claim: people are normally responsible for the readily foreseeable consequences of their actions. To begin with, the responsibility in question is moral. This means that the consequences for which people should be held responsible are the readily foreseeable effects of their actions on the well-being of others. Holding people morally responsible for their evil actions is to hold them liable to moral condemnation. There is a continuum of increasingly severe condemnations ranging from mild, unexpressed disapproval to generally felt outrage that unites members of a community in their reaction to the excesses and malevolence of evil actions. Condemnations express an attitude and a judgment consequent upon it. The attitude is a response to a violated expectation, and the judgment is directed against the person whose actions violate it.[2] Since the actions in question are evil, their condemnation should be severe. If this seems harsh, the concrete details of evil actions, such as those of the crusaders, Robespierre, Stangl, Manson, the dirty warriors, and the psychopath, should be vividly remembered. Evil, then, will not be just an ominous word but a reminder of the suffering of the tortured, mutilated, and murdered innocent victims.

The expectation whose violation provokes condemnation is that members of a society will respect the physical security of other members. This, of course, is not the only expectation fellow members have of one another, but it is perhaps the most basic. An essential part of the morality and the legal system of a society is to ensure that this expectation is generally met. Occasional violations of it do not endanger society itself, but if the violations are frequent, the society cannot count on the allegiance of its members. They can be held together by terror and propaganda, as numerous dictatorships have done, yet fear and insecurity will spread, and elementary self-interest will compel people to choose among actively or passively opposing the status quo, siding with the violators by becoming at least their tacit accomplices, and leaving the society if they can. Whatever they choose, they will worsen the already wretched state of their society.

Evil actions violate this expectation and spread insecurity. They seriously harm their victims, but they are also excessive and malevolent. Evil actions thus at once violate and show contempt for the expectation that must be met by any society with a legitimate claim to the allegiance of its members. The manner in which evil actions harm their victims undermines the foundation on which the society rests. It is, consequently, natural for evil actions to provoke severe condemnation. When they do not, there is something morally amiss with the individuals or the society that fails to react in this way. The condemnation, however, is not primarily of the evil actions, but of the people whose actions they are and for being the kind of persons they are. It holds them up as examples to avoid; teaches children not to be like them; unites uncorrupted members of the society by their shared convictions; motivates various forms of refusal to associate with them; aims to prevent them from getting into influential positions; and generally regards them as enemies of the society they have shown themselves repeatedly to hold in contempt. It also supports the legal system, where the moral condemnation of evildoers takes a judicial form and results in their punishment.

Holding evildoers morally responsible is thus holding them liable to such condemnation. The condemnation expresses a moral attitude, which is not a moralistic urge to vent indignation, but a desire to protect the physical security of people living together in a society and to identify and influence people whose actions threaten it. The attitude combines feelings and beliefs, facts and values, expectation and judgment. Like all attitudes, it can go wrong, and it has gone terribly wrong on numerous historical occasions as a result of misdirected feelings, mistaken beliefs, misperceived facts, false values, wrong expectations, and baseless judgments. But a society cannot protect the well-being of its members without such an attitude, and the most fundamental interest of its members dictates the effort to prevent it from going wrong.

Responsibility is thus the liability to condemnation imposed on evildoers. It has been rightly called a "reactive" attitude because it is a reaction to actions that violate the expectation that members of a society will respect one another's physical security.[3] Responsibility can be internalized. Evildoers, then, are not merely held to it by others. They feel it themselves, and would feel it even if their evil actions escaped detection and were not actually condemned. Regret, shame, guilt, and remorse are some of the feelings through which internalized responsibility may manifest itself. But responsibility has to be taught and learned. It is an attitude acquired from the outside. People can direct it toward themselves only because they learned to share the attitude of others who direct it toward evildoers. It is essential to understanding responsibility that people have it because they are held to it, not because they feel it, since they would be rightly held to it even if they did not feel it. It is good to feel it, and members of a society ought to feel it, but evildoers are not exempt from responsibility if they do not feel it. On the contrary, it makes them liable to even more severe condemnation, for if they do not feel responsible for their evil actions, they are more likely to repeat them.

Any account of responsibility as something ascribed to people, as a liability to which they are held, must explain how the distinction between justified and unjustified ascriptions of it should be drawn. Responsibility is not just for evil actions, because the insane and imbeciles are not, and should not be, held responsible for them. The justification of holding people responsible, therefore, must depend not only on their evil actions but also on some component of their psychological makeup that the insane and imbeciles lack. This component is being able to foresee the readily foreseeable consequences of one's actions.

The overwhelming majority of human adults are able to do this and constantly do it. It is like being able to speak one's mother tongue, imagine possible states of affairs, or recognize familiar faces that have not been seen for a while. Being able to do such things can be taken for granted; it requires no explanation; it is its lack that needs to be explained. Since actions and consequences are incalculably various, it is impossible to define what consequence of what action is readily foreseeable. But it is not hard to convey the basic idea. Jumping off a tower, putting one's hand in fire, being awake for forty-eight hours, driving a car into a crowd, dropping a large rock on someone's head normally have consequences that anyone acquainted with the facts could readily foresee. It would be absurd to claim that the immediate consequences of such actions were uncertain or difficult to predict. Of course, what holds normally does not hold necessarily. There may be unusual circumstances, technological manipulations, or interferences with perception or judgment that invalidate ordinary expectations. But if there are no unusual considerations and those considering the actions are not handicapped, the immediate consequences of the actions will be readily foreseeable by them.

The test of what these consequences are is to ask whether others in that situation would readily foresee them. What is readily foreseeable for a person is what would be readily foreseeable in normal circumstances by any unhandicapped person. This test is not foolproof because appearances could deceive. If some situation is supposed to be deceptive, then those who suspect deception owe an explanation of why the facts are contrary to appearances. Normally, the immediate consequences of evil actions are readily foreseeable. There can be no reasonable doubt that murder, torture, and mutilation constitute readily foreseeable serious harm. Normally, evildoers are readily able to foresee that, so they meet the psychological requirement of responsibility. It is, then, justified to condemn them for their evil actions.

This must be qualified, however, because although evildoers normally are able to foresee the consequences of their actions, in the circumstances preceding their evil actions they may not have been able to do so. As competent language users may be rendered speechless, or a normally imaginative person may have a psychological block against imagining some possibility, so evildoers may generally foresee what actions would cause serious harm and yet be prevented from foreseeing it in a particular situation. People in a blind rage, under much stress, in the face of great provocation, in a state of panic, under the influence of drugs, alcohol, or sleeplessness may not be able to foresee what normally they can readily foresee. This, however, is not the situation of the evildoers in the six cases, and it is not the usual situation of evildoers in general. For their evil actions are not isolated episodes that occur in exceptional circumstances, but habitual patterns. They cause serious harm regularly and predictably, and, it should be remembered, the harm is not only serious but also excessive and malevolent.

Passions prevented the crusaders, Robespierre, Stangl, Manson, the dirty warriors, and the psychopath from understanding the moral significance of their actions. They misunderstood the facts and reasons that led to their actions. But passions did not prevent them from foreseeing that their actions would cause serious harm. They all foresaw that, and many of them performed their actions precisely because they foresaw the serious harm they would cause. They believed—wrongly, of course—that their actions were justifiable or excusable. They could not have believed that, however, if they had not foreseen the serious harm their actions would cause. If responsibility is taken to depend on being able to foresee the readily foreseeable consequences of one's actions, then they are rightly held responsible. The insane and imbeciles are not able to do this, and that is why they should not be held responsible.

Putting all this together, my account is that normally evildoers should be held morally responsible and liable to severe condemnation if they cause serious, excessive, malevolent harm and their actions have that as a readily foreseeable consequence. They are held responsible by other members of the society because they have violated the expectation that members of the society will respect the physical security of other members. The reason for their severe condemnation is that the well-being of everyone in the society depends on the expectation's being generally met. One essential task of morality is to foster that.

This is not to deny that evildoers may have reasons for their actions. Faith, ideology, ambition, envy, honor, and boredom provided reasons for the crusaders, Robespierre, Stangl, Manson, the dirty warriors, and the psychopath for their evil actions. They also had reasons against them, namely, the expectation of their society that they will not act in those ways. But the evildoers acted as they did because their reasons for evil actions overrode their reasons against them. That is why their society held, or should have held, them morally responsible and severely condemned them. The evildoers knew that they were liable to such condemnation, and they could have counted that among their reasons. They had no reasonable complaint, therefore, when what they knew could happen did happen.

13.3 Excuses

There is one last component of this account that needs further elaboration. The ascription of moral responsibility to evildoers has throughout been qualified by saying that it is *normally* justified. This implies that there are cases in which it is not justified, cases in which evildoers should be excused from moral responsibility. In discussing what such an excuse might be, I shall assume that evildoers are causally responsible for patterns of evil action. Although the natural explanation of why people regularly cause evil is that they are evil people, this is not always so. There are three types of cases in which causally responsible evildoers should be excused from moral responsibility: they may be exempt from moral responsibility altogether; their actions may be morally justified; or their moral responsibility may be mitigated.

People should be exempted from moral responsibility if they are unable to foresee the readily foreseeable consequences of their actions. Examples already given of this are the insane and imbeciles. Children are more complicated because as they mature, they develop the ability. Their exemption from responsibility, then, is temporary and partial, depending on the stage of their maturity. More complicated still are cases in which people have the ability but are unable to use it in a particular case. Their responsibility, then, hinges on whether their episodic inability is their fault. Shock, deprivation, or stress may render most people unable to foresee much of anything, but if they have not brought it upon themselves, they should not be held responsible. If, however, they know or should know that alcohol or a particular drug deprives them of the use of their ability, yet get drunk or take the drug and temporarily lose the ability, then they should be held responsible because they made themselves unable to use their ability. Inability exempts only those who did not bring it upon themselves. The extent to which a person is responsible for a temporary inability may be unclear. Such unclarity, however, is not about what in general exempts people from responsibility, but about facts bearing on the presence or absence of known exempting conditions in a particular case.

The second type of excuse holds when patterns of evil action are morally justified. In such cases, exceptional circumstances demand that evil be done in order to prevent even greater evil. These are heartbreaking situations in which morally committed people must regularly violate their commitment. Here is an example. It was the official Nazi policy to demand that leaders of Jewish communities in occupied territories draw up successive lists of Jews to be transported to concentrations camps. There they were to be murdered immediately or more slowly by forced labor with minimal food, no sanitation, and brutal beatings by the guards. This was known to the Jewish leaders who faced the demands for the lists. The majority of them nevertheless met the demands because they hoped that they might slow down the process and bargain for lives as the Nazis had already lost the war and its end was just a matter of time. They accepted the terrible responsibility and sent thousands to their deaths believing that any alternative would hasten the process and result in even more murders. Thus they collaborated with the Nazis and became accessories to mass murder. There are serious questions about the success of their delaying tactics and the absence of alternatives, but let us suppose that these doubts are groundless and their actions saved many lives that would otherwise have been lost. Their patterns of evil actions, then, were morally justified. They deserve praise, not condemnation, for taking upon themselves the awful burden of making the choices involved in drawing up the lists.

Such cases are rare, but they exist. They show that the expectation to respect the physical security of other members of one's society is not unconditional. The protection of physical security in general may require the violation of the physical security of particular members. And these may not just be ones who have themselves violated or threatened others' physical security, but also totally innocent victims. These cases are terrible. Denying their existence, however, is to fail to recognize the seriousness of the burden of responsibility. Morality requires that evil be done if there is no other way of avoiding even worse evil.

The third type of excuse recognizes that there are degrees of responsibility and concentrates on cases in which there are extenuating conditions.

This type of excuse rests on the distinction between full and mitigated responsibility. I shall proceed by considering first conditions of full responsibility and then mitigated responsibility in which conditions of full responsibility are not met. The conditions of full responsibility depend on the consequences and context of evil actions and the character and motives of evildoers.

The consequences have to do with the serious harm caused by an evildoer's actions. If the harm is immediate and involves the violation of the victim's physical security, it is normally readily foreseeable. One condition of full responsibility is that a pattern of such actions has been done and the evildoer was readily able foresee that serious harm would be the result. If evildoers are murdering, torturing, or mutilating their victims, it is not difficult for them to foresee what effects their actions will have on their victims.

The context involves conditions ranging from the particular circumstances of the evildoers and their victims to the general state of their society. It is impossible to enumerate all these conditions because they vary with time, place, individuals, and societies. I shall focus instead on one particular and one general contextual condition, each normally central to the ascription of responsibility. The particular condition has to do with the interaction between the evildoers and the victims. It is one thing if the evildoers' actions are reactions to provocation, challenge, or threat by their victims, and quite another if their victims have done nothing to which the evildoers could reasonably react. It may also be that although the victims have in fact done nothing that would call for a reaction, the evildoers falsely believe that the victims have done something. The question in this case is how good were the evildoers' reasons for their false beliefs. One condition of full responsibility is that the victims have done nothing, the evildoers' reasons for believing otherwise were bad, and their evil actions were not reactions.

The general condition concerns the morality prevailing in the context of the evildoers' actions. The simplest case is when the prevailing morality protects the physical security of members of the society, the evildoers' actions violate their physical security, and the actions are therefore morally condemned. Another condition of full responsibility is then met. In more complicated cases, the prevailing morality is defective because it fails to extend protection to everyone and the evildoers' actions conform to the defective moral requirements. Their actions, then, are still evil, although they have reasons to believe that they are not. In such cases what needs to be determined once again is how good the evildoers' reasons are.

It is very unlikely, however, that anyone would have good reasons of this sort. For on the one hand, the evildoers have before them the suffering and mangled bodies of their victims. And what they have on the other hand is a morality at least nominally committed to the protection of everyone's physical security, while inconsistently making an exception for some. This requires justification. The usual ones either demonize the victims or deny their full humanity. Ideologies typically opt for the first, slaveholding and colonizing societies for the second. We have seen how untenable were the justifications the crusaders, Robespierre, and the dirty warriors supposed themselves to have, and the justifications of Nazis, Communists, and other ideologues are no better. The denial of the victims' full humanity is just as implausible because they look, act, and, especially, suffer like other humans. And what weakens further the reasons that may be given to remove the inconsistency is that it is virtually impossible for anyone to be ignorant of alternative moralities in which those victimized by the defective morality are not demonized or dehumanized, but treated in the same way as other members of the society.

The position of evildoers in the context in which the prevailing morality is defective is, then, as follows. They have to weigh the readily foreseeable consequences of their evil actions and their immediate experience of their victims' suffering over against bad reasons given to them by their moral authorities. If they follow the bad reasons, they are rightly held responsible, although their responsibility is mitigated. How mitigated it should be depends on numerous considerations, such as how defective the prevailing morality is, how bad the reasons are, how far can the questioning of local moral authorities go, how available are alternative moralities, and so forth. Their responsibility is full if they lack even bad reasons.

Another condition of full responsibility can be derived from the connection between the character of evildoers and their actions. We are proceeding on the assumption that their actions are evil and form a pattern. The question is whether these patterns reflect their character. Patterns of action usually do that, but there may be exceptions. Morally committed people may find themselves in circumstances where they have no reasonable alternative to becoming evildoers. They may have to do evil to survive or to protect those they love, and that requires radically altering their hitherto characteristic conduct. As Hume puts it on behalf of someone in these circumstances: "I shou'd be the cully of my integrity, if I alone shou'd impose on myself a severe restraint amidst the licentiousness of others."[4] People, then, may perform patterns of evil action, and yet the patterns reflect the adversity they face, not their character. A good reason for thinking that this is the case is that if the adversity passes, they revert to their usual morally committed conduct. Their responsibility for their evil actions, then, is mitigated. If, however, their evil actions form characteristic patterns, if they are not responses to circumstances in which evildoing is the norm, then another condition of their full responsibility is met.

This brings us to motives, the psychological causes of action. People usually have many motives, and they may or may not act on any of them. Motives may prompt actions simply because they are stronger than other motives, or because they have been endorsed after critical reflection, while competing motives have been decided against. Desires often form a large part of motives, but they need not because one may be motivated to suppress desires in order to do what reason, prudence, duty, or the law requires. People may or may not be aware of their motives, and they may or may not identify with or approve the motives of which they are aware. Motives play an important part in morality, but only because they lead to action. If it were not for their connection with actions, motives in themselves would be neither good nor bad. Their moral status derives from the actions to which they lead. If we call motives leading to good actions virtues and those leading to bad actions vices, then a further condition of full responsibility is that evildoers motivated by vices performed evil actions.

Motives and actions, however, can miscarry. Evil actions may be prompted by virtues or, indeed, by morally neutral or indeterminate motives. People may believe that they are acting on a virtue when, in fact, they are acting on a vice. They may decide upon critical reflection to endorse one of their vices and perform the actions it prompts, but the action may accidentally fail to be evil because the gun misfired or the bomb did not explode. In such cases, their responsibility is mitigated.

It is now possible to sum up the conditions of full responsibility. Evildoers should be held fully responsible for their patterns of evil action if they are able to foresee the readily foreseeable serious harm that results from their actions; if their victims have done nothing to provoke their actions; if their actions violate the moral requirement that prevails in their society and protects the physical security of its members; if their actions reflect their character; and if their actions are motivated by their vices. Since these conditions are met by the evildoers in the six cases we have been discussing, they should be held fully responsible.

Full responsibility allows for degrees. There are morally significant differences among fully responsible evildoers as a result of differences in the quantity and quality of serious harm they have caused and the nature of their motivation. The worst cases are moral monsters whose excesses and malevolence are great and deliberately cultivated. The crusaders, Robespierre, Stangl, Manson, the dirty warriors, and the psychopath are fully responsible, but they are not moral monsters because their vices were not deliberately cultivated and they did not do evil for its own sake.

They mistakenly thought that their actions were justified or excused because they were misled by their passions. I have endeavored to explain how this came about in each case, but explanation and understanding do not constitute justification or excuse. It is understandable why they were misled by their passions, but they ought not to have been misled. Although it is right to hold them fully responsible, it should be acknowledged that they could have been even more evil if they had done what they did without being misled.

If any one of the conditions of full responsibility is not met, the responsibility of evildoers is mitigated. Mitigated responsibility also involves degrees, and what the degree is depends on the circumstances. Mitigated responsibility ranges from warranting severe condemnation that falls only marginally short of full responsibility to mild condemnation barely distinguishable from exemption or justification. The recognition that some evildoers may have only mitigated responsibility does not mean, therefore, that they are not liable to condemnation; it means only that the condemnation is not as severe as it might be. Just how severe it should be must be judged individually and case by case.

The ascription of responsibility should proceed on the assumption that normally evildoers should be held fully responsible for their patterns of evil actions. If it is claimed that they should be excused, then reasons must be given to support this claim. These reasons may be that they should be totally exempt from responsibility because they lack the ability to foresee the readily foreseeable consequences of their actions; or that their actions are morally justified because they were the only ways in which much greater evil could be prevented; or that their responsibility was mitigated by extenuating circumstances.

The reason for holding evildoers responsible and liable to condemnation is that they violated the physical security of their victims and caused serious harm to them. A central task of morality is to prevent this from happening. The ascription of responsibility expresses a moral attitude formed of the expectation that individuals will conform to this basic moral requirement and of the judgment that those who fail to meet this expectation should be condemned. This attitude is not one of gratuitous moralizing, but a necessary condition of individual well-being. And that is the reason for it. This completes my account of responsibility.

13.4 Intention

One of the ways in which this account differs from most currently favored ones is that intention has no significant role in it, whereas these other accounts regard it as a necessary condition of responsibility. According to these accounts, people should be held responsible only for their intentional actions. Stuart Hampshire provides a particularly clear expression of the supposed connection between intention and responsibility: "A man becomes more and more a free and responsible agent the more he at all times knows what he is doing, in every sense of this phrase, and the more he acts with a definite and clearly formed intention. . . . If he in fact generally sets himself to do exactly that which he intended to do, and if he does not find his activities constantly diverted in a direction that he had not himself designed and thought of, he is fully responsible for his actions."[5]

How exactly intention should be understood is a very difficult question to which there is no generally accepted answer.[6] The basic idea, however, is that intention connects motive to action. Motives, in themselves, may or may not lead to action, but if a motive is conjoined with intention, then the agent has resolved to act on it on the basis of some reason. An intentional action, then, represents a reasoned decision of the agent. The analysis of reasoned decision is also controversial. It may be to evaluate one's first-order decisions about what to do by a second-order decision about wanting to be the kind of person who does that;[7] or to appreciate the force of reasons for and against one's action;[8] or to judge the importance of reasons;[9] or to respond to reasons for or against one's action.[10]

All these interpretations of what is involved in having an intention are unsatisfactory as identifications of a necessary condition of responsibility, for several reasons. First, they set the requirement too high and thereby wrongly excuse numerous evildoers from responsibility. They all deem evildoers responsible only if their evil actions were intentional, that is, only if they were based on reasoned decisions. This perhaps fits moral monsters who deliberately and knowingly set out to do evil, but most evildoers are not moral monsters. The evildoers in the six cases, for instance, were shown (in 8.3) not to act intentionally, in this sense, because their passions prevented them from making reasoned decisions. Their passions were aroused by what they mistook as attacks on their psychological security. As a result, they were grotesquely carried astray, falsified facts, misjudged the comparative importance of reasons, and failed to appreciate or be responsive to reasons. If intentional action were a requirement of the justified ascription of responsibility, it would be unjustified to hold responsible such evildoers as the crusaders, Robespierre, Stangl, the dirty warriors, Manson, and the psychopath. And that would make nonsense of the very idea of responsibility.

Second, if this view of the centrality of intention were correct, the overwhelming majority of humanity would not be responsible. For most human beings live and always have lived in ways in which the reasoned decisions in terms of which intention is analyzed are not valued at all or not nearly as highly as this view does. Devout Catholics, orthodox Jews, fundamentalist Protestants, or Shiite Muslims, people who live in traditional or tribal societies in which their status and role are defined very early on, those whose energies are taken up with securing the means of livelihood, and those who are long-term members of hierarchical organizations, which may be military, monastic, criminal, or corporate, are told what to do and they do it. They have not themselves "designed and thought of" their actions. They do what is expected of them. And if they are in doubt, they ask their superiors or moral authorities, and they tell them. The view that intention is necessary for responsibility inflates the moral importance of an ideal that appeals to many Western intellectuals (myself included, I should say) and falsely elevates it into a necessary condition of responsibility. Responsibility is primarily for the readily foreseeable consequences of one's actions, not for being motivated by a rare psychological process that presupposes leisure, reflectiveness, and self-analysis.

Third, the denial of responsibility for patterns of unintentional evil actions contradicts moral judgments held by virtually everyone. Consider the moral standing of the evildoers in the six cases. According to this view, they are not to be condemned because, lacking intention, they are only causally and not morally responsible for their actions. Now consider their counterparts on the opposite end of the moral spectrum: people who are decent, altruistic, and reasonable, but they too are acting unintentionally, perhaps because they have been indoctrinated by a benign creed. The implication of this view is that people who perform these good and evil actions have exactly the same moral standing: none, because they are only causal, not moral, agents. Neither are morally responsible because neither are acting intentionally. But who could believe this? How could it be reasonably denied that it is morally better to be decent, altruistic, and reasonable than to be like the evildoers in the six cases? To be sure, it is better still to possess and exercise virtues intentionally than unintentionally, but is it not obvious that, intentional or not, people who possess the virtues and perform good actions are morally better than evildoers motivated by vices to perform evil actions? Yet the denial of moral responsibility for unintentional actions leads to rejecting this obvious moral judgment.

Fourth, if moral responsibility holds only for intentional actions, it becomes crucial to realize that people ultimately have no control over their characters and circumstances on which intentions depend. For people can influence their political, social, or economic circumstances only in insignificant ways, if at all, and characters are contingent on inheritance, upbringing, and later conditions of life. Acting intentionally thus ultimately depends on the kind of character people have, but that is ultimately the product of conditions and circumstances over which they can exercise no intentional control. As a result, if it were inappropriate to ascribe moral responsibility to people who habitually and predictably cause nonintentional evil, it would also be inappropriate to ascribe it to those whose actions are intentional, since intentional actions ultimately depend on unintentional factors. If this argument were correct, the ascription of moral responsibility could never be appropriate. This difficulty is not one of the hoary problems raised by determinism, but that of inconsistency. For the refusal to ascribe moral responsibility for unintentional actions and the willingness to ascribe it only for intentional ones are incompatible, since intentional actions depend on unintentional factors. It is for these reasons that the psychological requirement of responsibility is not intention, but being able to foresee the readily foreseeable consequences of one's actions.

13.5 Shibboleths

The account of responsibility I have been giving is incompatible with several shibboleths that permeate contemporary moral sensibility. This is a mark in favor of the account, if it is true, as I believe, that there is much wrong with these shibboleths. Let us begin with sincerity. It is widely held that people deserve moral credit if what they say or do reflects their genuinely held beliefs. It is supposed to be praiseworthy to act in good faith, to be authentic, to be oneself. In contrast, hypocrisy, bad faith, insincerity, and phoniness are condemned. But this cannot be right because sincerity may involve expressing and acting on beliefs that are false, noxious, ignorant, destructive, and lead to evil actions. The world would be less bad if people were hypocritical and did not act on such beliefs. It is better to be inauthentic and refrain from doing evil than to be authentic and do it. The sincerity of the evildoers in the six cases did not make them less evil. Ignoring this obvious consideration against the cult of sincerity requires explanation, and the explanation is the influence of the Kantian view of morality.

According to this view, the moral rightness of an action depends solely on its being motivated by good will. It is a complex question what this involves, but whatever good will comes to, it is a psychological process internal to agents; requires acting on one's reasoned decisions, not following external influences; and excludes consequences as irrelevant to the moral rightness of actions. Morally praiseworthy actions are thus inner-directed rather than motivated by external influences or conse-quences. The cult of sincerity celebrates just this mode of self-expres-sion. The decisive objection to this view is that it excludes what is central to responsibility: holding people responsible for the readily foreseeable consequences of their actions. Part of the reason for holding people responsible is to protect the physical security of others from the conse-quences of their evil actions. Since the Kantian view disallows this essen-tial feature of responsibility, the incompatibility of my account with it is a strength, not a weakness.

Another shibboleth of the age is toleration. All right-thinking people favor it and recoil with horror at the persecution of those whose beliefs and actions have been formed by moral, political, religious, ethnic, or cultural traditions different from their own. People, they say, must learn to live together in peace, and that requires them not to interfere with one another. All should recognize that attitudes to sex, illness, death, children, God, food, authority, privacy, and so forth are culturally condi-tioned. This is as true of our own attitudes as of other people's. We may find attitudes different from ours distasteful, offensive, unreasonable, strange, or plainly wrong, but we should not get moralistic about this. For our attitudes may provoke in others similar negative reactions. They should not interfere with us, and we should not interfere with them. This is thought to be the civilized way of proceeding, the key to enabling people in large multicultural societies to live peacefully together. Toleration requires that we should not judge and condemn others, and this makes it incompatible with the account of responsibility I have been defending. It is intolerant to hold different people to the same expecta-tions or to blame them for not meeting ours. Let a hundred flowers bloom, live and let live, vive la différence, different strokes for different folks, people should do their own thing, and so on with these silly catch-phrases. What lies behind them, however, is not just a reluctance to think about the dark side of life, but an attitude that threatens the very possibility of civilized life to which toleration is supposed to be the key.

Slavery, clitoridectomy, blood feuds, assassination, terrorism, mutilat-ing criminals, persecuting religious dissenters, torturing captives, hold-ing innocent people hostage, dooming children to life as prostitutes or castrati are also culturally conditioned practices, but they are evil. The toleration of such evils, the implausible attempts to excuse them, and the reluctance to condemn them endanger civilized life by countenancing the violation of the physical security of their victims. Morally committed people ought to be intolerant of such evils. Those who mouth the catch-phrases of toleration avert their gaze from evil. Naive or morally obtuse innocents can avow the sentiment that nothing human is alien to them, but they should consider whether tolerating the evil actions of the crusaders, Robespierre, Stangl, Manson, the dirty warriors, and the psychopath would promote civilized life.

Yet countless people strive to be tolerant and feel guilty if they fail. One reason for this is that moral relativism has made them doubt their own moral views. According to relativists, morality is a cultural product. Good and evil, right and wrong, virtue and vice are merely conventional labels. Different social groups have different conventions, and the expectations, judgments, and condemnations of a group change with time and circumstance. There are no objective moral values. What makes something valuable is that some people value it. If this were so, and if people with different moral views wanted to live in peace, they would have to be tolerant of one another. That is what makes it reasonable to abandon the expectation, judgment, and condemnation that holding people responsible expresses and my account urges.

If moral relativism simply claimed that some values are conventional, it would be a truism not worth uttering. But it claims more, namely, that all moral values are conventional. And that claim is untenable. For morality is concerned with protecting the conditions of human well-being, some of its conditions are universal, and no reasonable conception of human well-being can ignore them. These universal conditions are the satisfaction of basic needs, including the protection of physical security. The requirement to satisfy them derives from the physical constitution of human beings, not from any convention that may be held. Their satisfaction is good regardless of what any convention holds. If any moral convention fails to recognize this, it is defective. Serious harm occurs if basic needs are not satisfied. If such harm is caused by human beings, if it is excessive and malevolent, if there is no justifying, exempting, or mitigating excuse for it, it is evil and those who cause it ought to be held responsible and condemned. To do this is a moral necessity, a requirement that follows from the very nature of morality. The toleration of such evils undermines morality and the conditions of human well-being that morality protects. All those right-thinking people who favor toleration and are horrified by intolerance should, therefore, think further and better.

The moral equality of all human beings is another thoughtlessly repeated shibboleth. People differ in power, intelligence, wealth, education, beauty, health, upbringing, and so forth, but from the moral point of view these differences are supposed to be irrelevant. Everyone should be accorded the same basic respect, the same rights, the same claim to the resources distributed by their society. For all human beings have the capacity to try to achieve a good life. Everyone is entitled to develop and exercise this capacity, and one person's efforts to do so are no less and no more valuable than any other person's. In this respect, all ought to count for one and no more than one. Therefore, everyone should have the freedom and resources needed to live a good life. A society is thought to be good to the extent to which it guarantees this by treating its citizens with equal respect.

People whose critical faculties have not been numbed by this familiar rhetoric dressed up as a moral imperative will ask, however, whether this implies that murderers and their victims, terrorists and their hostages, pedophiles and pediatricians, benefactors and scourges of humanity should be treated with equal respect. Does it imply that good and evil people should be guaranteed equal freedom and resources to live and act as they please? And, to come to the point that concerns us here, does it mean that the unequal respect implied by holding evildoers responsible and condemning them is unjustified? And if this shibboleth does not imply these absurdities, what does it imply?

It may be said in response that the claim to equal respect is prima facie and can be forfeited. People ought to be treated with equal respect until there are reasons for withholding it. For everyone has the capacity to try to achieve a good life, and everyone's efforts to do so should be supported equally unless they have shown themselves unworthy of it. But this response does not provide what is needed. There are obvious differences in the extent to which people possess and exercise this capacity, in the morality of the life they aim at, and in the rightness or wrongness of what they do to try to achieve it. Ignoring these differences will not make them disappear, and since many of them affect the well-being of others, morality prohibits treating good and evil people and actions with equal respect. The necessity of moral judgment consequently enters as soon as people exercise this capacity. If the judgment is adverse, as it often is, responsibility and condemnation are appropriate. What is prima facie, therefore, is the need for moral judgment, not the favorable moral judgment implied by equal respect. The assumption that the prima facie judgment should be favorable rests on an illusion that underlies and lends support to all three of the shibboleths I have been considering.

This illusion is that human beings are basically good and they do evil only because unjust political arrangements corrupt them. The illusion has been bequeathed to us by the Enlightenment. I have given reasons for rejecting it (in 9.5). I merely mention it here as a reminder that the illusion is untenable because the same evil actions recur under very different political arrangements; only some of those who live under the same political arrangements become evildoers; and political arrangements are evil only because evil people sustain them, so that evil political arrangements must be explained with reference to evil people, not the other way around. The illusion is nevertheless widely held, and it sustains the shibboleths. Sincerity is valued because it gives expression to human goodness; toleration is good because it enriches everyone by nurturing different ways in which human goodness shines forth; and moral equality is obligatory because of the respect owed to all on account of their basic goodness. The illusion and the shibboleths, however, are not harmless pipe dreams nurtured by naive do-gooders, but dangerous threats to human well-being because they deny the facts of evil and undermine the effort to face and combat them. Holding evildoers responsible and condemning them for evil actions is an indispensable part of this necessary effort. And that is what I have endeavored to show in this chapter.

Toward Elementary Decency

The notion of evil is the idea of a force, or forces, which are not merely contrary to all that is most praiseworthy and admirable and desirable in human life, but a force which is actively working against all that is praiseworthy and admirable. . . . Illiberal moralists . . . retain their hold on us, because they convey a vivid sense of the forces of destruction which are always at large and which have to be diverted and controlled if any kind of decent civilised life is to continue.

—STUART HAMPSHIRE, *Innocence and Experience*

14.1 The Secular Problem of Evil

Throughout the book I have argued that evil presents a fundamental difficulty for the religious world view. This is not exactly news since the difficulty has long been recognized by both defenders and critics of the religious approach. Perhaps it is less of a commonplace that the secular world view also faces a fundamental difficulty on account of evil. The difficulty is not to explain how evil fits into the world view, as it is for the religious approach, but to explain how natural conditions could be transformed so as to make evil less widespread. If the religious reliance on supernatural aid is groundless, and if the Enlightenment view that evildoing is necessarily irrational is also unwarranted, if the appeals to God and reason are both uncompelling, then what can be done to overcome the obstacle evil presents to the betterment of human lives? If, as I have argued, evildoing can be both a natural and a reasonable reaction to threatened psychological security, then what secular answer is there to the question why actual or potential evildoers should not do evil? Why, then, should evildoers be held responsible for doing what is natural and reasonable? The aim of this chapter is to answer these questions.

The discussion of the six cases in Part One was intended in part to explain how people motivated by faith, ideology, ambition, envy, honor, and boredom may become evildoers. These motives are understandable and very different ways of trying to achieve some measure of psychological security. I have endeavored to show that these motives provide a variety of reasons for evil actions, and that the conjunction of the evildoers' motives, weak prohibitions against evil, and the threats evildoers perceive to their psychological security explains why they habitually cause serious, excessive, malevolent, and inexcusable harm to their innocent victims.

The key to meeting the difficulty evil presents to the secular world view is to recognize that although reason may allow evil actions, reason does not require them, and that reason also allows refraining from evil actions. Coping with evil depends on making the reasons against evil actions stronger than the reasons for them. One central task of morality is to provide these stronger reasons, and the question before us is how that task can be performed. The mixed explanation of evil I have proposed and defended points toward the answer. Since evil is the result of internal and external conditions, the answer is to be found by weakening the causal efficacy of these conditions and strengthening the internal and external constraints prohibiting evil actions. Although this will go some way toward strengthening the reasons against doing evil and weakening the reasons for doing it, it will not go far enough unless supplemented by a version of secular morality. I now turn to this version.

14.2 Morality

Perhaps the simplest way to understand the secular approach to morality is through the Platonic explanation of evil I have criticized (in 11.1–2). Plato thought that morality consists in acting according to reason. Reason, in turn, provides knowledge of the good. If people are motivated by this knowledge, life will go well for them. The explanation of evil is that uncontrolled wants and emotions prevent the reasonable pursuit of the good. Plato's view assumes that the good exists in a supernatural world; it can be known, by those few who have the necessary talents and education to comprehend the supernatural world; it is independent of human wants and emotions; those who know the good cannot but be motivated by it; and lives are good to the extent to which they are guided by knowledge of the good. It is a consequence of these assumptions that people necessarily end up with what they deserve because their well-being is proportional to the extent to which they conform to the good. This necessity is guaranteed by the morally good supernatural order that permeates the scheme of things.

Plato's assumptions have been extensively criticized. There is no reason to believe that there is a morally good supernatural order; even if there were one, it could not be known by human beings; those who claimed to have the required knowledge have given many conflicting accounts of it; the good cannot be independent of human wants and emotions because human beings are the ultimate judges of the goodness of their lives and they must judge at least partly on the basis of the satisfaction of their wants and their emotional attitudes toward their lives; knowledge of the good often fails to motivate corresponding action; and human experience testifies against *the* good because individuals and societies can be good in many different ways. The cumulative effect of these and other criticisms is strong enough to warrant the rejection of Plato's view as the description of morality.

The criticisms, however, do not justify the rejection of Plato's view as the ideal of morality. The conviction is widely shared that the world ought to be such that people whose actions are reasonable and good have good lives, and miserable lives result from unreasonable or evil actions. Whatever may be the ultimate truth about a supernatural order, virtually no one believes that in life, as we know it in the natural world, people get what they deserve. The natural world is inundated with contingency. Good people often come to undeserved harm, and evildoers often enjoy undeserved benefits, even in the long run. Although it is generally acknowledged that this is so, it is generally wished that it were otherwise. The wish may take forms that range from moral outrage to resigned lament, but hardly any reflective person is without it. Plato's ideal of morality thus lives, even if his description of it does not.

The motivation behind the secular view of morality can now be seen as the endeavor to approximate the Platonic ideal—that the benefits people enjoy and the harms they suffer should be proportional to the moral quality of their actions—as closely as the contingency of life allows. Aristotle shared this ideal, as well as many of the doubts about Plato's account, and he took a significant step toward clarifying it. It is possible to extract from his *Nicomachean Ethics,* book V, the general formula that equals ought to treated equally and unequals unequally (1131a10–25). This Aristotelian formula, however, is too vague to be useful as it stands. It is a condition of the application of any rule in any context that the like cases that come under its purview should be treated alike and different cases differently. This is as true of classifying fauna, diagnosing illness, adding numbers, and so forth as it is of morality. The Aristotelian formula, therefore, is insufficiently informative about why some rules are rules of morality. Furthermore, for any two things it is always possible to find respects in which they are alike and respects in which they are different. Yet the Aristotelian formula fails to specify what respects are relevant to judging whether two things are equal or unequal. It correctly identifies consistency as necessary for a rule being moral, but it remains incomplete.

The way to complete it, however, follows from the Platonic ideal that benefits and harms should be proportional to how good or bad are the actions of the people who receive them. The Aristotelian formula is thus completed by the addition of desert. The secular view of morality should be understood, then, in terms of consistency and desert: equals should be treated equally and unequals unequally in respect to desert. The reason why some rules are rules of morality is that they are concerned with people getting the benefits and harms they deserve. The respects in which people are equal or unequal are their goodness or badness and the benefits and harms they enjoy or suffer. Consistency and desert, then, are individually necessary and jointly sufficient conditions of the moral entitlement to benefits and harms.

The *Oxford English Dictionary* (1961) gives the pertinent definition of "to deserve" as: "2. to have acquired, and thus to have, a rightful claim to; to be entitled to, in return for services or meritorious actions, or sometimes for ill deeds and qualities, to be worthy to have." The unabridged *Random House Dictionary* (1987) defines "to deserve" as "1. to merit, be qualified for, or have a claim to (reward, assistance, punishment, etc.) because of actions, qualities, or situations. . . . 2. to be worthy of, qualified for, or have a claim to reward, punishment, recompense, etc." If people deserve some benefit or harm, it must be because of some fact about them. This fact is the *basis* of desert. Their entitlement to some benefit or harm on that basis creates a *claim* of desert. Desert is thus relative to people because its basis is a fact about them and the claim is for some benefits or harms they ought to have. The fact that forms the basis of desert in general may be a character trait, such as a virtue or a vice, an excellence or a fault, a skill or a deficiency; or it may be a relation, like being a taxpayer, a competitor, a child of, or an employee; or it may be an explicit or implicit agreement, for instance, having made a promise, got married, or enrolled as a student; or it may be an action that is kind or cruel, thoughtful or unthinking, fair or unfair. The basis of desert, then, is some characteristic, relation, agreement, or action of a person. Since we are concerned with moral desert in particular, the centrally relevant bases are virtues, vices, and actions that reflect them.

The claim of desert is that the person in question ought to enjoy some benefit or suffer some harm on the relevant basis. The claim need not be made by someone concerned; indeed, it is not often that people lay claim to deserved harm. Nor need there be some institution or another person making the claim on someone else's behalf. The claim is the general one that someone has a certain benefit or harm coming and it would be good, right, or fitting for that person to receive it. The claim sometimes could and should be enforced, but it need not be. It need not even be enforceable because there are perfectly legitimate claims of desert that are not directed toward any person or institution, such as that evildoers do not deserve to live happily until they die of old age, or that good people do not deserve the misfortune that befalls them.

The ascription of desert is both backward- and forward-looking. It looks backward toward its basis, and it looks forward from there to lay claim to the appropriate benefit or harm. The ascription of desert thus requires a particular type of reason, and the claim it creates requires a particular type of justification. Both requirements are met by desert. It may thus be said that hard work deserves success, employees deserve wages from their employers, children deserve a decent upbringing from their parents, and acts of kindness deserve gratitude from their recipients, just as hypocrites deserve to be exposed, incompetent physicians deserve to lose their licenses, and criminals deserve punishment. The justification of these claims is to point at the relevant characteristic, relation, agreement, or action that provides the basis for claiming that the person to whom they are attached deserves the appropriate benefits or harms. If the required explanation is moral, it must point at some virtue, vice, or action that provides the basis for claiming that a particular person deserves some particular benefits or harms. But why should people get what they deserve? Why should benefits and harms be proportional to how good or bad their recipients are? The Platonic answer is that the morally good supernatural order makes that a requirement of human well-being. But this answer is based on the unacceptable assumption that such an order exists, so the question stands.

The secular answer is that the claim that people should get what they deserve is based on the expectation that actions conforming to practical reason will be successful. Consider typical patterns of human conduct. People have various *wants:* important and trivial, physiological and psychological, personal and social, long-term and temporary, and so forth. They make *choices* about satisfying or frustrating their particular wants. If their choices are reasonable, they take into account the larger *goals* they have, such as living a certain kind of life, being a certain kind of person, serving a certain cause, and so forth. The conjunction of wants, choices, and goals leads them to perform some *action* that reflects their choices and bridges the gap between their wants and goals. The pattern of wants, choices, goals, and actions is permeated with beliefs about what wants to satisfy, what choices to make, what goals to have, what actions to perform, and how to coordinate one's relevant activities with the similar activities of others. These beliefs may be reasonable or unreasonable. Mistakes may occur at each step along the way, not just because reasonable beliefs may turn out to be false, but also because there are numerous internal and external obstacles to forming reasonable beliefs. The task of practical reason is to help form reasonable beliefs and act on them.

Suppose this is done and the people in question hold and act on reasonable beliefs of the relevant sort. The expectation is that their actions, then, will be successful. Yet their actions may still fail through no fault of their own because various contingencies may place obstacles in their way. If this happens, the expectation is disappointed and gives rise to the belief that since they have done everything they reasonably could, they ought to have succeeded. This expectation and belief are the sources of the claim that people should get what they deserve. They should get it because they have followed practical reason, and that is what practical reason is meant to provide for those who follow it. The lamentable fact remains, however, that people often fail to get what they deserve even though they are guided by practical reason. One task of morality, the law, and other conventional systems created by humanity is to close this gap. These systems are imperfect secular substitutes for a morally good supernatural order. They attempt to approximate this ideal order regardless of whether it actually exists. The secular answer, then, to the question why people should get what they deserve is that the ideal of morality requires it. One main aim and one main justification of morality is the pursuit of this ideal.

Its pursuit takes place in a wide variety of contexts. There are complicated questions and contested answers regarding what people deserve politically, economically, personally, professionally, legally, as citizens, consumers, parents, children, married or unmarried partners, patients, competitors, and so on and on. There are also various degrees of urgency with which these questions arise and need to be answered. Morality is complex, and nothing I have said about the centrality of desert to it is meant to deny this. But since my concern is with evil, which is only a part of morality, I can fortunately avoid these complexities because the question of what desert comes to in the context of evil is not complicated. Morality has some universal requirements. Among them is the protection of conditions required for the well-being of all human beings simply in virtue of their humanity. Evil violates these conditions. Its victims do not deserve the serious, excessive, malevolent, and inexcusable harm inflicted on them. If evildoers are or should be able to foresee the readily foreseeable consequences of their actions, and yet habitually do evil, they deserve to be held responsible. Innocent people do not deserve to be murdered, tortured, or mutilated. Those who do this to them deserve moral condemnation. Protection against evil is thus a requirement of elementary decency and a central, perhaps the most important, task of morality.

There can be no morally acceptable reason for violating elementary decency and causing evil. As I have repeatedly argued, however, this does not exclude the possibility of there being nonmoral reasons. Faith, ideology, ambition, envy, honor, and boredom may provide such reasons, as we have seen in the six cases of evildoing. The question we need now to consider is whether or not reasons against doing evil are stronger than reasons for doing it.

These reasons may be internal or external. Internal reasons are moral or nonmoral psychological scruples that may lead people to refrain from evil actions even if they have reasons for doing them. External reasons are social prohibitions of evil actions. They are backed by coercion that ranges from the threat of public disapproval to serious punishment. Internal and external reasons, of course, are connected. External reasons may be internalized; the scruples people have may be social prohibitions they have been taught to observe. And external reasons may be the publicly accepted expressions of the promptings of influential moral exemplars' and their followers' conscience. But whether internal or external, the reasons against evil actions express limits that ought not to be transgressed because they protect minimum requirements of human well-being and conformity to them is a requirement of elementary decency. Evil actions violate this requirement through the inexcusable excess and malevolence of the serious harm they cause. That is why evil actions are much worse than simply morally bad and why they provoke outrage for transgressing limits in a manner that threatens the very possibility of civilized life. They provoke the thought that if the horrors the crusaders, Robespierre, Stangl, the dirty warriors, Manson, and the psychopath have caused are possible, then there are no limits, anything may happen, and counting on security, order, and trust is folly because the bulwark against barbarism has been breached.

14.3 Internal Reasons

The question before us now is whether there are psychological considerations internal to actual or potential evildoers that would make the reasons against habitual evildoing stronger than the reasons for it. Clarity about these reasons requires distinguishing between what reasons there are for and against evildoing and what reasons evildoers have for or against their actions. If evildoers were perfectly reasonable, the reasons there are and the reasons they have would be the same. But of course, they, like others, are not perfectly reasonable, so these two sets of reasons do not coincide. The result is that it makes good sense to ask about evildoers whether or not the reasons they have are the reasons they would have if they were more attentive to reasons. Perhaps evildoing only seems reasonable to them because they ignore the reasons against it. Or perhaps the reasons against evildoing are not available to evildoers because circumstances for which they cannot be blamed prevent it. Be that as it may, before we can ask whether evildoers have the reasons they should have, we must get clear about what reasons there are for or against evildoing, and that is what I shall now endeavor to do. It makes an important difference whether the evildoing in question is intentional or unintentional. I shall discuss unintentional evildoing first.

The cases in point are the six I have been considering throughout the book. These cases deal with habitual but unintentional evildoers. The evil they caused was unintentional because they did not understand that what they were doing was evil. They mistakenly believed either that their actions were not evil, or that, although they recognized that actions such as theirs are normally evil, they were justified or excused by special circumstances. In each case, however, the belief was false. The evildoers came to hold these false beliefs because their passions obscured from them the truth, and their passions were aroused because they felt that their psychological security was threatened. The various forms the supposed threats took were the internal components of the causes whose effects were their habitual but unintentionally evil actions and the real reasons that explain why they did what they did.

The crusaders were devout Christians who believed that the Cathars jeopardized the faith on which everyone's salvation depends. Robespierre was a committed revolutionary who believed that his opponents were attacking the ideology that was the key to the well-being of humanity. The dirty warriors were patriots who believed that honor and duty required them to defend their country against enemies dedicated to its subversion. Stangl believed that his evil actions were coerced and thus excused. Manson believed that his actions caused justified harm to people who usurped the success that he was unjustly denied. And the psychopath believed that the harm his actions caused was justified because it made interesting his otherwise boring life.

The reasons these evildoers had were deficient, quite apart from moral considerations, partly because they were based on false beliefs, which the evildoers should have known to be false. The Cathars were naive simpletons who meant to be good Christians. Thousands of those Robespierre had murdered as opponents were actually sympathetic to the ideology he was defending. Substantial portions of the supposed enemies against whom the dirty warriors were protecting Argentina were ordinary citizens who had no connection with subversion. Much of what Stangl took to be coercion was in fact inducement to satisfy his ambition. Manson's victims had nothing whatever to do with his lack of success. And the psychopath could easily have made his life interesting in other ways than through mayhem. Each was in a position to form true beliefs rather than the false ones they in fact formed, and the true beliefs would have deprived them even of the deficient reasons they had for their evil actions.

Let us suppose, however, that this is not so, that they had no reasonable alternatives to the false beliefs from which reasons for their evil actions could be derived. Their reasons would still have been deficient because the protection of their psychological security did not require the excessive and malevolent harm they caused. They could simply have murdered their victims; there was no need to torture and mutilate them beforehand. The serious harm they caused was in each case more than was warranted by the deficient reasons they had. And their actions in each case revealed a pent-up malevolence that was disproportionately greater than what could have been provoked by the threat they falsely believed was directed against their psychological security. It was this malevolence that partly explains why they were so indiscriminate in the selection of victims as to murder, mutilate, and torture people who were innocent even if the false beliefs of the evildoers had been true and their deficient reasons had been much less so.

I conclude that the reasons these evildoers had for their unintentionally evil actions were not the reasons they ought to have had. But this is not enough to show what needs to be shown, namely, that the reasons against their evil actions were stronger than these deficient reasons. One clue to these stronger reasons against evil actions is that all we know about these evildoers' attitude to their own lives indicates that—with the exceptions of the crusaders, about whom not enough is known—they were deeply dissatisfied with their lives, which were, and were regarded by them as, miserable failures.

Robespierre saw his fellow Jacobins reject his ideology and have him executed. He realized that the Revolution had lost its momentum, his ideology was being repudiated, his murder of thousands was for naught, and none of his important goals had been achieved. He had no friends, no lovers, no intimate relationships; his life was devoid of enjoyment, his execution was widely celebrated, and he died knowing that all he lived for was lost. Stangl, after years of prevarication and denial, came to the conclusion in the jail to which he was sentenced for life that "I should have killed myself in 1938"[1] rather than accept the inducements he was offered to become a mass murderer. Before he died he repudiated his life and was wracked by guilt for the way he lived during the crucial years. The dirty warriors were haunted by what they did. Some turned to religion, others publicly confessed, more than a few resigned from the military and gave up the life on which their honor depended. Most felt tainted by the murders and tortures they had inflicted on their victims. As one of them says: "We are condemnable. We've killed people without trials. . . . As a good Christian I have problems of conscience. . . . We must condemn torture . . . although we tortured."[2] Manson is in jail for life. He has no hope. He sees himself as a failure whose musical ambition had been scorned and who is unfit for normal life. "I realize," he says, that "I am only what I've always been . . . 'a half-assed nothing'"; "my ego has been crushed."[3] And the psychopath, since his early thirties confined to a wheelchair, paralyzed from the waist down, impoverished, having spent fourteen of his thirty-three years in jail, his days filled with the boredom he tried so hard to avoid, says: "I get tremendously bored. Sometimes I stay in the house two, three weeks, doing nothing but looking out the window."[4]

It would be wishful thinking to infer from the miserable failures of these evildoers' lives that just as virtue leads to a good life, so vice leads to a bad one. The lives of these evildoers were bad. What made them so, however, was not their vices, but the false beliefs they cultivated about themselves and their surroundings. These beliefs, infused with their passions, prevented them from seeing their actions as evil, and thus made them unintentional evildoers.

I have argued that their beliefs were false because their passions led them to misinterpret the facts, and their passions were aroused by what they wrongly supposed were threats to their psychological security. The result of this tangled web of falsification was that they were deceived both about their own motives and about their surroundings. They did not see that alongside the faith, ideology, ambition, envy, honor, and boredom that motivated them there was also a great fear of losing their psychological security, if they still had it, or a great resentment, if they lacked it. Nor did they see that their victims were not their enemies, that there was no conspiracy against the cause they favored, that no one was trying to frustrate their efforts, that their division of the people they encountered into "us" and "them," or "I" and my "friends" and "enemies," was wrong. No wonder, then, that they reacted inappropriately and, as a result, failed to achieve what they themselves regarded as most important, namely, the psychological security of a life worth living.

These considerations provide reasons for preventing their passions from obscuring from them the true nature of their actions, and thus reasons against being unintentional evildoers. These reasons, however, need not be reasons against being an evildoer; they may just be reasons against being an unintentional one. If these evildoers had been more attentive to reasons, they might have transformed themselves into intentional evildoers rather than cease to be evildoers. The question, then, is whether there are stronger reasons against being an intentional evildoer than there are reasons for not being an evildoer at all.

In order to answer this question, let us suppose that the evildoers in the six cases acted intentionally. They, then, understood that what they were doing was evil, and they meant to do it. What reasons might they have had for it? Consider their motivation, about which we are now supposing them to be clear-sighted. They believe that living a worthwhile life depends on living and acting according to the dictates of their faith, ideology, ambition, or honor, or on reacting to their worthless lives either by blaming others rather than themselves or by seeking thrills to make their worthless lives more interesting. But, being clear-sighted, they also believe that this is not all that motivates them, that they also have strong fears about losing what gives them psychological security or strong resentments on account of having already lost it. These feelings grow into passions, which they realize also motivate them. Their habitual evil actions are, then, the outcomes of these motives, they recognize this about themselves, and they nevertheless persist in continuing their pattern of evildoing. Their reasons for doing so is that acting otherwise would jeopardize their psychological security or would leave them with the enormous frustration of unexpressed and unassuaged fears or resentments, making their lives even worse. They judge it reasonable to protect their psychological security or cope with its loss even at the cost of causing serious, excessive, malevolent, and morally inexcusable harm to their victims. These are their reasons for being intentional evildoers.

There are also, of course, reasons against it. The chief among them is the suffering of the innocent victims. Even intentional evildoers are unlikely to be totally indifferent to it, especially since they unavoidably witness it as they murder, torture, and mutilate their victims. But we must take care not to suppose that what morally committed people find a decisive reason against such actions would also be found such by intentional evildoers. For the question is whether intentional evildoers have stronger reasons for committing themselves to morality than for continuing to do evil. The reasons derivable from morality are, of course, the strongest for those who have committed themselves to it. Intentional evildoers, however, have not done so. Saying that if they had made that commitment, they would have decisive reason against doing evil does not provide the slightest reason for making it.

A much better reason is that it is very difficult to be an intentional evildoer. It takes great strength of character to violate consistently and knowingly the moral prohibitions to which most people in the evildoer's society profess to be committed. There are legal sanctions against violating these prohibitions, and the public opinion that surrounds the evildoer strongly condemns them. Intentional evildoers, therefore, must hide their actions; if suspected, they must deny they have done them; and they cannot be honest with anyone lest they be exposed and punished. They must, therefore, run the constant risk of exposure, and they cannot rely on anyone but themselves. There may be some exceptional moral monsters who have the strength to live with the constant risk, the isolation, and the barriers to intimate relationships, but there cannot be many who have the capacity to live such a life. The suffering of their victims, the difficulty and the cost of such a life, and the risk of exposure, then, may be adduced as nonmoral reasons against being an intentional evildoer.

As intentional evildoers weigh the respective importance of the reasons for and against their evil actions, they will consider, if they are reasonable, the particular circumstances of their lives and of the society in which they live. Perhaps they can risk having intimate relationships because they can rely on the loyalty of some few friends, family members, or fellow evildoers. Perhaps their society is in a state of chaos, the legal sanctions against evil are not dependably enforced, and the chances of getting away with evil actions are good. Perhaps their victims are generally despised, feared, or persecuted by others in their society and the evil they inflict on them does not outrage or is actually welcomed by their fellow citizens. From these considerations two conclusions follow. First, there are internal reasons both for and against being an intentional evildoer, and neither is necessarily stronger than the other. Considering only internal reasons, therefore, allows but does not require both being and not being an intentional evildoer. Second, whether or not the reasons against being an intentional evildoer are stronger than the reasons for it depends not only on the respective strengths of the internal reasons, but also on such external reasons as may follow from the context in which evildoers live. Let us now consider these external reasons.

14.4 External Reasons

In contrast with internal reasons, which are psychological, external reasons are social. They depend on the strength of the prevailing social prohibitions of evil actions. If the prohibitions are reliably enforced, they provide strong external reasons for actual or potential evil-doers to refrain from evil actions. I have argued (in 10.3–4 and 12.5) that reason requires a society to have and enforce such prohibitions, but I need to restate the main point here. One main expectation people have of their society is the protection of their physical security. The prohibition of evil actions is necessary for meeting that expectation, and that is why it is a requirement of reason. I must stress that what reason requires is the prohibition only of evil actions, that is, of actions that are contrary to elementary decency and violate fundamental conditions of human well-being. Societies may also prohibit other actions, and this may or may not be required or allowed by reason. But whatever reason there may be for or against the prohibition of other actions is irrelevant to reason requiring the prohibition of evil actions.

The requirements of reason, however, do not automatically carry over from societies to individuals because their aims often diverge. It is true that individuals cannot very well pursue their aims unless their physical security is protected as much as possible. Individuals, therefore, would want to live in a society where elementary decency prevails. But that does not mean that individuals cannot have political, religious, or personal reasons for evil actions. It can and often does happen that the pursuit of individual aims involves inflicting evil on other people who are, or are seen as, obstacles to the achievement of these aims. This is just what happened in the six cases. And when it happens, individuals have external reasons for evil actions.

Individuals, of course, also have external reasons against them. They want to live in a society where physical security is protected. Yet the external reasons individuals have for evil actions may outweigh their external reasons against them when two conditions obtain. One is that they rightly or wrongly see their society as defective and undeserving of their allegiance. The other is that they regard their own aims as having overwhelming importance. It lends extra strength to these conditions if the society is seen by individuals as defective precisely because it prevents the pursuit of their political, religious, or personal aims. When these conditions obtain, individuals may have stronger reasons for evil actions, even if they risk jeopardizing their own physical security, than external reasons against them deriving from the requirements of elementary decency. They may say to themselves—rightly or wrongly—that it would be unreasonable for them to act as elementary decency requires when its requirements are routinely violated by numerous people in their society.

This, however, is not the last word, but merely one relevant consideration, regarding the relative strengths of external reasons for and against evil. For it must be remembered that societies do not merely prohibit evil but also enforce the prohibitions. If evildoers are reasonable, they must consider this in their deliberations. If the threat of moral and legal sanctions is serious enough, it may tilt the balance between the requirements of elementary decency and the pursuit by individuals of contrary political, religious, or personal aims toward the former. Individuals motivated by their vices may then conclude that the combination of the security of living in a society where elementary decency generally prevails, the possibility of pursuing their aims less uncompromisingly or in ways that do not involve evildoing, and the threat of sanctions makes it reasonable for them to refrain from evildoing.

They *may* conclude this, or they may not. What conclusion is reasonable depends on the strength of their internal and external reasons, which, in turn, depends on contingent and variable considerations, such as how serious are the perceived threats to their psychological security, how satisfied they are with their lives, how strong are their commitments to their political, religious, or personal aims, how reliably enforced are the sanctions against evildoing, how widespread are the violations of elementary decency, and so forth. The balance of these considerations varies with individuals, contexts, and times. There always is a reasonable decision that particular individuals can make in their particular context at a particular time, since it is most unlikely that considerations for or against evildoing will be evenly balanced, but that decision cannot be automatically carried over to other individuals, contexts, and times.

We must conclude, then, that neither internal nor external reasons are by themselves sufficient to make evildoing necessarily irrational. Although the combination of external and internal reasons may strengthen the case against evildoing, it may also do the opposite. The regrettable fact is that reason alone does not require individuals to refrain from evildoing. Reason requires societies to prohibit evil actions and to enforce the prohibitions reliably. But societies are made up of individuals, and a society doing this or that means that individuals acting in or on behalf of a society do this or that. Since individuals are not required by reason to avoid evildoing, they may not prohibit or enforce the prohibition of evil. The threat of evil, therefore, is permanent. Even if the balance of internal and external reasons tells against evildoing, the balance may shift in favor of evildoing as circumstances change. It must also be remembered that individuals are rarely motivated only by the force of reasons. Their fears, resentments, and other passions often lead them to ignore or misjudge the strength of reasons available to them and do evil contrary to reason. This is a conclusion with ominous implications and therefore hard to accept. But it is better to face the truth than to sentimentalize the facts and nurture illusions that prevent coping with the problem.

14.5 The Permanent Threat of Evil

Coping with the problem requires supplementing the insufficient internal and external reasons against evildoing with commitment to the ideal of morality that people should get what they deserve. That commitment would provide sufficient reason against evildoing because inflicting serious, excessive, malevolent, and inexcusable harm on people is not to treat them as they deserve. It follows, therefore, from the commitment that evil should be prohibited and elementary decency upheld. If that commitment were made, coping with evil would be possible, but why make the commitment? Reason allows but does not require it, and it also allows not making it. What could be said to those who hesitate or refuse to make it? If reason does not require it, and if supernatural considerations are uncompelling, then what remains is to appeal to the well-being of humanity. Those who care about it will commit themselves to avoiding evil, treating people as they deserve, and upholding elementary decency. The appeal, then, is to a feeling, which, in conjunction with external and internal reasons, calls for making the commitment.

Most people have this feeling to some extent. Not many people are indifferent to whether the hammer they wield hits a nail or someone's head, or whether it is a rodent or a child they run over while driving a car. There is a widely shared fellow feeling that leads people, in normal circumstances, when nothing momentous is at stake, to wish well, or at least not ill, for others. The feeling is often weak, some are altogether without it, and the ones who have it also have other feelings and interests that may prove stronger than their fellow feeling. Those who have the feeling to a sufficient extent and are reasonable enough to be guided by external and internal reasons will commit themselves to morality.

But what about those whose fellow feeling is weak or nonexistent, or who are not guided by reasons? To them the following can be said. Being as you are, lacking in feeling and heedless of reason, you pursue your own well-being as well as you can without sufficient regard for others. Your first preference is to be left unhindered in your pursuit. But we shall not let you proceed unhindered, and we shall do what we can to make you act with due regard for others. You have the choice of cooperating with us and acting as elementary decency requires, or you can oppose us, and then we will fight you. If you cooperate you will have to give up your first preference, but you will be able to have the second, which is to pursue your well-being only in ways that avoid inflicting evil on others. You will be somewhat curtailed in what you can do, but you will not have to fight and risk losing all. The choice is yours.

What the reasonable choice is depends on various and changing conditions: the strength of those who are committed to protecting elementary decency; the extent to which one's well-being is thought to involve evildoing; one's attitude to risks and one's estimate of the chances of winning or losing; the hold the conception of well-being that involves evildoing has on one and the availability of attractive alternatives to it; the extent to which one is without fellow feeling and is unwilling to be guided by reasons against evildoing; the prevailing state of one's society; and so on. It is by no means a foregone conclusion that the reasonable choice is to avoid evildoing because these conditions vary with individuals, societies, and times, and they also change. That is why evil is a permanent threat. The secular problem of evil, therefore, does not have a solution, if by that is meant finding something that would once and for all remove the threat of evil. But if by solution is meant finding ways of coping with evil and reducing the threat it presents, then there is a solution, which is the topic of the final chapter.

Conclusion: What Is to Be Done?

Defenseless under the night
Our world in stupor lies;
Yet, dotted everywhere,
Ironic points of light
Flash out wherever the Just
Exchange their messages:
May I, composed like them
Of Eros and of dust,
Beleaguered by the same
Negation and despair,
Show an affirming flame.

—W. H. AUDEN, "September 1, 1939"

Coping with evil depends on changing the conditions that cause it. Since these conditions are partly internal and partly external, changing them requires proceeding in two directions. I shall consider internal conditions and how they can be changed first, and external conditions next.

15.1 Changing Internal Conditions

The internal conditions include both motives actively prompting evil actions and passive resistance to recognizing that the actions are evil. Since these conditions vary with individuals and circumstances, discussion of them must be particular. This is why I have kept returning to the six cases again and again, and why I must do so once more.

The active motives for the evil actions in the six cases were faith, ideology, ambition, honor, envy, and boredom. These motives need not always prompt evil actions, although they easily do so, and there are also other motives that may lead to evildoing. It would be futile to try to eliminate from the human repertoire the motives for evildoing because many of them are natural reactions. Faith and ideology give meaning and purpose to life; ambition is the drive to succeed; honor is to be true to one's values; and envy and boredom are reactions to one's unsatisfactory life. Each is connected with psychological security, and each leads easily to evil actions when that security is felt to be threatened. The perceived threat provokes passionate defense, which, in turn, prevents the recognition that the defensive actions are evil. What can be done to change the internal conditions of evil actions is to cultivate moral imagination and thereby overcome the passive resistance to seeing one's actions as they are.

Moral imagination is the attempt to appreciate other ways of life by coming to understand them from the inside as they appear to those who are actively engaged in them. The benefits of moral imagination are many, but three of them are particularly important in the context of coping with evil. First, the evildoers in the six cases thought that their actions were not evil partly because they grotesquely misperceived their victims. The crusaders saw the Cathars as bent on the destruction of Christendom; Robespierre saw those who were not his wholehearted supporters as enemies of humanity; the dirty warriors saw the people they tortured and murdered as terrorists bent on subversion; Stangl saw men, women, and children about to be gassed as cattle; Manson saw his targets as scorning him while usurping the fame and wealth he deserved; and the psychopath saw the people he shot, beat, and robbed as means to having fun. If these evildoers had the imaginative understanding that they so conspicuously lacked, and saw their victims' lives as their victims saw them, they could not have misperceived their victims as badly as they did. They would, then, have seen the Cathars as naive simpletons, political opponents as disagreeing about how human well-being is best pursued, suspected terrorists as ordinary citizens, those on the way to the gas chamber as persecuted human beings, murder victims as scorning and usurping nothing, and their means to alleviating boredom as bleeding human beings. This is not to say, of course, that if moral imagination had prevented evildoers from misperceiving their victims, then they would not have inflicted serious, excessive, malevolent, and inexcusable harm on them. They might still have done so by turning into intentional evildoers, and thus moral monsters. But they were unintentional evildoers, not moral monsters, because they believed, albeit falsely, that their actions were justified or excused.

Moral imagination would have deprived them of the supposed excuse and justification, and given the difficulty of being a moral monster, it would have made it less likely that they would do evil intentionally.

A second benefit derivable from moral imagination is growth in self-knowledge. The evildoers in the six cases systematically misunderstood not only their victims but also their own motives. They were seriously dissatisfied with their lives partly because the misunderstandings they had cultivated led them to respond inappropriately to their circumstances. They did the wrong things, for the wrong reasons, to the wrong people partly because they were deficient in self-knowledge. Moral imagination would have alleviated this deficiency by prompting these evildoers to see themselves from the outside as others might see them. They would, then, have acquired a point of view, in addition to the flawed self-understanding with which they had begun, from which they could have raised critical questions about the accuracy of their view of themselves and their motives. As it actually was, their passions prevented them from questioning the accuracy of their self-understandings. They were so taken up with protecting their own psychological security from supposed threats that they left themselves no opportunity to understand what they were doing. Moral imagination would have provided that opportunity.

They might, then, have asked themselves whether they were indeed defenders of the faith rather than persecutors of innocents; incorruptible revolutionaries rather than cruel tyrants; coerced into committing crimes rather than driven by ambition; honorable patriots rather than sadistic torturers; victims of unjust persecution rather than envious failures; or rebelling against stifling boredom rather than amusing themselves by inflicting pain on others. This is not to say, of course, that if moral imagination had given them the opportunity to ask such questions, they would have recognized or accepted the true answers and ceased to be evildoers. They may have continued as before, but they would have had the possibility, which they previously lacked, of understanding their motives. It would have become more difficult for them to cultivate their self-imposed misunderstandings and thus more difficult to continue to do evil unintentionally. Perhaps this difficulty—in conjunction with their dissatisfactions with their lives, the obstacles to being an intentional evildoer, the prohibitions against evil actions, and such fellow feeling as they may have had— would have motivated them to refrain from evildoing.

The actualization of this possibility would have been made more likely by the third benefit that may be gained from moral imagination. It is much easier to change one's evildoing ways if one is aware of attractive alternative possibilities. Moral imagination provides such alternatives by acquainting one with other ways of living and acting. It enriches and empowers those who have it by expanding the range of their choices and thus increasing the control they have over their lives. If the evildoers in the six cases had been able to see that their version of faith was not the only way to live a good life, that Jacobin ideology was not the only recipe for the betterment of humanity, that honor and the ambitious pursuit of status was not the only means to a worthwhile life, that resentment or mayhem was not the only response to the success of others or to boredom, then they would have been less determined evildoers. And if the possible alternatives moral imagination had provided for them were more attractive and less risky to pursue than the one they did pursue, then, once again, they might have been motivated to alter their ways.

It is reasonable to conclude, then, that if moral imagination had enabled evildoers to understand better their victims and their own motives and to realize that they had attractive alternatives to evildoing, then they would have been less likely to become or to continue as evildoers. This reduced likelihood, however, need not have moved them in the direction of elementary decency; it might have led them instead to intentional evildoing. But as we have seen, it is difficult and risky to be an intentional evildoer, especially if the external conditions are changed in the way I indicate in the next section. The better people's moral imagination is, the better are their reasons against evildoing. These reasons are not conclusive, even in the best circumstances, but they carry enough weight to make moral imagination a force for the good.

Moderately intelligent people have the capacity of moral imagination, but like other modes of imagination, it has to be cultivated. This requires, in the first instance, becoming familiar with an increasingly wider range of possible ways of living and acting. The process no doubt begins as individuals try to pay attention and understand others in their immediate context. But personal acquaintance is limited, and the range of possible ways of life is much wider than anyone could appreciate on the basis of personal contacts alone. Literature, history, ethnography, drama, religion, and philosophy can expand this range by depicting admirable and deplorable lives. These lives, then, may come to serve as thought experiments in living whereby individuals try to discover what it would be like to adapt these possibilities to their own character and circumstances.

The time-honored role of the humanities and liberal education has been to acquaint the young with these possibilities and to teach them through a complex mixture of example, cajolery, inspiration, and challenge to begin to use and then expand their moral imagination. The vehicles of such teaching have been the classics, works that have stood the test of time through many centuries because they achieved the evocative depiction of some possibilities of life that have endured through great changes. These possibilities have become cultural icons to which literate people can react critically or sympathetically, and which provide them with a shared moral vocabulary and shorthand references dense with significance. Becoming acquainted with the classics and then acquiring the facility of using them in private reflection and public discussion is the process of initiation and eventually of participation in a common cultural tradition formed of the inherited riches of human experience.

The cultivation of moral imagination in this way provides not only personal enrichment but also a moral force that can help make lives better and cope with evil. By increasing self-knowledge, presenting attractive alternatives to evildoing, and providing a basis for the comparison, contrast, and criticism of one's own way of being and acting, moral imagination helps to avoid the falsifications involved in unintentional evildoing. And by helping to make clear to intentional evildoers what is really involved in their actions, how their victims are affected, and why others are horrified by evildoing, it helps to make intentional evildoing less likely.

Finally, I must add that recent attacks on the cultural tradition that nourishes moral imagination encourage evil, even if they do so unintentionally. For deconstruction, relativism, radical feminism, postmodernism, and similar ways of scorning the achievements of dead white European males undermine the possibilities that not only present attractive alternatives to the inexcusable excess and malevolence that characterize evil, but may also make life worth living. In one way or another these deplorable attempts at unmasking, based on the false belief that to see is to see through, deny the reality of evil. They thus refuse to face its threat to elementary decency and to human well-being.

15.2 Changing External Conditions

Moral imagination helps to cope with evil, but it cannot by itself prevent it. For it may be deficient or unused, or it may merely help to transform unintentional evildoers into intentional ones. The chances of coping with evil are improved, however, if moral imagination is supplemented with strong prohibitions of evil actions. These prohibitions set limits in order to protect the physical security of people living together in a society. Thus they protect conditions on which the well-being of all human beings depends simply in virtue of their humanity, and quite independently of how they conceive of their well-being. Murder, torture, mutilation, for instance, violate these conditions. What I have called elementary decency requires the prohibition of such actions.

Evildoers are what they are because they habitually violate these prohibitions. That is why a society must not only have prohibitions, perhaps in the form of pious homilies or earnest disapprovals, but also enforce them by threatened or actual legal punishment. In these days when toleration, pluralism, and the protection of rights are regarded as central civic virtues, talk about strong prohibitions and their enforcement is likely to raise hackles. But perhaps they will subside if it is realized that what I am talking about is limiting evil, not interfering with people's sex lives, parenting, religious practices, or political views. The strong prohibitions are of actions that cause serious, excessive, malevolent, and inexcusable harm. And the moral and legal enforcement of these prohibitions is necessary for the protection of civilized life in which toleration, pluralism, and rights can flourish. Elementary decency, therefore, marks the boundary within which civilized life can be lived and on the outside of which barbarism reigns.

The means for enforcing strong prohibitions of evildoing is punishment. If it is swift, predictable, and severe, its threat may be reason enough to deter evildoers. But the passions that form part of their motivation may be so strong as to be undeterred by mere threats, and then actual punishment must follow. The purpose and justification of punishment in general is a complex question that need not be considered here because the purpose and justification of the punishment of evildoing are simple. They are to protect the physical security of members of a society against the depredations of evildoers. How severe justified punishment ought to be is guided by the moral ideal of coming as close as the contingencies of life allow to treating people as they deserve and not treating them as they do not deserve. There is, therefore, a good reason both for punishing evil actions and for keeping the punishment within morally acceptable limits. This purpose and justification of punishment serve as guides to finding reasonable answers to the many questions of detail that inevitably arise: Should punishment involve execution, imprisonment, expulsion, fine, or something else? Who has the authority and what method should be used to adjudicate disputes? What procedures should be followed for arrest, prosecution, defense, trial, and appeal? What may excuse or justify actions that are normally evil? What may be done to apprehend evildoers and how far may appropriate authorities go in trying to prevent evil actions? and so on. These are questions that legislators and officers of criminal law must ask and answer, and I shall say no more about them.

There is, however, an essential aspect of punishment that requires further discussion here. This is that although punishment is *for* evil actions, punishment must be *of* evildoers, since actions can only deserve, but not receive, punishment. If there is to be punishment, it must be of the people who performed the punishable actions. From this follows the reciprocal transitivity that holds between evildoers and evildoing. Normally, evildoers will do evil, and evildoing will be done by evildoers. What happens normally, of course, does not happen necessarily. Evildoers may occasionally do what is morally good, and the evil actions of a person may be uncharacteristic, accidental, or forced. Normally, however, people act in characteristic ways. Evildoers are evildoers because their habitual actions are evil, and patterns of evildoing by people indicate that they are evildoers. Given the transitivity of evil, it is normally justified to punish people for their evil actions.

As we have seen in the discussion of responsibility (in 13.4), however, there is a prevalent tendency to deny the transitivity of evil because only intentionally evil actions are thought to deserve punishment. I have argued at length that responsibility is for the readily foreseeable consequences of one's actions, not for intentional actions. Many evil actions are unintentional because the evildoers failed to understand what they were doing. But evildoers are often blameworthy for their lack of understanding because they should have understood what they did not. They should have been more thoughtful, attentive, or patient; they should have been less self-centered, preoccupied with trivial concerns, or contemptuous of their victims. From the fact that a person's action is unintentional it does not follow, therefore, that it should be excused, for its being unintentional may be the person's fault. If it is, and the action is evil, then the person should be held responsible and punished for it. The prevalent tendency to deny this is not only mistaken but also a serious obstacle to coping with evil. Changing the external conditions of evil depends on removing the obstacle and avoiding the mistake.

If it is true that many evil actions are unintentional (which I accept), and if it is true that people should not be held responsible and punished for their unintentionally evil actions (which I deny), then a society could not cope with many evil actions. Since these actions violate elementary decency, the society could not defend a condition that justifies its existence. It would have given up enforcing its own moral and legal prohibitions and would thereby leave its members unprotected against many evil actions. It would, in effect, encourage unintentional evildoing by removing moral and legal prohibitions of it.

Changing the external conditions requires, therefore, the enforcement of the prohibition of evildoing regardless of whether or not it is intentional. This would not be a regression to the barbaric practice of strict liability, since unintentionally evil actions may be excused if the evildoers were, through no fault of their own, incapable of foreseeing the readily foreseeable consequences of their actions. Imbecility, insanity, or debilitating stress would excuse them. But murder, torture, and mutilation are rarely actions whose direct consequences are not readily foreseeable. The evildoers' immediate experience of the bleeding bodies of their victims provides them with undeniable knowledge of the consequences of their actions. It would be exceptionally difficult for them to escape having this knowledge.

The evildoers in the six cases certainly had it, but they ignored or misperceived the moral significance of the knowledge they had. Since they were clearly not insane, imbecilic, or irresistibly stressed, they had no acceptable excuse. That they were blinded by faith, ideology, ambition, honor, envy, or boredom is a psychological explanation of the causes of their evil actions, not an excuse for them. They were quite capable of judging the comparative moral significance of the justifications they believed they had and their immediate experience of the suffering they caused their victims. And they did judge, but their judgments were depraved. That makes them deserving of more, not less, severe punishment.

Coping with evil depends, then, on combining the cultivation of moral imagination and the enforcement of moral and legal prohibitions by punishment. Changing in this way only the internal or the external conditions of evil would not suffice, for even a well-cultivated moral imagination may be unused or put to evil uses, and passions generated by self-serving falsifications may be powerful enough to ignore the likelihood of even severe punishment. The best hope of coping with evil is to change both internal and external conditions, and to keep doing it in response to ever-changing circumstances and contingencies even though nothing can expel evil from human life. For evil is the result of natural human motives, and these motives will prompt evil actions that jeopardize the efforts to cope with it. Evil is a permanent threat to human well-being because human actions both constitute the threat and are the only means of countering it.

15.3 Summary

My aim in the book has been to explain why people do evil. In closing, I shall state bluntly, without restating the supporting arguments, the conclusions I have reached. Some of these conclusions are critical, others constructive. I begin with the critical ones.

Evil is not:

- deviation from a morally good supernatural order because there is no good reason to believe that there is such an order;

- contrary to the requirements of reason because evil actions are often allowed by reason;
- the result of motivation alone because external conditions crucially influence what motives evildoers act on;
- the result of external conditions alone because motivation plays a central role in how evildoers respond to their circumstances;
- the unnatural violation of biological requirements because different psychological propensities, all of which conform to biological requirements, decisively influence people's actions;
- the passive failure to understand internal motives or external conditions because there are motives and circumstances that actively promote evil;
- an active internal or external force because the passive failure of evildoers to understand their motives and/or circumstances is necessary for evil;
- the effect of some single cause because evil has many forms and each has different causes.

I now turn to the constructive conclusions, beginning with the general and going on to particular ones.

The explanation of evil has the following general characteristics: it is

- mixed because it involves the combination of internal-active, internal-passive, external-active, and external-passive conditions;
- multicausal because the conditions that jointly cause it vary with individuals, societies, times, and places;
- particular because it involves the detailed consideration of conditions that differ from case to case.

The explanation of evil has the following particular characteristics:

- if evil is unintentional, the explanation must identify the particular motive (internal-active condition), failure of understanding (internal-passive condition), circumstances eliciting response (external-active condition), and weak prohibitions of evil (external-passive condition) that jointly are the causes of evil;
- if evil is intentional, the explanation must identify the motive and the circumstances eliciting response, but there will be no failure of understanding, and prohibitions of evil may not be weak.

Given this explanation, coping with evil has the following requirements:

- the cultivation of moral imagination because it changes the internal conditions and makes evildoing less likely;
- the enforcement of strong prohibitions because it changes the external conditions and may deter evildoing;
- enforcement by threatened or actual punishment for violations;
- holding evildoers responsible for both their intentional and unintentional violations, provided they have the capacity to foresee the readily foreseeable consequences of their actions; or excusing them if they lack the capacity.

Coping with evil depends on meeting these requirements, but meeting them will not make evil disappear once and for all because human motivation and the contingencies of life make evil a permanent threat to human well-being.

Notes

1. Introduction: The Problem and the Approach

1. For a similar account of evil, see Claudia Card, *The Atrocity Paradigm* (New York: Oxford University Press, 2002). On evil in general and on its difference from what is merely bad, see Adam Morton, *On Evil* (New York: Routledge, 2004); Marcus G. Singer, "The Concept of Evil," *Philosophy* 79 (2004): 185–214.

2. E.g., Robert Conquest, *The Great Terror* (New York: Oxford University Press, 1990); Jonathan Glover, *Humanity* (New Haven: Yale University Press, 2000); Philip Gourevitch, *We wish to inform you that tomorrow we will be killed with our families* (New York: Farrar, Straus & Giroux, 1998); and Raul Hilberg, *The Destruction of the European Jews* (New York: Holmes & Meier, 1985).

3. Immanuel Kant, *Religion within the Limits of Reason Alone* [1794], trans. T. M. Greene and H. H. Hudson (New York: Harper & Row, 1960), p. 38. See also note 5 in chapter 8 of the present work.

4. Candace Vogler, *Reasonably Vicious* (Cambridge, Mass.: Harvard University Press, 2002), p. 37.

5. Two outstanding examples are Richard J. Bernstein, *Radical Evil: A Philosophical Interrogation* (Cambridge: Polity Press, 2002), and Susan Neiman, *Evil in Modern Thought: An Alternative History of Philosophy* (Princeton: Princeton University Press, 2002).

2. The Sleep of Reason

1. For the history, beliefs, and persecution of the Cathars, I rely on Stephen O'Shea, *The Perfect Heresy* (New York: Walker, 2000), hereafter referred to as PH; and Jonathan Sumption, *The Albigensian Crusade* (London: Faber & Faber, 1978), hereafter referred to as AC; both are cited directly in the text.

2. See Norman Cohn, *Europe's Inner Demons* (London: Paladin, 1976), pp. 22 and 55.

3. Thomas Aquinas, *Summa Theologiae*, 2, 2, qu. xi, art. 3, quoted and translated by R. W. Southern, *Western Society and the Church in the Middle Ages* (Harmondsworth, U.K.: Penguin, 1970), p. 17; hereafter referred to as WSC and cited in the text.

4. Robert I. Moore, *The Formation of a Persecuting Society* (Oxford: Blackwell, 1987), p. 5.

5. Deuteronomy 13.12–16 (King James Version).

6. Southern, *Western Society and the Church*. See also R. W. Southern, *The Making of the Middle Ages* (1953; New Haven: Yale University Press, 1970).

7. *Catholic Encyclopedia,* edited by Catholic University of America (New York: McGraw-Hill, 1967–79), 17 vols., s.v. "Faith."

8. Exodus 20.13.

9. Matthew 5.7.

10. Soren Kierkegaard, *Fear and Trembling* [1843], trans. Walter Lowrie (Princeton: Princeton University Press, 1974), p. 69.

11. These remarks owe a great deal to Isaiah Berlin's work. See especially *Four Essays on Liberty* (Oxford: Oxford University Press, 1969).

12. In this, and much else, I follow Stuart Hampshire, *Innocence and Experience* (London: Allen Lane, 1989), p. 8.

3. Perilous Dreams

1. Stanley Loomis, *Paris in the Terror* (Philadelphia: Lippincott, 1964), p. 82; hereafter referred to as Loomis and cited in the text.

2. James Matthew Thompson, *Robespierre*, 2 vols. (New York: Appleton-Century, 1936), 1:273, 275; hereafter referred to as Thompson and cited in the text.

3. Simon Schama, *Citizens* (New York: Knopf, 1989), pp. 782–83; hereafter referred to as Schama and cited in the text.

4. Norman Hampson, *The Life and Opinions of Maximilien Robespierre* (London: Duckworth, 1974), p. 263; hereafter referred to as Hampson and cited in the text.

5. These convictions are most illuminatingly discussed in Alfred Cobban, *Aspects of the French Revolution* (New York: Braziller, 1968), chaps. 8–9; hereafter referred to as Cobban and cited in the text.

4. A Fatal Fusion

1. Gitta Sereny, *Into That Darkness* (London: Andre Deutsch, 1974; London: Pimlico, 1995). Quotations are from the Pimlico edition, hereafter referred to as D and cited in the text.

2. Gitta Sereny, *The Healing Wound* (New York: Norton, 2001), first published as *The German Trauma* (London: Norton, 2000), hereafter referred to as W and cited in the text.

5. The Revenge of Ruined Pride

1. For the facts of the case, I rely on Vincent Bugliosi and Curt Gentry, *Helter Skelter* (New York: Norton, 1974), hereafter referred to as HS and cited in the text. Bugliosi prosecuted Manson and the others for the murders; his book is based on the multitude of facts the investigations revealed and which became part of the official record. For Manson's comments on himself and the facts, I rely on Nuel Emmons, *Manson in His Own Words* (New York: Grove, 1986), hereafter referred to as MW and cited in the text. Emmons was a reformed fellow convict of Manson and trusted by him. The book is based on many hours of Emmons's interviews with Manson while he was serving the sentence of life imprisonment. The purpose of the interviews and the book is to allow Manson to tell his side of the story. The final version of the book was approved by Manson.

2. Ed Sanders, *The Family*, rev. ed. (London: Nemesis, 1989), p. 454.

3. For a general account of envy, see Helmut Schoeck, *Envy* (1966; Indianapolis: Liberty Fund, 1987). For an analysis of the overlapping notion of *ressentiment*, see Max Scheler, *Ressentiment* [1912], trans. Lewis B. Coser and William W. Holdheim (Milwaukee:

Marquette University Press, 1994). For a literary study, see Michael Andre Bernstein, *Bitter Carnival: Ressentiment and the Abject Hero* (Princeton: Princeton University Press, 1992).

4. William L. Davidson, "Envy," in *Encyclopedia of Religion and Ethics* (New York: Scribner's, 1925–35).

5. See, e.g., Robert Nozick, *Anarchy, State, and Utopia* (New York: Basic Books, 1974), chap. 8, and Schoeck, *Envy*, chap. 12 and on.

6. See, e.g., John Rawls, *A Theory of Justice* (Cambridge, Mass.: Harvard University Press, 1971), secs. 80–81, and Ronald Dworkin, *Sovereign Virtue* (Cambridge, Mass.: Harvard University Press, 2000), chap. 2.

6. Wickedness in High Places

1. Mark J. Osiel, *Mass Atrocity, Ordinary Evil, and Hannah Arendt* (New Haven: Yale University Press, 2001), pp. 13–14; hereafter referred to as Osiel and cited in the text. See also references in the notes of Osiel's book.

2. Horacio Verbitsky, *The Flight: Confessions of an Argentine Dirty Warrior*, trans. Esther Allen (New York: New Press, 1996), pp. 25 and 37; hereafter referred to as Verbitsky and cited in the text.

3. The Report of the Argentine National Commission on the Disappeared, *Nunca Más* (New York: Farrar, Straus & Giroux, 1986), hereafter referred to as Report and cited in the text. The original Spanish edition was published in Buenos Aires in 1984.

4. See, e.g., Ronald Dworkin's Introduction to Report.

5. Carlos Santiago Nino, *Radical Evil on Trial* (New Haven: Yale University Press, 1996), p. 51; hereafter referred to as Nino and cited in the text.

6. For a scholarly account of the activities of the guerillas, see Maria José Moyano, *Argentina's Lost Patrol* (New Haven: Yale University Press, 1995).

7. Quoted in Tina Rosenberg, *Children of Cain* (New York: Morrow, 1991), p. 123; hereafter referred to as Rosenberg and cited in the text.

8. Hannah Arendt, *Eichmann in Jerusalem: A Report on the Banality of Evil*, rev. ed. (New York: Viking, 1965).

9. Stanley Milgram, *Obedience to Authority* (New York: Harper, 1974).

10. It has been labeled *corporatism*. See, e.g., Howard J. Wiarda, *Corporatism and Comparative Politics* (New York: Sharpe, 1997).

7. Disenchantment with Ordinary Life

1. John Allen, *Assault with a Deadly Weapon*, ed. Dianne Hall Kelly and Philip Heymann (New York: Pantheon, 1977). References in the text are to the pages of this book.

2. *Diagnostic and Statistical Manual of Mental Disorders*, 4th ed. (Washington, D.C.: American Psychiatric Association, 1994), pp. 645–50.

3. Robert B. Edgerton, "The Study of Deviance," in *The Making of Psychological Anthropology*, ed. George D. Spindler (Berkeley: University of California Press, 1978), p. 471. See also his "Deviant Behavior and Cultural Theory," in *Current Topics in Anthropology* (Reading, Mass.: Addison-Wesley, 1973), 7:1–40.

4. Hervey Cleckley, *The Mask of Sanity* (New York: New American Library, 1982), pp. 241–43, 251. The book has gone through many editions and revisions.

5. Bertrand Russell, *The Conquest of Happiness* (1930; London: Routledge, 1993), p. 44.

6. Martin Heidegger, "What Is Metaphysics?" in *Existence and Being*, ed. W. Brock (Chicago: Regnery, 1949), pp. 364, 366.

7. Sean Desmond Healy, *Boredom, Self, and Culture* (Cranbury, N.J.: Associated University Presses, 1984), p. 15.

8. Ralph Linton, *The Study of Man* (New York: Appleton-Century, 1936), p. 90.

9. Karl E. Scheibe, *The Drama of Everyday Life* (Cambridge, Mass.: Harvard University Press, 2000), p. 19.

10. O. E. Klapp, *Overload and Boredom* (Westport, Conn.: Greenwood, 1986), pp. 11–12.

11. Reinhard Kuhn, *The Demon of Noontide* (Princeton: Princeton University Press, 1976), p. 331.

12. Jacques Barzun, *From Dawn to Decadence* (1949; New York: HarperCollins, 2000), pp. 788, 801.

13. Ecclesiastes 1.1–18, 3.16, 4.2–3.

14. Kuhn, *Demon of Noontide*, pp. 40, 45, 52. See also Michael L. Raposa, *Boredom and the Religious Imagination* (Charlottesville: University Press of Virginia, 1999), and Patricia Meyer Spacks, *Boredom* (Chicago: University of Chicago Press, 1995).

15. Johan Huizinga, *The Waning of the Middle Ages* (1949; New York: Doubleday, 1954), pp. 9–10.

16. See Haskell E. Bernstein, "Boredom and the Ready-Made Life," *Social Research* 42 (1975): 512–37.

17. These attitudes are discussed in greater detail in my *Art of Life* (Ithaca: Cornell University Press, 2002), chaps. 9–10.

8. Taking Stock

1. Primo Levi, *The Drowned and the Saved*, trans. Raymond Rosenthal (New York: Vintage, 1989), pp. 48–49.

2. This point has been made familiar by G. E. M. Anscombe, *Intention* (Oxford: Blackwell, 1957).

3. The characterization is in Peter Strawson, "Freedom and Resentment," in *Freedom and Resentment and Other Essays* (London: Methuen, 1974).

4. Pierre Bayle, *The Great Contest of Faith and Reason* [1740], trans. Karl C. Sandberg (New York: Unger, 1963), p. 108.

5. "The rational origin of . . . the propensity to evil remains inscrutable to us." Immanuel Kant, *Religion within the Limits of Reason Alone* [1794], trans. Theodore M. Greene and Hoyt H. Hudson (New York: Harper, 1960), p. 38. "Radical evil seems to surpass the boundaries of moral discourse; it embodies a form of life and a conceptual scheme that is alien to us. We seem unable to evaluate such acts from a moral vantage point because they are as incomprehensible to us as would be the behavior of people who did not share our concepts of time and space." Carlos Santiago Nino, *Radical Evil on Trial* (New Haven: Yale University Press, 1996), p. ix. "Men are unable to forgive what they cannot punish and they are unable to punish what has turned out to be unforgivable. This is the true hallmark of those offenses which . . . we call 'radical evil' and about whose nature so little is known. . . . They . . . transcend the realm of human affairs and the potentialities of human power." Hannah Arendt, *The Human Condition* (Chicago: University of Chicago Press, 1958), p. 241. "There is really nothing that provides enlightenment on the eruption of radical Evil in Germany. . . . This Evil really is singular and irreducible in its total inner logic and its accursed rationality. For this reason all of us are faced with a dark riddle." Jean Amery, *At the Mind's Limits*, trans. S. Rosenfeld and S. P. Rosenfeld (New York:

Schocken, 1986), p. xviii. "Where the Holocaust is, *no* thought can be, and where there is thought it is in flight from the event." Emil L. Fackenheim, *To Mend the World* (New York: Schocken, 1982), p. 200. "The need to affirm what reason finds offensive makes me speak of mystery, but not because I believe our limited understanding is defeated, that perhaps other beings with vastly superior intelligence and knowledge could better comprehend these things. I mean by mystery something which no power of understanding can penetrate, not because it is so difficult . . . but because the mystery of good and evil is not contingent on our limited cognitive powers." Raimond Gaita, "Evil beyond Vice," in *A Common Humanity* (London: Routledge, 1998), pp. 38–39. "A gap has opened up between our awareness of evil and the intellectual resources we have for handling it." Andrew Delbanco, *The Death of Satan* (New York: Farrar, Straus & Giroux, 1995), p. 3. "The whole intellectual tradition of modernity can be written as a growing incomprehension of evil, of our inability adequately to understand both the evils we mean to oppose, and those in which we find ourselves implicated." Charles T. Mathewes, *Evil and the Augustinian Tradition* (New York: Cambridge University Press, 2002), p. 3. "The ultimate ground for the choice between good and evil is inscrutable." Richard J. Bernstein, *Radical Evil: A Philosophical Interrogation* (Cambridge: Polity Press, 2002), p. 235. "My conclusion is that it is ultimately not possible to understand evil." Lance Morrow, *Evil* (New York: Basic Books, 2003), p. 3.

6. The central works are Friedrich Nietzsche, *On the Genealogy of Morals* and *Beyond Good and Evil*, in *Basic Writings of Nietzsche*, trans. Walter Kaufmann (New York: Modern Library, 1966). Illuminating interpretations are in Richard Schacht, ed., *Nietzsche, Genealogy, Morality* (Berkeley: University of California Press, 1994), especially essays 1–3, and Simon May, *Nietzsche's Ethics and His War on "Morality"* (Oxford: Clarendon Press, 1999).

7. For the Stoic view, see Julia Annas, *The Morality of Happiness* (New York: Oxford University Press, 1993), and Martha C. Nussbaum, *The Therapy of Desire* (Princeton: Princeton University Press, 1994); for a contemporary restatement, see Lawrence C. Becker, *A New Stoicism* (Princeton: Princeton University Press, 1998). For the Spinozistic view, see Baruch Spinoza, *Ethics*, parts 3–4, in *The Collected Works of Spinoza*, ed. and trans. Edwin Curley (Princeton: Princeton University Press, 1985), and Stuart Hampshire, *Spinoza* (Harmondsworth, U.K.: Penguin, 1951), chap. 4.

8. E.g., Gordon Graham, *Evil and Christian Ethics* (Cambridge: Cambridge University Press, 2001).

9. External Explanations

1. Alexander Pope, "Essay on Man," *Selected Poetry and Prose* (New York: Holt, Rinehart & Winston, 1951).

2. Gottfried Wilhelm Leibniz, *Theodicy* [1875–90], trans. E. M. Huggard (LaSalle Ill.: Open Court, 1985). Leibniz's view of evil is discussed by Susan Neiman, *Evil in Modern Thought: An Alternative History of Philosophy* (Princeton: Princeton University Press, 2002), pp. 21–29; my discussion is much indebted to hers; by Bertrand Russell, *A Critical Exposition of the Philosophy of Leibniz* (London: Allen & Unwin, 1937), pp. 197–202; and by R. C. Sleigh, Jr., "Leibniz," in *Encyclopedia of Ethics*, 2d ed., ed. Lawrence E. Becker and Charlotte B. Becker (New York: Routledge, 2001), which has useful references to other treatments of the topic.

3. Georg F. W. Hegel, *Reason in History* [1840], trans. Robert S. Hartman (New York: Liberal Arts, 1953), p. 26.

4. John Stuart Mill, *The Subjection of Women* [1869] (Arlington Heights, Ill.: AHM, 1980), p. 1.

5. Jean-Jacques Rousseau, *Emile* [1780], trans. Barbara Foxley (London: Dent, 1974), p. 1.

6. The changes from Rousseau through the Enlightenment to Kant are superbly traced by Jerome B. Schneewind, *The Invention of Autonomy* (New York: Cambridge University Press, 1998). The changing conceptions of evil that have occurred throughout this process are most illuminatingly discussed in Neiman, *Evil in Modern Thought*. A general history of the idea of human perfectibility is John Passmore, *The Perfectibility of Man* (London: Duckworth, 1970).

7. Immanuel Kant, "What Is Enlightenment?" [1784], in *Perpetual Peace and Other Essays*, trans. Ted Humphreys (Indianapolis: Hackett, 1983), p. 41.

10. A Biological Explanation

1. Philippa Foot, *Natural Goodness* (Oxford: Clarendon Press, 2001). Parenthetical references in the text are to the pages of this book.

2. For a parallel argument about the connection between biology and morality, see Anthony O'Hear, *Beyond Evolution* (Oxford: Clarendon Press, 1997).

3. This distinction is indebted to Bernard Gert, *The Moral Rules* (New York: Harper & Row, 1966), substantially revised as *Morality* (New York: Oxford University Press, 1988). Candace Vogler, *Reasonably Vicious* (Cambridge, Mass.: Harvard University Press, 2002), following a different line of argument, also finds Foot's argument inadequate.

4. For numerous illustrations, see Robert E. Edgerton, *Sick Societies* (New York: Free Press, 1992) and Lyall Watson, *Dark Nature: A Natural History of Evil* (London: Hodder & Staughton, 1995).

11. Internal Explanations

1. Plato, *Meno*, 77e, trans. W. K. C. Guthrie, in *The Collected Dialogues of Plato*, ed. Edith Hamilton and Huntington Cairns (Princeton: Princeton University Press, 1989).

2. There is an immense literature on this. I found G. M. A. Grube, *Plato's Thought*, chap. 7 (London: Methuen, 1935), and Gregory Vlastos, *Socrates, Ironist and Moral Philosopher* (Ithaca: Cornell University Press, 1991), most helpful.

3. Augustine returns to the discussion of evil again and again in his works. The central text is perhaps his *Confessions* [397], trans. E. B. Pusey (London: Dent, 1907). The best discussion I know of his view of evil is G. R. Evans, *Augustine on Evil* (Cambridge: Cambridge University Press, 1982). A contemporary Augustinian approach to evil is Charles T. Mathewes, *Evil and the Augustinian Tradition* (New York: Cambridge University Press, 2002). Aquinas' writings on evil are most usefully collected in John A. Oesterle and Jean T. Oesterle, ed. and trans., *On Evil: St. Thomas Aquinas* (Notre Dame, Ind.: University of Notre Dame Press, 1995). Good contemporary discussions of Aquinas' view are in F. C. Copleston, *Aquinas* (Harmondsworth, U.K.: Penguin, 1955), and John Finnis, *Aquinas* (Oxford: Oxford University Press, 1998). For a most interesting consideration of Aquinas' account of evil from a secular point of view, see Candace Vogler, *Reasonably Vicious* (Cambridge, Mass.: Harvard University Press, 2002). The various Christian approaches to evil are well summarized in the preface of Evans, *Augustine on Evil*. See also Mary Midgley, *Wickedness* (London: Routledge, 1984); John Hick, *Evil and the God of Love* (New York: Harper & Row, 1966); and Marilyn McCord Adams, *Horrendous Evils and the Goodness of God* (Ithaca: Cornell University Press, 1999).

4. This version has been recently formulated and defended by Denis de Rougemont, *La part du diable* (1945; Paris: Gallimard, 1982); R. G. Collingwood, "The Devil," in *Concerning Prayer*, ed. B. H. Streeter (London: Macmillan, 1931), reprinted in *Religion and Understanding*, ed. D. Z. Phillips (Oxford: Blackwell, 1967); and Gordon Graham, *Evil and Christian Ethics* (Cambridge: Cambridge University Press, 2001). Quotations from Collingwood and Graham are cited in the text by page number.

5. Hannah Arendt, *Essays in Understanding, 1930–1954*, ed. Jerome Kohn (New York: Harcourt, 1993), pp. 134–35.

6. Aristotle, *Nicomachean Ethics*, trans. W. D. Ross, rev. J. O. Urmson, in *The Complete Works of Aristotle*, ed. Jonathan Barnes (Princeton: Princeton University Press, 1984), 1094a1–3.

7. G. E. M. Anscombe, *Intention* (Oxford: Blackwell, 1957), pp. 75–76.

8. E.g., Peter Byrne, *The Moral Interpretation of Religion* (Grand Rapids, Mich.: Eerdmans, 1998), pp. 44–47; Nancy Sherman, *The Fabric of Character* (Oxford: Clarendon Press, 1989), chap. 3; and Susan Wolf, *Freedom within Reason* (New York: Oxford University Press, 1990), especially chap. 4.

9. Thomas Hobbes, *Leviathan* [1651] (London: Dent, 1962), The First Part: Of Man. A recent interpretation is David P. Gauthier, *The Logic of Leviathan* (Oxford: Clarendon Press, 1969). Joseph Butler, *Fifteen Sermons* [1726], (London: Bell, 1953). Excellent commentaries are Austin Duncan-Jones, *Butler's Moral Philosophy* (Harmondsworth, U.K.: Penguin, 1952), and Terence Penelhum, *Butler* (London: Routledge, 1985). Immanuel Kant, *Religion within the Limits of Reason Alone* [1794], trans. T. M. Greene and H. H. Hudson (New York: Harper, 1960). Of the numerous contemporary works, I found most useful John R. Silber, "The Ethical Significance of Kant's *Religion*," in Kant, *Religion;* Richard J. Bernstein, *Radical Evil: A Philosophical Interrogation* (Cambridge: Polity Press, 2002), chap. 1; Susan Neiman, *Evil in Modern Thought* (Princeton: Princeton University Press, 2002), pp. 57–84; Francis Herbert Bradley, *Ethical Studies,* 2d ed. (Oxford: Clarendon Press, 1927), essay 7; and Richard Wollheim, "The Good Self and the Bad Self," in *The Mind and Its Depth* (Cambridge, Mass.: Harvard University Press, 1993). Sigmund Freud, *Civilization and Its Discontents* [1930], trans. James Strachey (New York: Norton, 1961), and *Beyond the Pleasure Principle* [1920], trans. James Strachey (New York: Bantam, 1959). For an overview of Freud on evil, see Bernstein, *Radical Evil*, pp. 132–60; Adam Morton, *On Evil* (New York: Routledge, 2004).

10. Hobbes, *Leviathan*, p. 49.

11. Sigmund Freud, *Thoughts for the Times*, in *Standard Edition of the Complete Psychological Works of Sigmund Freud*, 24 vols., ed. and trans. James Strachey (London: Hogarth, 1974), 14:281.

12. Colin McGinn, *Ethics, Evil, and Fiction* (Oxford: Clarendon Press, 1997), 4. Further quotations are cited by page number in the text.

13. The general discussion is Hannah Arendt, *The Origins of Totalitarianism* (1951; New York: Harcourt, 1968), hereafter referred to as OT and cited in the text. The particular discussion is Hannah Arendt, *Eichmann in Jerusalem: A Report on the Banality of Evil* rev. ed. (1963; New York: Penguin, 1994), hereafter referred to as EJ and cited in the text. I found the following works illuminating on Arendt. Bernstein, *Radical Evil;* Neiman, *Evil in Modern Thought;* and Dana R. Villa, *Politics, Philosophy, Terror: Essays on the Thought of Hannah Arendt* (Princeton: Princeton University Press, 1999).

12. The Mixed Explanation

1. John Godfrey Saxe, "The Blind Men and the Elephant," in *The Poems* (Boston: Osgood, 1871), pp. 259–61.

13. Responsibility

1. See Saul Friedlander, *Kurt Gerstein: The Ambiguity of Good,* trans. Charles Fullham (New York: Knopf, 1969).

2. For a similar approach to expectation, see R. Jay Wallace, *Responsibility and the Moral Sentiments* (Cambridge, Mass.: Harvard University Press, 1996), especially chap. 2.

3. This way of thinking about responsibility is indebted to and follows several writers, such as Joseph Butler, "Upon Resentment," in *Fifteen Sermons* [1726] (London: Bell, 1953); Peter Strawson, "Freedom and Resentment," in *Freedom and Resentment and Other Essays* (London: Methuen, 1974); Jonathan Bennett, "Accountability," in *Philosophical Subjects,* ed. Zak van Straaten (Oxford: Clarendon Press, 1980); Gary Watson, "Responsibility and the Limits of Evil," in *Responsibility, Character, and the Emotions,* ed. Ferdinand Schoeman (New York: Cambridge University Press, 1987); and Wallace, *Responsibility and the Moral Sentiments.*

4. David Hume, *A Treatise of Human Nature* [1739], ed. L. A. Selby-Bigge (Oxford: Clarendon Press, 1960), p. 535.

5. Stuart Hampshire, *Thought and Action* (London: Chatto & Windus, 1960), pp. 177–78.

6. These difficulties are surveyed by Bruce Aune, "Intention," in *The Encyclopedia of Philosophy,* vol. 4, ed. Paul Edwards (New York: Macmillan, 1967); Ann Bumpus, "Intention," in *Encyclopedia of Ethics,* 2d ed., vol. 2, ed. Lawrence C. Becker and Charlotte B. Becker (New York: Routledge, 2001); Robert Dunn, "Intention," in *Routledge Encyclopedia of Philosophy,* ed. Edward Craig (London: Routledge, 1998); and the essays in *Moral Responsibility,* ed. John Martin Fischer (Ithaca: Cornell University Press, 1986); see especially Fischer's introduction.

7. E.g., Harry G. Frankfurt, "Freedom of the Will and the Concept of a Person," in *The Importance of What We Care About* (New York: Cambridge University Press, 1988), and Charles Taylor, "Responsibility for Self," in *The Identities of Persons,* ed. Amelie Rorty (Berkeley: University of California Press, 1976).

8. E.g., Susan Wolf, "Sanity and the Metaphysics of Responsibility," in Schoeman, *Responsibility, Character, and the Emotions.*

9. E.g., Patricia Greenspan, "Unfreedom and Responsibility," in Schoeman, *Responsibility, Character, and the Emotions.*

10. E.g., John Martin Fischer, "Responsiveness and Moral Responsibility," in Schoeman, *Responsibility, Character, and the Emotions.*

14. Toward Elementary Decency

1. Gitta Sereny, *Into That Darkness* (1974; London: Pimlico, 1995), p. 39.

2. Tina Rosenberg, *Children of Cain* (New York: Morrow, 1991), pp. 125–26.

3. Nuel Emmons, *Manson in His Own Words* (New York: Grove, 1986), pp. 26, 64.

4. John Allen, *Assault with a Deadly Weapon,* ed. Dianne Hall Kelly and Philip Heynmann (New York: Pantheon, 1977), p. 226.

Works Cited

Adams, Marilyn McCord. *Horrendous Evils and the Goodness of God*. Ithaca: Cornell University Press, 1999.

Allen, John. *Assault with a Deadly Weapon*. Edited by Dianne Hall Kelly and Philip Heynmann. New York: Pantheon, 1977.

Amery, Jean. *At the Mind's Limits*. Translated by S. Rosenfeld and S. P. Rosenfeld. New York: Schocken, 1986.

Annas, Julia. *The Morality of Happiness*. New York: Oxford University Press, 1993.

Anscombe, G. E. M. *Intention*. Oxford: Blackwell, 1957.

Aquinas, Thomas. *On Evil: St. Thomas Aquinas*. Edited and translated by John A. Oesterle and Jean T. Oesterle. Notre Dame, Ind.: University of Notre Dame Press, 1995.

Arendt, Hannah. *Eichmann in Jerusalem: A Report on the Banality of Evil*. Rev. ed. New York: Penguin, 1965.

———. *Essays in Understanding, 1930–1954*. Edited by Jerome Kohn. New York: Harcourt, 1993.

———. *The Human Condition*. Chicago: University of Chicago Press, 1958.

———. *The Origins of Totalitarianism*. 1951. New York: Harcourt, 1968.

Aristotle. *Nicomachean Ethics*. Translated by W. D. Ross. Revised by J. O. Urmson. In *The Complete Works of Aristotle*, edited by Jonathan Barnes. Princeton: Princeton University Press, 1984.

Augustine. *Confessions*. 397. Translated by E. B. Pusey. London: Dent, 1907.

Aune, Bruce. "Intention." In *The Encyclopedia of Philosophy*, vol. 4, edited by Paul Edwards. New York: Macmillan, 1967.

Barzun, Jacques. *From Dawn to Decadence*. New York: HarperCollins, 2000.

Bayle, Pierre. *The Great Contest of Faith and Reason*. 1740. Translated by Karl C. Sandberg. New York: Unger, 1963.

Becker, Lawrence C. *A New Stoicism*. Princeton: Princeton University Press, 1998.

Bennett, Jonathan. "Accountability." In *Philosophical Subjects*, edited by Zak van Straaten. Oxford: Clarendon Press, 1980.

Berlin, Isaiah. *Four Essays on Liberty*. Oxford: Oxford University Press, 1969.

Bernstein, Haskell E. "Boredom and the Ready-Made Life." *Social Research* 42 (1975): 512–37.

Bernstein, Michael Andre. *Bitter Carnival: Ressentiment and the Abject Hero*. Princeton: Princeton University Press, 1992.

Bernstein, Richard J. *Radical Evil: A Philosophical Interrogation.* Cambridge: Polity Press, 2002.

Bradley, Francis Herbert. *Ethical Studies.* 2d ed. Oxford: Clarendon Press, 1927.

Bugliosi, Vincent, and Curt Gentry. *Helter Skelter.* New York: Norton, 1974.

Bumpus, Ann. "Intention." In *Encyclopedia of Ethics,* 2d ed., edited by Lawrence C. Becker and Charlotte E. Becker. New York: Routledge, 2001.

Butler, Joseph. "Upon Resentment." 1726. In *Fifteen Sermons.* London: Bell, 1953.

Byrne, Peter. *The Moral Interpretation of Religion.* Grand Rapids, Mich.: Eerdmans, 1998.

Card, Claudia. *The Atrocity Paradigm.* New York: Oxford University Press, 2002.

Catholic Encyclopedia. 17 vols. Edited by Catholic University of America. New York: McGraw-Hill, 1967–79.

Cleckley, Hervey. *The Mask of Sanity.* New York: New American Library, 1982.

Cobban, Alfred. *Aspects of the French Revolution.* New York: Braziller, 1968.

Cohn, Norman. *Europe's Inner Demons.* London: Paladin, 1976.

Collingwood, R. G. "The Devil." In *Concerning Prayer,* edited by B. H. Streeter. London: Macmillan, 1931. Reprinted in *Religion and Understanding,* edited by D. Z. Phillips. Oxford: Blackwell, 1967.

Conquest, Robert. *The Great Terror.* New York: Oxford University Press, 1990.

Copleston, F. C. *Aquinas.* Harmondsworth, U.K.: Penguin, 1955.

Davidson, William L. "Envy." In *Encyclopedia of Religion and Ethics.* New York: Scribner's, 1925–35.

Delbanco, Andrew. *The Death of Satan.* New York: Farrar, Straus & Giroux, 1995.

Diagnostic and Statistical Manual of Mental Disorders. 4th ed. Washington, D.C.: American Psychiatric Association, 1994.

Duncan-Jones, Austin. *Butler's Moral Philosophy.* Harmondsworth, U.K.: Penguin, 1952.

Dunn, Robert. "Intention." In *Routledge Encyclopedia of Philosophy,* edited by Edward Craig. London: Routledge, 1998.

Dworkin, Ronald. *Sovereign Virtue.* Cambridge, Mass.: Harvard University Press, 2000.

Edgerton, Robert B. "Deviant Behavior and Cultural Theory." In *Current Topics in Anthropology* 7:1–40. Reading, Mass.: Addison-Wesley, 1973.

——. *Sick Societies.* New York: Free Press, 1992.

——. "The Study of Deviance." In *The Making of Psychological Anthropology,* edited by George D. Spindler. Berkeley: University of California Press, 1978.

Emmons, Nuel. *Manson in His Own Words.* New York: Grove, 1986.

Evans, G. R. *Augustine on Evil.* Cambridge: Cambridge University Press, 1982.

Fackenheim, Emil L. *To Mend the World.* New York: Schocken, 1982.

Finnis, John. *Aquinas.* Oxford: Oxford University Press, 1998.

Fischer, John Martin. "Responsiveness and Moral Responsibility." In *Responsibility, Character, and the Emotions,* edited by Ferdinand Schoeman. New York: Cambridge University Press, 1987.

Fischer, John Martin, ed. *Moral Responsibility.* Ithaca: Cornell University Press, 1986.

Foot, Philippa. *Natural Goodness.* Oxford: Clarendon Press, 2000.

Frankfurt, Harry G. "Freedom of the Will and the Concept of a Person." In *The Importance of What We Care About.* New York: Cambridge University Press, 1988.

Freud, Sigmund. *Beyond the Pleasure Principle.* 1920. Translated by James Strachey. New York: Bantam, 1959.

——. *Civilization and Its Discontents.* 1930. Translated by James Strachey. New York: Norton, 1961.

——. *Standard Edition of the Complete Psychological Works of Sigmund Freud.* 24 vols. Edited and translated by James Strachey. London: Hogarth, 1974.

Friedlander, Saul. *Kurt Gerstein: The Ambiguity of Good.* Translated by Charles Fullham. New York: Knopf, 1969.

Gaita, Raimond. "Evil beyond Vice." In *A Common Humanity.* London: Routledge, 1998.

Gauthier, David P. *The Logic of Leviathan.* Oxford: Clarendon Press, 1969.

Gert, Bernard. *The Moral Rules.* New York: Harper & Row, 1966. Substantially revised as *Morality.* New York: Oxford University Press, 1988.

Glover, Jonathan. *Humanity.* New Haven: Yale University Press, 2000.

Gourevitch, Philip. *We wish to inform you that tomorrow we will be killed with our families.* New York: Farrar, Straus & Giroux, 1998.

Graham, Gordon. *Evil and Christian Ethics.* Cambridge: Cambridge University Press, 2001.

Greenspan, Patricia. "Unfreedom and Responsibility." In *Responsibility, Character, and the Emotions,* edited by Ferdinand Schoeman. New York: Cambridge University Press, 1987.

Grube, G. M. A. *Plato's Thought.* London: Methuen, 1935.

Hampshire, Stuart. *Innocence and Experience.* London: Allen Lane, 1989.

——. *Spinoza.* Harmondsworth, U.K.: Penguin, 1951.

——. *Thought and Action.* London: Chatto & Windus, 1960.

Hampson, Norman. *The Life and Opinions of Maximilien Robespierre.* London: Duckworth, 1974.

Healy, Sean Desmond. *Boredom, Self, and Culture.* Cranbury, N.J.: Associated University Presses, 1984.

Hegel, Georg F. W. *Reason in History.* 1840. Translated by Robert S. Hartman. New York: Liberal Arts, 1953.

Heidegger, Martin. "What Is Metaphysics?" In *Existence and Being,* edited by W. Brock. Chicago: Regnery, 1949.

Hick, John. *Evil and the God of Love.* New York: Harper & Row, 1966.

Hilberg, Raul. *The Destruction of the European Jews.* 1949. New York: Holmes & Meier, 1985.

Hobbes, Thomas. *Leviathan.* 1651. London: Dent, 1962.

Huizinga, Johan. *The Waning of the Middle Ages.* 1949. New York: Doubleday, 1954.

Hume, David. *A Treatise of Human Nature.* 1739. Edited by L. A. Selby-Bigge. Oxford: Clarendon Press, 1960.

Kant, Immanuel. *Religion within the Limits of Reason Alone.* 1794. Translated by T. M. Greene and H. H. Hudson. New York: Harper & Row, 1960.

——. "What Is Enlightenment?" 1784. In *Perpetual Peace and Other Essays,* translated by Ted Humphreys. Indianapolis: Hackett, 1983.

Kekes, John. *The Art of Life.* Ithaca: Cornell University Press, 2002.

Kierkegaard, Soren. *Fear and Trembling.* 1843. Translated by Walter Lowrie. Princeton: Princeton University Press, 1974.

Klapp, O. E. *Overload and Boredom.* Westport, Conn.: Greenwood, 1986.

Kuhn, Reinhard. *The Demon of Noontide.* Princeton: Princeton University Press, 1976.

Leibniz, Gottfried Wilhelm. *Theodicy.* 1875–90. Translated by E. M. Huggard. LaSalle, Ill.: Open Court, 1985.

Levi, Primo. *The Drowned and the Saved.* Translated by Raymond Rosenthal. New York: Vintage, 1989.

Linton, Ralph. *The Study of Man.* New York: Appleton-Century, 1936.

Loomis, Stanley. *Paris in the Terror.* Philadelphia: Lippincott, 1964.

Mathewes, Charles T. *Evil and the Augustinian Tradition.* New York: Cambridge University Press, 2002.

May, Simon. *Nietzsche's Ethics and His War on "Morality."* Oxford: Clarendon Press, 1999.

McGinn, Colin. *Ethics, Evil, and Fiction.* Oxford: Clarendon Press, 1997.

Midgley, Mary. *Wickedness.* London: Routledge, 1984.

Milgram, Stanley. *Obedience to Authority.* New York: Harper, 1974.

Mill, John Stuart. *The Subjection of Women.* 1869. Arlington Heights, Ill.: AHM, 1980.

Moore, Robert I. *The Formation of a Persecuting Society.* Oxford: Blackwell, 1987.

Morrow, Lance. *Evil.* New York: Basic Books, 2003.

Morton, Adam. *On Evil.* New York: Routledge, 2004.

Moyano, Maria José. *Argentina's Lost Patrol.* New Haven: Yale University Press, 1995.

Neiman, Susan. *Evil in Modern Thought: An Alternative History of Philosophy.* Princeton: Princeton University Press, 2002.

Nietzsche, Friedrich. *Beyond Good and Evil.* 1886. In *Basic Writings of Nietzsche,* translated by Walter Kaufmann. New York: Modern Library, 1966.

———. *On the Genealogy of Morals.* 1887. In *Basic Writings of Nietzsche,* translated by Walter Kaufmann. New York: Modern Library, 1966.

Nino, Carlos Santiago. *Radical Evil on Trial.* New Haven: Yale University Press, 1996.

Nozick, Robert. *Anarchy, State, and Utopia.* New York: Basic Books, 1974.

Nussbaum, Martha C. *The Therapy of Desire.* Princeton: Princeton University Press, 1994.

O'Hear, Anthony. *Beyond Evolution.* Oxford: Clarendon Press, 1997.

O'Shea, Stephen. *The Perfect Heresy.* New York: Walker, 2000.

Osiel, Mark J. *Mass Atrocity, Ordinary Evil, and Hannah Arendt.* New Haven: Yale University Press, 2001.

Passmore, John. *The Perfectibility of Man.* London: Duckworth, 1970.

Penelhum, Terence. *Butler.* London: Routledge, 1985.

Plato. *Meno.* Translated by W. K. C. Guthrie. In *The Collected Dialogues of Plato,* edited by Edith Hamilton and Huntington Cairns. Princeton: Princeton University Press, 1989.

Pope, Alexander. "Essay on Man." In *Selected Poetry and Prose.* New York: Holt, Rinehart & Winston, 1951.

Raposa, Michael L. *Boredom and the Religious Imagination.* Charlottesville: University Press of Virginia, 1999.

Rawls, John. *A Theory of Justice.* Cambridge, Mass.: Harvard University Press, 1971.

Report of the Argentine National Commission on the Disappeared. *Nunca Más.* Buenos Aires, 1984. New York: Farrar, Straus & Giroux, 1986.

Rosenberg, Tina. *Children of Cain.* New York: Morrow, 1991.

Rougemont, Denis de. *La part du diable.* 1945. Paris: Gallimard, 1982.

Rousseau, Jean-Jacques. *Emile.* 1780. Translated by Barbara Foxley. London: Dent, 1974.

Russell, Bertrand. *The Conquest of Happiness.* 1930. London: Routledge, 1993.

———. *A Critical Exposition of the Philosophy of Leibniz.* London: Allen & Unwin, 1937.

Sanders, Ed. *The Family.* Rev. ed. London: Nemesis, 1989.

Saxe, John Godfrey. "The Blind Men and the Elephant." In *The Poems.* Boston: Osgood, 1871.

Schacht, Richard, ed. *Nietzsche, Genealogy, Morality*. Berkeley: University of California Press, 1994.

Schama, Simon. *Citizens*. New York: Knopf, 1989.

Scheibe, Karl E. *The Drama of Everyday Life*. Cambridge, Mass.: Harvard University Press, 2000.

Scheler, Max. *Ressentiment*. 1912. Translated by Lewis B. Coser and William W. Holdheim. Milwaukee: Marquette University Press, 1994.

Schneewind, Jerome B. *The Invention of Autonomy*. New York: Cambridge University Press, 1998.

Schoeck, Helmut. *Envy*. 1966. Indianapolis: Liberty Fund, 1987.

Sereny, Gitta. *The Healing Wound*. New York: Norton, 2001. First published as *The German Trauma*. London: Norton, 2000.

———. *Into That Darkness*. London: Pimlico, 1995. First published 1974 by Andre Deutsch.

Sherman, Nancy. *The Fabric of Character*. Oxford: Clarendon Press, 1989.

Silber, John R. "The Ethical Significance of Kant's *Religion*." In Immanuel Kant, *Religion within the Limits of Reason Alone*, translated by T. M. Greene and H. H. Hudson. New York: Harper & Row, 1960.

Singer, Marcus G. "The Concept of Evil." *Philosophy* 79 (2004): 185–214.

Sleigh, R. C., Jr. "Leibniz." In *Encyclopedia of Ethics*, 2d ed, edited by Lawrence E. Becker and Charlotte B. Becker. New York: Routledge, 2001.

Southern, R. W. *The Making of the Middle Ages*. 1953. New Haven: Yale University Press, 1970.

———. *Western Society and the Church in the Middle Ages*. Harmondsworth, U.K.: Penguin, 1970.

Spacks, Patricia Meyer. *Boredom*. Chicago: University of Chicago Press, 1995.

Spinoza, Baruch. *Ethics*. 1669. In *The Collected Works of Spinoza*, edited and translated by Edwin Curley. Princeton: Princeton University Press, 1985.

Strawson, Peter. "Freedom and Resentment." In *Freedom and Resentment and Other Essays*. London: Methuen, 1974.

Sumption, Jonathan. *The Albigensian Crusade*. London: Faber & Faber, 1978.

Taylor, Charles. "Responsibility for Self." In *The Identities of Persons*, edited by Amelie Rorty. Berkeley: University of California Press, 1976.

Thompson, James Matthew. *Robespierre*. 2 vols. New York: Appleton-Century, 1936.

Verbitsky, Horacio. *The Flight: Confessions of an Argentine Dirty Warrior*. Translated by Esther Allen. New York: New Press, 1996.

Villa, Dana R. *Politics, Philosophy, Terror: Essays on the Thought of Hannah Arendt*. Princeton: Princeton University Press, 1999.

Vlastos, Gregory. *Socrates, Ironist and Moral Philosopher*. Ithaca: Cornell University Press, 1991.

Vogler, Candace. *Reasonably Vicious*. Cambridge, Mass.: Harvard University Press, 2002.

Wallace, R. Jay. *Responsibility and the Moral Sentiments*. Cambridge, Mass.: Harvard University Press, 1996.

Watson, Gary. "Responsibility and the Limits of Evil." In *Responsibility, Character, and the Emotions*, edited by Ferdinand Schoeman. New York: Cambridge University Press, 1987.

Watson, Lyall. *Dark Nature: A Natural History of Evil*. London: Hodder & Staughton, 1995.

Wiarda, Howard J. *Corporatism and Comparative Politics.* New York: Sharpe, 1997.

Wolf, Susan. *Freedom within Reason.* New York: Oxford University Press, 1990.

———. "Sanity and the Metaphysics of Responsibility." In *Responsibility, Character, and the Emotions,* edited by Ferdinand Schoeman. New York: Cambridge University Press, 1987.

Wollheim, Richard. "The Good Self and the Bad Self." In *The Mind and Its Depth.* Cambridge, Mass.: Harvard University Press, 1993.

Index